Teaching, Learning, and Loving

Teaching, Learning, and Loving

Reclaiming Passion in Educational Practice

Daniel Liston
and Jim Garrison
Editors

ROUTLEDGEFALMER
NEW YORK AND LONDON

Published in 2004 by
RoutledgeFalmer
29 West 35th Street
New York, NY 10001
www.routledge-ny.com

Published in Great Britain by
RoutledgeFalmer
11 New Fetter Lane
London EC4P 4EE
www.routledgefalmer.com

RoutledgeFalmer is an imprint of the Taylor and Francis Group.

Printed in the United States of America on acid-free paper.

10 9 8 7 6 5 4 3 2 1

Library of Congress Cataloging-in-Publication data is available on file.

ISBN 0-415-94514-3 (hbk.)
ISBN 0-415-94515-1 (pbk.)

Contents

Acknowledgments

We would like to thank Zaha Alsuwailan, Sue Arnold, Derya Cobanoglu, Laura Creighton, Leslie S. Daniel, Beth Dorman, Shanan Fitts, Kim Geil, André M. Green, Daneille Harlow, Virginia Knapp, Karin Kuffner, Kathleen Luttenegger, Mary Pittman, Michelle Reidel, Ann Mary Roberts, Michele Seipp, Suzanne P. Shelburne, Lourdes Lucía Travieso-Parker, Jennifer Urbach, Tamara K. Wallace, and the contributors to this collection for comments and suggestions on earlier drafts of this work.

Introduction
Love Revived and Examined

DANIEL LISTON
AND JIM GARRISON

Love binds us to the abode of life and everything in it we call good or beautiful. Those who feel the call to teach, who sense teaching is a profoundly meaningful part of their life, have a passion for teaching. Exactly what that passion is, though, they often cannot name. We think they are in love; they are in love with some aspect of teaching; perhaps they are in love with everything about it. The good that comes of connecting with students and transforming their lives attracts many people, the creative possibilities of teaching appeal to others, while some respond to the allure of the beauty found in their subject matter. The promise of these possibilities is immense; not all of them are lovely, however, because there are many corruptions of love in teaching, as elsewhere. The papers comprising our collection strive to reveal the wonder while exposing the distortions of love in teaching and learning. Institutional constraints silence the discourse of passion and love in the public realm of teaching and learning. This collection seeks to end the silence by speaking loudly in public about what many think should only be spoken about softly in private.

Love Revived

Unfortunately, many teachers teach without passion, without a love of ideas or a felt concern for students. We think it's one of the tragedies of our age. Daily, it seems, students are spoon-fed "educational" material, not to

1

satiate their learning hunger but rather to meet the mandates of the state. Sometimes the directives are explicit. These days practicing teachers and future teachers are told to never touch their students and, at times, to overlook the lives their students lead so as to teach to the test. At other times this neglect seems to be the outcome of simply trying to 'meet' the new state standards. Increasingly, and in effect, we are asked to disavow our loves, our love of learning, our passion for teaching, our care and concern for our students so as to meet federal, state, and district requirements. We are being "asked" to dismantle the vocation and profession of teaching. Teaching and learning are activities that work best when we work through our hearts as well as our heads. Teachers have known that for a long time. It is time for the academy to allow, even invite, the emotions, and more specifically love, into our understanding and practice of teaching.

In *Teaching, Learning, and Loving: Reclaiming Passion in Educational Practice* we reassert and re-insert the passions, the loves, the emotions back into teaching, and, as a result, recognize their role in learning. We do this because love, in all its forms and facets, is so integral to teaching. It is a creative, critical, and disruptive force in teaching and learning. In an era that would have us hive off two-thirds of our humanity (keeping the mind but disavowing our bodies and emotions), embracing love in teaching reconnects us not only with our forgotten parts and pasts, but also with the students and colleagues with whom we interact. Operating with these loves we become more creative, affirming, and caring in our interactions with others. Seeing the students before us as whole human beings in search of meaning is the kind of understanding that a loving perspective affords teachers. Seeing the hurt and the pain that inevitably arise from daily life is another such recognition. Love makes us vulnerable and that vulnerability invites loss and grief. These are the necessary shadows, the natural corollaries to a loving engagement. Learning how to deal with these losses is part of life and ought to be part of learning—if we are learning to be creative, human, and wise.

This sort of learning and teaching will not be produced by the instrumental, patriarchal logic of a bureaucratic, linear means–ends rationality, one that demands teachers unquestionably accept preassigned ends (e.g., curriculum objectives) and the means for obtaining them (hence the supposedly "teacher proof" curricula). When higher test scores are the preoccupation and bureaucratic strategies are the means, love and passion are discouraged, even denounced. Our preferred "teacherly" approach to students will not result when our eyes are on the assessment prize. We all need standards of achievement; they are integral to individuals, society, and most any worthwhile human endeavor, but the caring, loving eye tailors the standards to fit the student instead of the student to the one-size-fits-all standard. We need to expect much of others and ourselves. But the obsession with and the instrumental logic of the bureaucratic testing can not produce the kind of future family members or citizens we want. When only what is measurable is considered "real," the discourse of love is suppressed. When teachers are told that they have to get scores higher or their schools will be closed, staffs deliberate and "perseverate" over how to increase individual and aggregate scores. When math and reading are the areas that count in the assessment mandate, other subjects like the imaginative arts and physical education are dropped from the curriculum. When the instrumental logic that fuels current teaching and assessment reigns, we forget our love of inquiry; we no longer see students richly and fully; instead of unique individual selves, we see standardized, universal ciphers. Under such oppressive circumstances, we can no longer see the beauty in science or math, and our classroom communities become settings of control, not communities of engaged learning.

Love, as a yearning to connect with our natural and social worlds in a meaningful fashion, can fuel our critical intent to act against the structures that block an abundant and engaged approach to teaching and learning. When institutions significantly constrain the shared creation of meaningful lives, when structures of inequality enable some but not others to pursue full and rich lives, this love can become a critical lens and a powerful force. With this critical capacity, love can disturb and disrupt the reigning order, not in a violent or harmful fashion, but with creative and caring energies.

All too often, emotions are taken as affective upheavals in an otherwise smoothly functioning and reasonable process. Love, especially in its romantic variations, is viewed as reason abandoned and passion fulfilled. But what learner and what teacher, enthralled and engaged with their topic, would wish to reduce their inquiry to outcomes on a standardized test? What teacher would want to live disconnected from their subject or their students? Sometimes it is reasonable for emotions to disrupt the imposed norms and practices that constrain schooling. Our loving engagement with learning and our loving involvement with others can guide the disruptions that need to occur. Love, in most all of its forms, is a practice that honors individual insights and affirms shared struggle. We need this creative, critical, and disruptive energy. We need the creative energy to reaffirm and recreate our shared humanity, and we need the critical and disruptive energies to speak truth to a power that denies this life force. Teaching is emotional and intellectual work; so is learning. Love, in its various forms, offers invaluable benefits to teachers and students.

The benefits of love's discourse and practices are loudly declaimed by many, even while they are silently lived by many more. Love, as a concept, has seemed terribly suspect, irrational, somewhat out-of-bounds, and a bit too unwieldy. And this scholarly disdain for love is actually a small subset of a much larger issue. The larger issue is the purported antimony between reason and emotion. Rarely have modern scholarly analyses seemed adept at handling the stuff of feelings except, perhaps, in clinical texts. Reason and emotion have tended to be viewed as mortal enemies rather than helpful companions. It has not always been this way. In the history of philosophy, Aristotle, William James, John Dewey, Jean Paul Sartre, Simone Weil, and Iris Murdoch[1] have focused on the logic of emotion and the passion for logic. More recently, philosophers in the analytical tradition have argued for the rationality and reasonableness of emotions (e.g., Ronald deSousa, Patricia Greenspan, Robert Solomon, Amelie Rorty, William Lyons, and George Turski).[2] Post-modern/structural writers have attempted to dispel binary influences on our ways of thinking and being in the world (e.g., Michel Foucault, Homi Bhabha, and Eve Sedgwick).[3] Feminist analyses by Sara Ruddick, Alison Jaggar, and Sandra Bartky[4] have explored and critiqued the patriarchal bifurcation of thinking and feeling. In sociology Max Scheler, Norman Denzin, and Arlie Hochschild have contextualized the analyses of emotion.[5] We think and feel in social contexts and grow to develop and interpret those emotions. In academic psychology, Carol Gilligan; George Mandler; and Andrew Ortony, Gerald Clore, and Allan Collins have utilized various distinct frameworks to meld cognition and affect.[6] And as a result of recent advances in neuroscience, as explained by Joseph LeDoux and Antonio Damasio,[7] we are beginning to discern neurological bases of various emotions and of our thinking through and acting on those emotions. These scholars reject the reason–emotion opposition and affirm the need to see the relationship with greater complexity and subtlety.

Within educational scholarship recent work has underscored the need to explore the ways in which our thinking and feeling intermingle. Jane Roland Martin's work on the head and the heart in teaching, Nel Noddings' thoughts on caring, Megan Boler's analyses of feeling and power, Daniel Goleman's work on emotional intelligence, Andy Hargreaves' explorations of teaching as emotional labor, Parker Palmer's holistic approach to teaching, and Vivian Gussin Paley's reflections on her teaching[8]—all of these individuals have provided needed reorientations. These scholars' (and others') inquiries into the affective and deliberative terrain enlarge the boundaries of what is considered acceptable scholarship. Their reasoned discourse on the complex ways in which the head and the heart intermingle and on teaching's emotional attractions has engaged scholars, teachers, and even a few members of the general public. But those boundaries, once stretched, pulled, and ever so slightly enlarged, seem to have a way of rebounding back to their original shape—back to old comfort levels. Perhaps it is a natural proclivity to shy away from the perceived messiness of affect and its embodiment, or perhaps it is a product of a cultural tendency to view emotions as suspect, or it may be simply the cost of doing educational business with the state. But affect and emotions can neither be banished from the classroom nor easily put into the service of promoting standardized tests and higher test scores.

For too long we have left emotions in the ontological basement of educational scholarship, to be dragged up and out only when a particular topic necessitated it (e.g., classroom management, student motivation, or teacher 'burnout'). That seems ill advised, and it is time to rebuild our academic house. When we teach, we teach with ideas and feelings. When we interact with students, we react and they respond with thoughts and emotions. When we inquire into our natural and social worlds, we do so with desire and yearning. Many teachers and teacher educators know that their work, instruction, and profession require a complex interaction between their heads and their hearts, their thoughts and feelings. Teaching is an activity that brings one's emotions and mind to bear on subject matter and students and on connecting students with the subject matter. Our time in the classroom has very distinct moods, feels, and ruminations. When it is engaging, the time in the classroom is frequently alive with passion, purposefulness, and involvement and moves quickly. When it is boring, engagement is absent, the minutes pass slowly, and the mind and heart hibernate. Classroom efforts to manage, instruct, and direct groups of twenty to thirty students frequently require a feeling for others and an intuition that connects teacher to student and to subject matter. For the new teacher the multiple tasks entailed in this activity can be overwhelming. For the experienced teacher they can seem almost unconscious.

Slowly we are acknowledging these cognitive and emotional dynamics and focusing on the role of love and eros in education. Within the last decade (and more intensely during the last five years), scholars have begun to explore aspects of this terrain. Megan Boler, Kerry Burch, Michael Dale, Ann Diller, Jim Garrison, Lisa Goldstein, Ursula Kelly, Rachael Kessler, Dan Liston, Jane Roland Martin, and Elaine J. O'Quinn[9] have examined features of this terrain. Each of these authors recognizes the complex interactions among thoughts and feelings in educational settings, and many have explored the ways in which love works within them. All these individuals will contribute essays to this volume. When scholars begin to acknowledge the role of emotion in classrooms and in teaching, the discourse on love does not seem far behind. A significant number of teachers talk of love as a guiding metaphor in their work. They talk of their love of learning, their love of students, their love of subject matter, and their love of teaching. Love's presence in the classroom can be a powerful dynamic, one that links teachers and students with the grace of great things. But our loves are not always bridges to blessings and enrichment. Our desires, our yearning to connect with others and other worlds can be distorted, manipulated, and malformed. In this collection, we examine and explore further the contours of love in teaching, learning, and teacher education.

Our authors write about and bear witness to aspects of daily educational practice all too often overlooked by theorists and educational researchers, though well known to practitioners. These include such topics as love, along with the related concepts of the pursuit of happiness, domestic tranquility, critical hope, vulnerability, compassion, risk, and mystery—topics that are almost never the subject of educational research, though they are the daily companions of good educational practice. They also include grief, despair, discomfort, acceptance of ignorance, and loss of hope. These papers explore regions outside the bounds of the explicit, cognitive, and categorical. Their motivations, however, are familiar; they include the desire to create hope, meaning, and mutual understanding in the pursuit of better classrooms, more equitable education, and more effective teacher education. They help map for educational researchers and theorists terrain that is familiar to, but sometimes not articulated by, practitioners. To chart this territory, though, our authors move through regions of practice beyond those circumscribed by the cognitive bias that pervades the field of educational research, a bias that is already beginning to recapture the discourse about caring and emotions.

The essays in this collection concentrate on the creative, critical, disruptive, and destructive dimensions of cognitively engaged, emotionally charged, and loving relationships with content and with students. These essays recognize that these relationships are fraught with problems, but then all relationships encounter hazards. Many of the authors devote considerable effort to discussing these dangers and their potentially destructive elements. Some dispositions and engagements that might be called "love" are inappropriate, even harmful. Love as a doting, preoccupied, and dependent relationship seems inappropriate. Romantic love as sexual intimacy between teacher and student is simply improper, harmful, and morally unacceptable. Nonetheless, there are other kinds of love teachers should and do practice in their classrooms regularly. We are confident that a loving relationship with students that supports mutual inquiry and questioning is an ideal many teachers embrace and pursue in their daily classroom practice. Although often unobtainable, it is an ideal that nonetheless provides guidance to good practice, if we guard against the dangers.

In this edited collection we explore further these loves, to understand better our engagements and their dangers. Teaching is an emotional and a cognitive endeavor. If we are going to understand our practices and our teaching, then we need to explore the affective and rational contours of this terrain. Our authors in this collection attempt to do just that and quite a bit more.

Love Examined

Love has had a prominent place in the discourse of the West from the beginning. Certainly, it has exercised an immense influence on western philosophy and theology. Today, representation by popular media conceals most of that discourse, though its influence on our thoughts, attitudes, and emotions remains immense. Not knowing the cultural structures that organize and give meaning and value to our lives does not make us free and independent of them. Actually, it means we forfeit ourselves to them in the most hopeless and helpless way. Any penetrating examination of the nature of teaching and learning requires exposing this hidden discourse of love. Once uncovered, we may wish to criticize and recreate it. That, in fact, is what several papers in this collection have already begun to do.

Four basic ideas of love have emerged in western history. They are eros, agape, philia, and romantic love. We will initially use these conceptions as if they were four points of a compass to orient ourselves. But we will not find ourselves, in any of the chapters that follow, heading in a particularly "true" direction. None of our authors employ a "true" and unsullied version of eros or philia or any of the other conceptions of love. In today's discourse our loves are far more complicated than that. However, it is important to realize that any human relationship is capable of evolving into any or all of these intensely binding expressions of human attachment. Teaching and learning are no exception. In what follows we hope to offer a rough map, one that represents the initial understandings of love in teaching and learning: love as we've inherited it within the western tradition.

In the first paper in this collection, Jane Roland Martin lists the various forms love can take, all of which fall either under the four basic forms or at their interspaces. Yet, as she notes, "the kind [of love] with special relevance to education is either missing, subsumed under some category, or treated as an afterthought." Our book was designed to help identify and remedy that oversight. Like all systems of categories, the four basic forms of love in the West conceal as much as they reveal; and if we look carefully, we may expose whose interests and purposes constructed these categories. We might then wish to deconstruct and reconstruct them to serve better purposes. If we are to recreate these loves, though, we must first recognize them. Martin identifies and examines what she calls "the love gap in the educational text." This gap in the educational text, this lack of discourse about love in teaching, is eerily strange. It is odd that love cannot speak its name aloud in education. Martin maintains that culture has confined talk of love in teaching and learning to the private realm of women's work.

One of the things that will become increasingly apparent as we go is that the construction of love and emotion in the western world is extraordinarily gender biased, even patriarchal. This bias comes in many guises, which act to suppress the public discussion of feeling, caring, nurturance, healing, and connecting. When such matters enter the public domain, there is a tendency to dismiss them, denigrate them, or praise them as women's work. Many male teachers, especially in the lower grades, feel they suffer a diminution in social status due to their calling. Frequently female elementary teachers feel their work is undervalued. Many teachers, at all levels, despair and leave. It is time we speak aloud the terms and relations that motivate teachers in their work, that guide the profession and constitute essential elements in their vocation—their calling. Reliance on technical instrumental rationality often suppresses the values that personally sustain male and female teachers alike. Since only one of our authors explicitly thematizes gender bias as the source of the love gap in education, we will not dwell on the theme, but astute readers will have no trouble recognizing it as a subtext in many of the papers that follow. We believe any successful introduction of love into the public discourse of education will eventually require recreating the concepts of love we have inherited from the distant past. Many papers in this collection have, *de facto*, begun such recreation.

Eros

Eros is the most ancient type of love. We best understand the nature of eros by beginning with its emergence in the West. Hesiod's Theogeny (c. 700 B.C.E.) personifies Eros as among the first generation born of Chaos, the opening or matrix from whence Cosmos (ordered existence) is progressively articulated. Unlike his siblings (e.g., his sisters Night and Earth), Eros is a primordial force of creation or procreation and not a state of being. In the Orphic cosmogonies of about the same time, Eros is the motivating power uniting all and from whose unions are born the increasingly more intelligible and fulfilled states of creation.

In the process of rendering Chaos into Cosmos, Eros may overwhelm every intelligent purpose, whether well or ill-conceived: "Eros, who is love, handsomest among all the immortals, who breaks the limbs, who in all gods, in all human beings overpowers the intelligence in the breast, and all their shrewd planning."[10] From the beginning, Eros is as ambivalent as he is all-powerful. This ambivalence persists in subsequent ideals of love that evolve from primeval Eros. As an irresistible force, Eros breaks the bounds of every rational category that would arbitrarily constrain it. We cannot enclose its force, but we may learn how to use it well. Intelligent, truly rational practice channels the flow of Eros so that it carries us where we should go, which is not always where we want to go. Those who overcome the false dualism between reason and emotion recognize that the two can cooperate and work well together; reason and love can guide us in our creative, critical, and disruptive engagements.

Effectively employed, eros helps overcome the limits established by the concepts, rules, and regulations of technocratic rationality. For instance, one of our authors, Kerry Burch, calls upon the boundlessness of eros as a way of breaking through institutional boundaries that repress educating for the pursuit of happiness promised in the Declaration of Independence of the United States. He also sees it as a "counterpoise to the cult of [instrumentalist] efficiency that dominates the current educational climate" that makes students and potential future democratic citizens "human capital" for the production function, thereby serving the desires of the nation's plutocracy.

Our book understands eros not as a personification (hence the lowercase *e*), but in the more ordinary sense of "passionate desire." Nonetheless, we believe the ambivalence attending its birth as a personification of creative force is still with us. Eros is the idea of love that seeks to possess what it passionately desires, whether it is the necessities of life, such as food and water, or those things that make life worth living, such as a mate, children, and the education of children. The danger in eros is that its desire to possess what it lacks may crush all uniqueness and difference in others in an effort to reduce them to something that satisfies its demands. Erotic love is often conditional, and readily withdrawn when others fail to satisfy our needs and desires. In their essay, Elaine J. O'Quinn and Jim Garrison call attention to the tragic consequences of this kind of conditional love and caring in the classroom and help us to envision a more compassionate classroom setting characterized by more truly loving relations. Conditional love is controlling, and when teachers exercise such love, the effect on their students may be coercive and even cruel. Nonetheless, many teachers experience a self-transcending eros that desires the good of the students more than their own good. The teaching eros often involves the need to be needed. One of the dangers of passionate teaching is that it can tend toward self-sacrifice rather than self-understanding.

Tragedy and comedy commonly occur within the travails of a single school year as loving, caring teachers strive to transform the chaos of the first day into a cosmos of learning, caring, and connecting in the classroom community. The essays in our book offer ample testimony to the ambivalence, paradoxes, ironies, and dangers as well as the joys and creative possibilities hidden in teaching and learning in loving relationship. Today, overzealous legislators, technocrats, and parents who rightly fear the excesses of eros strive to suppress its every expression in teaching and learning in our nation's schools. As they do, they also suppress the creative force of eros that brings connection, community, and cosmos. The high tragedies of the classical Greeks were almost all tragedies of hyper-rationality. They chronicle the disasters that befall those who presume that the force of unaided reason alone is enough to prevail over madness. Tragedies of technocratic hyper-rationality stalk students, teachers, and administrators moment by moment in our schools. Teachers have loving, caring, and connecting reasons for doing things mere instrumental rationality will never know.

There is profundity to the fact that the ancients who imparted the rational tradition to the West also imparted tragedy and comedy to help reconcile us to the limits of its use. Moderns and post-moderns alike have yet to learn the lesson. Our book strives to provide some useful insights about teaching, learning, and loving while warning of love's dangers and respecting the reciprocality constituting human relations that join reasoning to loving. We believe that for those individuals wise in the practical arts of teaching the two are really one.

In Plato's dialogue the *Symposium*, eros serves as a "harmony of opposites" unifying emotional intuition with rational comprehension.[11] Plato provides eros with educational, moral, and epistemological dimensions that became a permanent part of Western philosophy and Christianity. The *Symposium* describes the education of eros; the education of a person's passionate desire teaches them to discriminate things assumed good immediately and unreflectively from those that prove good upon intelligent assessment. In his essay, Daniel Liston examines our cognitive engagements with, and emotional attractions to, the allure of beauty (including lovely ideas) and the pain and harm of injustice. He illustrates how beauty and pain move us along our educational paths, in our yearning desire to know and act in the world.

The *Symposium* comprehends eros as a passionate desire seeking to possess the good for itself. It describes not only an ascent in the individual's moral quest for the good, but the epistemological expedition to possess knowledge as well. For Plato, the erotically mediated epistemological quest begins by knowing ordinary, everyday objects that exist in space and time, such as tables and chairs, and ends when it reaches the transcendent and eternal ontological Forms—the immutable objects of knowledge subsisting outside space and time. For Plato, though, wisdom was beyond knowledge, for it involved the Good that lies beyond the Forms, illuminates them, and harmonizes them. As students ascend the Platonic hierarchy, they learn to assess the exact value of every assumed good they encounter. The greatest Good lies beyond knowledge alone. In harmonizing the

Forms, it harmonizes the cosmos that is built by copying them; and since such harmony is the very definition of beauty for Plato, the Beautiful, the Good, and the Harmonious were one for him.

For the ancient Greeks the primary educational function was the education of eros, for they believed that once we knew what was truly good for us, we would desire it with determination. Today, there is almost no discourse among educators about how to educate our students to desire the genuinely good. Instead of educators focusing on the good and desirable, our advertising media spend tens of billions of dollars targeting young people to lure them into buying the goods of commerce. Therein lies one of the great tragedies of our hyper-rationalized technocratic education. While legislators and technocrats talk of test scores and accountability, they entirely ignore those actually educating the eros, including the sexual eros, of the nation's youth.

Agape

Diotima, a prophetess whose name means "cherished of God," taught Socrates the higher mysteries of love we have been discussing. Near the end of her lesson, she conveys to Socrates that those who come to possess the Good "shall be called the friend of God, and if ever it is given to man to put on immortality, it shall be given to him" (*Symposium,* 212a). The early church fathers, especially Saint Augustine, transformed Plato's education of eros to transcend the worldly realm in search of the Good into humankind's quest for union with God.

In Christianity, eros becomes the passion directing us to seek union with God. However, the Christian tradition added two remarkable properties to the idea of the Platonic eros. First, it personified the Good as a living God. Second, it developed the concept of loving bestowal, of creatively imparting value upon others regardless of their assessed worth. For the Christian, God's love, or agape, is unconditional love freely given to all. Ideally, such love should circulate through every member of the community (e.g., "love thy neighbor as thyself") before returning to God, the creator of all. However, agape, like eros, risks reducing all difference to the self-sameness of a central agent's norms and values, and therein lies one of its paradoxical dangers. Agape distributes itself and must flow if it is to strengthen and replenish; otherwise, it may deplete the community. Ann Diller's paper in this volume explicitly seeks to identify and overcome the barriers to the wise, clarifying flow of love in teaching and learning. These include such obvious feelings as hatred and cruelty but also subtle emotions such as attachment and pity.

Even considered apart from its theological implications, love as agape has remarkable properties that far exceed eros. Eros is acquisitive desire and longing that seeks to possess for itself what it appraises as valuable; the education of eros teaches individuals to make discerning discriminations. By contrast, agape is ideally self-transcending and giving. As Irving Singer points out, agape as loving bestowal is "a new creation of value" that for humankind at least is "an artifact of the human imagination."[12] Teaching attracts those hoping to find the creative autonomy necessary to create a classroom community, one that allows them to connect with their students, and their students with each other, so that the teacher may impart the goods and values of learning. There is danger here, too, though, for what the teacher finds of value for the student may not only vary from what the student finds valuable, but from those goods that would actually bestow value upon them. Lisa Delpit, for instance, has shown that the cultural assumptions guiding white, liberal-minded, suburban teachers can be harmful to the inner-city students when they impose their middle class norms and values.[13] If teachers are to respond to their students' needs and desires well, they must first know them. When love, as agape, is wise, it strives to know and understand its object.

Philia

The third idea of love in the Western tradition is philia, or friendship. Aristotle originally developed the idea by distinguishing three kinds of friendship. The first two are strictly instrumental, wherein we use friends as means to a worthy end. First, we may use friends for their practical utility; for instance, a novice teacher might cultivate a friendship with an experienced teacher who serves as a mentor, offering useful advice that helps the beginner achieve the end of becoming a good teacher. Friends may also serve as a means to the end of pleasure and enjoyment; morale-boosting relations with fellow teachers is an example of this second variation.

Aristotle calls the third and highest ideal of friendship "perfect friendship." In such friendship, we delight in our friends' companionship while appreciating and caring for their welfare because of who they are in themselves, not as instrumental means to our ends. Aristotle argues that only the morally virtuous are capable of perfect friendship. In such friendship, the friends love not so much the individuality in the other, but their embodiment of universal moral ideals and virtues.

The selection of friends is largely a matter of cold appraisal of the potential friends' virtue because philia, for Aristotle, eschews emotionality. Singer remarks: "love [eros as well as philia] might be a way of bestowing value upon the object . . . is as foreign to Aristotle as it was to Plato."[14] Theories of friendship (and eros), medieval or modern, remain remarkably cognitive, calculative, hyper-rationalized, or reductive.[15] Such a construction of friendship will never do for teachers who dedicate their professional lives to imparting meaning and value. As with eros, teaching and learning require a model of friendship that is more altruistic and thoughtfully intelligent and less egotistic and hyper-rationalistic. The gender bias in Aristotle on friendship is also strikingly plain.

Aristotle allows for friendship between unequals, for example, between beginning teachers and highly competent, experienced teachers. Philia may sometimes extend to students as well. His idea is that we may render the relationship proportioned to its merit. Teachers who enjoy a mentoring friendship with a much more capable teacher may reciprocate in different ways, including respect, appreciation, and youthful energy. Aristotle's ideal of moral community requires properly proportionate friendship. Again, it is a rather cold and calculating concept of friendship. Singer finds that "Aristotelian philia idealizes that conformity to reigning ideals which constitutes a sense of social importance."[16] It is an aristocratic version of friendship. Friendship in a democracy should sustain shared critical and creative reflection upon the social order, including the function of institutionalized teaching and learning, not docile compliance.

Singer states well what is wrong generally with the classical concepts of love in Aristotle or Plato: "They think of love as a response to an objective goodness which is prior to that response and independent of it."[17] Both classical and modern theories of philia are reductive, detached, or calculating. Good teachers will never accept such a construction because they are committed to the ideal that their responses to their students may not only see the good within but also impart something of value not previously there.

In her contribution, Rachael Kessler goes far beyond anything Aristotle and most modern theorists ever consider by providing guidance in how we may make friends with our own grief at the loss of love, so we may learn to love again. Those teachers who make this healing journey are prepared to help others do the same. Such friendship requires intelligently reaching out to others who may befriend us for help. Kessler teaches us how to creatively nurture and impart value to ourselves by emotionally relying on others for help. Learning to care for oneself properly is an important part of learning to care for others that too many teachers ignore because they often think they are supposed to be self-sacrificing. Those teachers who learn to make friends with their grief learn how to be a friend to their grieving students. By refusing to calculate proportion, call for appraisal, require conformity, or pursue reductive explanations, Kessler presses the concept of friendship beyond the breaking point of the traditional analysis. In doing so, she not only challenges the subtle gender biases hidden in the traditional concept of philia, she also challenges what Martin calls the "education-gender system" that would confine emotions such as grief to women's work, to be performed at home and with the family, while the rational work of men, such as technocratic administration of standards and tests, is the business of public schools. Kessler implicitly rejects the public-versus-private dualism as well as the gender divide. We believe learning to love, nurture, and care for students' emotions, as well as for their thoughts and actions, is everyone's work in every sphere. We think Kessler illustrates just one of the many ways thinking about the virtues of good teaching not only breaks the bounds of traditional thinking about loving, but of learning as well.

Romantic Love

Romantic love emerged in southern France around A.D. 1100 as part of early medieval humanism. Today, it entirely dominates the popular cultural conversation as it continues to evolve. Romantic love seeks to ennoble intimate union, aesthetically and morally, while idealizing a form of love reserved only for one unique individual to the exclusion of all others. It often sublimates sexual union (a form of eros) to release the imagination. We may also romantically sublimate the passions found in other forms of eros in similar ways; we believe the romance of knowledge, our love of learning, is one of these. In part, romantic love was a transgressive reaction against the hypocrisy of the medieval church's economic and political contrivances, and it has never lost its tendency toward rebellion. It seeks to preserve a realm of personal intimacy outside the bounds of institutional purposes and regulations. Romanticism has many other properties, but we will concentrate on its sense of insurgence.

Significantly, institutional norms neuter teachers, students, and curriculum in an effort to regulate sexual and other impulses. Yet, as any teacher in middle school or beyond knows, schools are highly sexualized and impulsive places where contemporary versions of romantic love play themselves out constantly. Ironically, the students, all of whom engage in some sort of libidinal practice, must turn to popular media to receive instruction in "proper" participation. If there is "sex education," it is curiously cognitive, disembodied, and dispassionate; there is nowhere in the curriculum where one might learn anything about how to experience loving intimacy in mutually caring, self-understanding, and devoted ways. Under such conditions, the ideal of sublimating primordial passions to release artistic creativity and moral responsibility is impossible.

Today romantic love remains a private refuge from public institutional control. In a sense, the discourse of love in teaching has likewise sought refuge in the private. Institutions contain passions and desires they cannot acknowledge and of which their officials are often unaware. Our book seeks to dissolve the dualism of public and private in the discourse of love by bringing private conversations into the public domain. Love has, we believe, a discipline of emotional thought that could alter the structure of the public sphere of education, making it more accommodating to those who care for and nurture the growth and development of students.

The four major ideas about love overlap in complex ways. They display as many differences in detail of expression as there are individuals who embody these western cultural constructions and practices of love both in their habits and attitudes. There are no necessary and sufficient conditions for any of the ideal types. Further, the actual interpretations of love we encounter in education, such as love of subject matter, love of learning, teacherly love of students, love of democratic community, or even "loving teacher education" (as Lisa Goldstein titles her paper—thereby expressing well love's ambivalence and multiple meaning), vary considerably. The loves of teaching and learning usually occur in between the four historical types of love. To recognize our educational loves, we will have to look carefully to begin mapping the terrain. Oftentimes these loves interact in complex and multi-layered ways. As Ursula Kelly remarks in her contribution, "the best teaching and learning will reach for this ultimate achievement of love." Such reaching involves various kinds of love. Many teachers passionately desire (eros) that students learn the values (perhaps a passion for learning) they seek to impart (agape); this is especially so when we feel particularly friendly (philia) toward them, even to the point of talking to them about their personal romantic lives. Such passions dangerously defy institutionalized norms of instrumental rationality. Those who passionately love teaching appear to break institutional rules daily, rather than harm individual students. Most teachers will admit in private that at some point in their career they have experienced a teacherly love this complex and defiant. We want to discuss such matters in public.

Love with its nuance and variety is far too complex, primitive, and common a quality of human existence to confine itself to the four basic categories used to construct it in the West. For example, almost every adult in almost every culture will have felt sexual attraction under some or another interpretation. For some, it is temptation to sin; for others it is an opportunity for religious practice; and yet for others it is a passionate, consuming, and sensual commingling with another. Several papers in our collection burst the cultural bounds of Western thinking about love by looking eastward, especially to Buddhism. Daniel Liston turns to the Buddhist contemplative tradition to better understand the relation between listening, learning, and emotional engagement. Megan Boler finds Buddhism helps us move beyond disabling binaries (of hope and despair) along with enabling teachers to follow students' affect and not simply their words. She specifically turns our attention to compassion and hope, so as to respond to the discomfort caused by a genuinely critical pedagogy. Ursula Kelly also discusses a form of Buddhist meditation that helps us see ourselves and others more compassionately. And Ann Diller devotes herself entirely to explicating the Buddhist Brahmaviharas in inviting ways that carry us completely beyond the bounds of ordinary western thought. All these authors are wise to seek alternatives to western wisdom, but we should not forget that those educated in western ways of loving inevitably bring their prejudgments to the interpretation of other cultural practices and attitudes.

Knowing the basic types of love that structure our thoughts, feelings, and action regarding love in the West will help us understand ourselves better and avoid misunderstanding others. It edifies us to remember that from the beginning, love in the West knew no bounds and always overpowered those intelligent forms of rationality that sought to suppress and confine it rather than use it wisely. Such a force cannot be constrained even by the cultural forces and intelligence that called it into existence.

PART **1**

Loving Gaps and Loving Practices

In this section, Jane Roland Martin draws on her extensive work entailed in rethinking education to identify a strange omission in our educational thinking, the love whose focus is the growth and development of children. Such love is, in part, a form of bestowal, a part of the teaching eros; that is, in teaching we affirm the value that exists in the world and we create value anew. Echoing the title of one of her earlier books, we might say Martin seeks to change the educational landscape by reconstructing the cultural fences that arbitrarily separate the private domain of the home from public institutions, including not only schools but also many other social institutions. As she has done in so much of her work, Martin shows that these fences form the social contours of gender segregation and discrimination. These fences also function to confine the flow of love to the private sphere of the home, where it is women's work to nurture and socialize children but not educate them (which remains a public function). She helps us understand why we never think of love and passion as a public concern, hence a concern of educators. The irony is that many teachers experience the call to teach as a call to connect with students in loving, caring, and creative ways that help them learn and grow. Yet, there is no official space inside our educational institutions for teachers to talk about these loves. Martin calls on us to create that space.

Following Martin, Lisa Goldstein concentrates on the role of love in teacher education, but, as she indicates in her paper: "The teacherly love we feel for our preservice teacher education candidates is very much akin to the more widely acknowledged teacherly love we felt for our young students when we were classroom teachers." As an experienced teacher, Goldstein can assume such a thing among those who have answered the call to teach. Unfortunately, as Martin explained, such love is not widely acknowledged in the official technocratic discourse of schools. To bridge this gap, Goldstein appropriates a general theory of loving that assumes a triadic relation among passion, commitment, and intimacy. Recognizing that intimacy as ordinarily understood, especially in the romantic tradition, is inappropriate for teaching, Goldstein reconstructs it as "intimacy-in-community," by which she means "creating a caring community of learners who work, dialogue, and explore together." She is cautious about claiming that her model provides a comprehensive understanding of loving teacher education. And in her conclusion, she urges us to see passion, commitment, and intimate community as cornerstones in a much larger and more elaborate edifice that each teacher education program must construct for themselves given their resources. Because teacher education is a public enterprise, what Goldstein says about loving and teacher education supports and supplements Martin's insights in many important ways.

After Goldstein, Elaine J. O'Quinn and Jim Garrison examine some of the conditions, complexities, and dangers involved in creating "intimacy-in-community." They begin by expressing concern regarding how standardization, fixed categories, and "sameness" force school communities into controlling rather than creative relations. O'Quinn and Garrison concentrate on building loving relations across difference, claiming that controlling relations tend to suppress diversity while creative relations support it. They question the notion teachers must always "know" students well to teach them well. They insist that we create understanding more often than we discover it, so they strive to show how we may "condition" classrooms for the creative possibility of loving relations. We cannot make people understand or love each other, but we may create conditions making it increasingly possible. Aware that conditioning easily slides into conditions of control, O'Quinn and Garrison identify three serious dangers before offering insights into the creation of shared classroom meaning. They conclude by contrasting the ethos of business and industry, dictated to classrooms by the ethos of a standards-driven technocracy, with the ethos of love in the classroom; and they observe that all they have said also applies to any community, including our democratic nation.

Concluding this section, Michael Dale shows how the standardized discourse of business and industry that controls public education is "a blinding story" of economic calculation that supplements bureaucratic control in ravaging narratives of loving, caring, and connection. In this manner he identifies another significant source for the strange omission in our educational thinking of any narrative of love regarding the growth and development of students. Like Lisa Goldstein, Michael Dale concentrates on teacher education, specifically the teaching of social and philosophical foundations; but what he says applies equally well to elementary, middle-, and high-school classrooms. Drawing on the work of Martha Nussbaum, among others, Dale shows that by turning directly to literary narrative, we can provide our students with an alternative vocabulary with which to see and describe their personal and professional lives. His insights arise from the fact that teaching is "intimately tied to the understanding and telling of stories." Dale shows us that when we lend our stories moral and emotional allegiance, the kinds of stories we tell determine the kind of teachers we become. In his paper, he reflects on student reactions to his own teaching to show how student teachers may learn to revise their teaching stories through encounters with rich and rewarding literary narratives, including powerful works such as Anne Michael's *Fugitive Pieces* and Dorothy Allison's disturbing *Bastard Out of Carolina*. Dale shows how we may use the moral, aesthetic, and passionate vocabulary of literature to help construct teaching identities committed to creating intimacy-in-community.

CHAPTER 1

The Love Gap in the
Educational Text

JANE ROLAND MARTIN

Introduction

The ancient Greeks acknowledged several forms of love, among them: sexual passion; parental, filial, and conjugal affection; fraternal feeling; friendship; love of country; love of wisdom.[1] An anthology of philosophies of love distinguishes six varieties in western thought: romantic love, eros, agape, Tristanism and chivalric love, friendship, fellow feeling.[2] A three-volume work on historical ideas of love discusses sexual love, courtly love, romantic love, married love, and religious love and makes passing reference to mother love, father love, and family love.[3] And a 2002 essay on teaching the philosophy of love calls friendship, romantic love, the love of parents for children, and the love of humanity the most basic forms of love.[4]

Despite the general acknowledgment that love takes many different forms, the kind with special relevance to the education of children is either missing from the lists, subsumed under some other category, or treated as an afterthought.[5] It has been said that commentators on Plato's *Symposium* ignore that this dialogue is about passionate love.[6] This philosophical neglect pales in comparison to the neglect of the kind of love whose object is the growth and development of children. In what follows I will first trace the fate of this love in the history of educational thought, then ask why the neglect, and finally show that it matters.

In focusing on the love whose object is the growth and development of children, I will leave open the question of whether other forms of love also have relevance for educational contexts. This issue is too huge, complicated, and controversial to be entered into here. However, because the sexual abuse of children is so pervasive a disorder of contemporary culture that any serious discussion of love for children is liable to be misunderstood, let me insist that there is no room for abuse of any kind in the form of love I will be discussing.[7]

My inquiry will also leave open the question of the precise nature of the love that has alternatively been called preservative, attentive, maternal, parental.[8] Interpretations of this love will vary, and it is beyond the scope of this paper to decide among them, just as it is beyond its scope to choose between competing visions of what counts as growth and development. Does the love whose object is children's growth and development share some of the characteristics of agape? Does it involve elements of romantic love, fellow feeling, or both? Are there perversions other than sexual abuse that need to be guarded against?[9] How does this form of love relate to the caring that feminist psychologists and philosophers have associated with women's experience?[10] It would lead too far afield to undertake an exploration of these and all the other vital issues regarding my subject.[11]

The Strange Fate of Home and Family in the History of Educational Thought[12]

With few exceptions, western thought has assumed that the natural site of the love that aims at the growth and development of children is the world of the "private house," to use Virginia Woolf's apt phrase.[13] Since that "world" has suffered from philosophical neglect, it is hardly surprising that this form of love has too.

Like other philosophical narratives, the strange story of the fate of home and family in the history of educational thought begins with Plato. Maintaining in the *Republic* that the institutions of private home, marriage, family, and child rearing will tear a city apart, Plato envisioned a state in which these social arrangements are abolished, at least for the guardian class. True, the guardians of his Just State are supposed to consider themselves one big family, and so "will think of the same thing as their own, aim at the same goal, and, as far as possible, feel pleasure and pain in unison."[14] But even if this is counted a form of love, it is very different from the kind under discussion here. The love that Plato's guardians feel for one another—assuming for the sake of argument that it is love—is a reciprocal affair between equals. Reciprocity and equality do not characterize the love that seeks the welfare of young children.

Given the *Republic*'s disregard for the private home in general and for its parent/child relationships in particular, it is scarcely surprising that Aristotle, whose philosophy so often countered Plato's, began his *Politics* with a treatment of it.[15] Remarkably enough, however, after making the household a basic constituent of the polis, and then discussing slavery and the art of acquisition in some detail in Book I while devoting only a single sketchy paragraph to a man's rule over wife and children, Aristotle quit the subject. Although he promised to return later to the topics of marriage and parenthood, he did not. More interesting still, when he discussed education in Books VII and VIII of the *Politics*, Aristotle was strangely silent about both the educative activities of the household and the interpersonal relationships these involve. He pointed out that children can easily learn what they should not—especially from slaves. But instead of crediting the household members in whose care he placed children up to age seven with showing affection for their charges and playing a positive role in furthering their charges' growth and development, he ignored these educational agents altogether.[16]

The educative aspects of home and family disappear in Rousseau's philosophy, too, as do home's domestic affections. In *The Social Contract*, published in 1762, this other philosopher who reacted so strongly to Plato's social policies called families the first model of political societies. In *Emile*, published that same year, he presented the private home as a necessary foundation of a healthy state and discussed the relationship between husband and wife, parent and child. Yet Rousseau was of two minds about the claims of home and family. Although in the last book of *Emile* he said that the love of one's nearest is the principle of the love one owes the state, the treatise begins with the orphaning of a newborn child. Our hero's parents are not dead. For the sake of education, the author has simply dismissed them from Emile's life, putting him instead in the hands of an unmarried male tutor with whom he is to live in virtual isolation.

Rousseau's ambivalence toward home and family was marked. Acknowledging in *Emile* that there is "no substitute for maternal solicitude,"[17] he dismisses Emile's mother from the scene. Insisting that it is "the good son, the good husband, and the good father who make the good citizen,"[18] he removes mother love and family affection from Emile's childhood. He also says that because a man does not know how to love his children, one of a woman's duties is to teach her husband to love them. Yet he puts Emile in the hands of the tutor and tells his readers how important it is for Jean-Jacques and Emile "to make himself loved by the other."[19]

The love that Rousseau wants Jean-Jacques to feel for Emile is not romantic love or sexual passion. Rather, he likens it to the tenderness and care a father feels for his children. However, according to the theory of gender relations Rousseau propounds in Book V of *Emile*, an unmarried man does not know how to love a small child in this way. If Jean-Jacques had a spouse, she could teach him to love Emile. But Jean-Jacques is a bachelor.

Perhaps—and this is stretching a point—if Emile and his tutor were to make their permanent home with the wet nurse Jean-Jacques is compelled to hire, she could perform this part of a wife's services. But Rousseau wants Jean-Jacques and Emile to set up house for themselves as soon as they can. Assuming they accede to his wishes, the tutor will not be able to do the very thing that Rousseau believes is so critical to a child's early education—love Emile.

In *Leonard and Gertrude,* a pedagogical novel published in 1781, Johann Heinrich Pestalozzi has no trouble remembering the "world" that the much-admired Rousseau tried so hard to forget. When in *Leonard and Gertrude* Cotton Meyer is asked how a "true" school—one that would "develop to the fullest extent all the faculties of the child's nature"[20]—could be established, he advises the village lord and his aide to visit Gertrude's home and observe how she teaches her children. The impression Gertrude's teaching makes can scarcely be exaggerated. Before the aide opens his eyes the next morning, he murmurs: "I will be schoolmaster!" Returning to Gertrude's house, he asks her if it would be possible to follow in a regular school the method she uses at home, and he requests her help in so doing. "There can be no substitute for your mother's heart, which I must have for my school," he says.[21]

Authors of texts and anthologies in the history of educational thought have neglected the gender reversal that distinguishes Pestalozzi's work on education from Rousseau's. Whereas Rousseau made a man his model educator, Pestalozzi bestows that honor on a woman. In consequence, commentators have not seen, or else have been unwilling to report, the domesticity at the very center of his educational philosophy. These oversights are more than matched by Pestalozzi's own ambivalence, however. In 1801 *How Gertrude Teaches Her Children* was published. Gertrude's name is not mentioned in this abstract, didactic work, nor is a mother in evidence until the last fifteen pages. The mother's appearance is so long delayed and so brief that few readers will take seriously Pestalozzi's protestations about the importance of her educational role. His stereotypical portrayal of her as a creature "forced by the power of animal instinct"[22] and his appropriation for himself of the methods she follows all but guarantee that she will not be given credit for the accomplishments Pestalozzi says are hers.

The mother one meets in *How Gertrude Teaches Her Children* is the direct opposite of the Gertrude of *Leonard and Gertrude.* The latter is a tower of strength, a repository of good sense, and a model of self-discipline. The former is a woman whose heart is detached from her hearth and whose love for her children is devoid of intelligence. It seems that, without ever announcing the switch, in *How Gertrude Teaches Her Children* Pestalozzi cast another woman—one who conforms to Western culture's standard image of an irrational female—in the good mother role. Having done so, he then felt free to represent himself as the sole authority on teaching.

Whereas Pestalozzi recognized the educational significance of rational mother love and of domestic environments, only to allow them to disappear from his philosophy, in *The School and Society,* first published in 1900,[23] John Dewey repressed domesticity from the start. Looking back at the home of preceding generations—one might almost say the home of Leonard and Gertrude—Dewey saw a household whose every member shared in its work. Directing attention to the discipline and character building of that earlier form of life, Dewey asked if the teachings that used to be acquired there were becoming available elsewhere. His answer was that they were not.

Aware of the effects of the Industrial Revolution, a lesser thinker might have proposed measures for making schools more efficient sites for training the new factory workers. From the changing home and developing factory system Dewey derived a different educational message: If home is no longer a center of occupations and, as a consequence, a unique source of educational value has been lost to us, let school become such a center; let it not become a place where children are trained *for* work, but what home used to be—a place *of* work.

As large as Dewey's educational vision was, however, in *The School and Society* it did not encompass mother love, father love, or family affections more generally. Although the first three chapters of this book give the impression that the home of the past was educative in the broadest possible sense, Dewey's conception of that home was highly selective. In his eyes it was a place of work. Of course it was, but it was also a site of the shared day-to-day living; the family relationships; and, in the best of cases, the affections that constitute domesticity. Furthermore, while changes in the American home provided Dewey's point of departure, the attention he paid home in *The School and Society* was short-lived. Read the first few pages and one wonders why the word *home* is not included in the title. Read on and one realizes that the gap is in the text.[24]

In contrast to Dewey, in *The Montessori Method,* first published in 1912,[25] Maria Montessori built domesticity into the very concept of school. Following Gertrude's advice that the aide do for the children in his school what their parents failed to do for them, she designed the Casa dei Bambini as a surrogate home for children. More often than not, texts and anthologies devoted to the history of educational thought have neglected Montessori's contributions. But even those commentators who have acknowledged these have ignored her radically different idea of school. Her translators bear some responsibility for this lapse. In a 1907 address,

Montessori made the point that the word *casa* has come to have for Italians the significance of the English word *home*.[26] Nevertheless, English translators rendered Casa dei Bambini as House of Childhood or Children's House. Ignoring the domestic metaphor at the heart of her philosophy of education, neither they nor the majority of Montessori's interpreters seem to have realized that in a Casa dei Bambini family affection is supposed to govern relations between the "directress" and the children and among the children themselves.

Why the Gap in the Text?[27]

The ambivalence toward home, family, and love persists to this day, and well it might. Common sense dictates that all three fall within education's purview, yet western culture's most basic educational assumptions banish home, family, and love from the educational realm. Thus, home is said to "nurture" and "socialize," not "educate" children. And it is taken for granted that to acquire an education children must leave home—or, as in the case of home schooling, that home must model itself on school.

In the last several decades, feminist scholars have quite rightly denied the descriptive adequacy of the public/domestic dichotomy. The fact remains, however, that the educational theory and practice of western culture have long been predicated on this split. Implicitly dividing social reality into the world of the private home and the world of work, commerce, politics, and the professions, just about everyone takes it for granted that the function of education is to transform children who have heretofore lived their lives in the one place into members of the other. Assuming that the private home is a natural institution and that membership in it is a given rather than something one must achieve, we see no reason to prepare people to carry out the tasks and activities associated with it. Perceiving the public world as a human creation and membership in it as something at which one can succeed or fail and therefore as problematic, we make the business of education preparation for carrying out the tasks and activities associated with it.

Now culturally speaking, the public world and the world of the private home are gender-coded. Indeed, given that the one is considered men's domain and the other is considered women's, and that education's ideology and practices are predicated on this dichotomy, gender becomes a basic dimension of the whole system. Comprising this culture's dominant educational practices and ideology, our *education-gender system* includes institutional forms and structures; accepted pedagogies; standard approaches to curriculum and organizations of subject matter; definitions of the function of school; conceptions of an educated person; and much, much more.

The love at issue here is a case in point. The assumption that becoming educated is a process of acquiring new ways of thinking, feeling, and acting might appear to be gender-neutral. However, given our education-gender system, it is not. If education is to be "rational," these new ways must be functional—or they must be thought to be functional—in relation to life in the public world. But this is to say that they must be functional in a world that, historically speaking, was a male preserve and still reflects this fact. Furthermore, there is no need at all for the newly acquired ways of thinking, feeling, acting to be—or to be considered—functional in relation to the world of the private home, a world whose inhabitants are presumed to be female. Since these two worlds are culturally represented as polar opposites, preparation for life in the one will not be expected to foster ways of thinking, feeling, and acting that are functional in the other.

· Woolf said that life in the world of work, politics, and the professions is competitive and that the people there have to be pugnacious and possessive in order to succeed.[28] We in the West signify our agreement by assuming that because love is associated with the world of the private home—and, of course, with women—it runs counter to education's raison d'être. Indeed, we consider love such an obstacle to the achievement of the objective of preparing children for life in the public world that we make one of early schooling's main tasks that of casting off the attitudes and values, the patterns of thought and action associated with home, women, and domesticity.

It is no accident that the reports periodically published on the condition of American education give home the silent treatment. Viewing children as travelers to the public world, their authors see school as the place children stop en route to acquiring the knowledge, skill, attitudes, and values that they presumably will need when they reach their destination—a kind of wayside inn. Once children enter school, they do not go home again in this unexamined scenario, not even as adults. The authors of such volumes forget that life is lived in both places. They fail to recognize that the love whose object is the growth and development of children needs to become an integral part of both. They overlook the fact that this kind of love deserves a central place in the educational process.

Why is the amnesia is so widespread? In *Deschooling Society,* Ivan Illich maintained that schooling perpetuates itself through a hidden curriculum that teaches dependency on schools. Confusing process and substance, school transmits the lesson that to get an education you must go to school.[29] Our education-gender system perpetuates itself, too. I do not mean that educated people become addicted to education, although this may be true. Rather, school transmits a hidden curriculum in "domephobia"—the devaluation of and morbid anxiety about things domestic. Through the silences of the liberal curriculum on the subject of home and the negative attitudes toward domesticity embedded especially, but not exclusively, in the disciplines of history, literature, and the social sciences,[30] school perpetuates the existing education-gender system.

One thinker who unequivocally acknowledged the educational importance of the kind of love whose object is the growth and development of children is the early twentieth century feminist writer and lecturer Charlotte Perkins Gilman.[31] As might be expected, her contributions to education have seldom been recognized. Indeed, even those late twentieth century feminist scholars who unearthed Gilman's works and celebrated her literary achievements tended to ignore the educational significance of her utopian novel *Herland*.

Published in serial form in 1915, *Herland* echoes the *Republic* in abolishing the world of the private home. But Gilman's utopia—Herland by name—is an all-female society whose shared ideal is "to make the best kind of people."[32] The Herland dream is, in turn, the growth and development of children.

One way to view the adults of Herland is as surrogate mothers to all children, not in the contemporary sense of putting their wombs in the service of another but in the old-fashioned sense of loving and serving children to whom they have not given birth. This is the sense in which Pestalozzi's Gertrude is a mother to the neighbor children she takes into her home. It is the sense in which the adults in Montessori's Casa dei Bambini relate to the children in their care. An equally valid way to view Gilman's women is as educators who place children's growth and development at the very heart of their practice.

The question is: Can the Herland Dream prevail in actual societies that include males as well as females? Gilman made it clear that the love that characterizes Herland is a social construction, not a female biological imperative; and she also rejected the standard two-sphere analysis of society that removes love from the realm of education. In effect, then, *Herland* can be read as one woman's attempt to dismantle our education-gender system. But then, just as the many women in Herland who never bear children are nonetheless dedicated to the growth and development of all children, so men can enact this ideal.

Rousseau might disagree with this conclusion. But Gilman constructed an all-female society in order to expose the stereotypical thinking about gender that Rousseau promoted. Assume as he did, and as our education-gender system does, that individual traits and qualities are divided up between the sexes and that the love of children is strictly a female capacity. Then the Herland Dream will be inapplicable to half the population of real life societies. Assume that reason is strictly a male affair. Then even if all the women in everyday society dedicate themselves to the growth and development of all children, they will botch the job because of their lack of rationality. But reject the ideology of two opposing spheres and its gender stereotypes as Gilman would have us do. Then both sexes can love—or can learn to love—all children in the way the women of Herland do.

Maintaining that Gilman sentimentalizes the love whose object is the growth and development of children, some might reject the Herland Dream out of hand. But supposing Gilman does sentimentalize, there is still much to be learned from her vision of an ideal social order. Moreover, one wonders if the charge of sentimentality does not say more about the way Gilman's critics see the world than about her own philosophy. Would not any proposal that projects love onto the "public" sphere seem overly sentimental or romantic to those who have been told since day one that the world is a harsh, competitive place where people have to be pugnacious and possessive in order to succeed?

The Difference a Gap Makes[33]

Does the love gap in the education text matter? Were it simply a historical curiosity, it might not. But love is missing today from public discourse about education in general and schooling in particular. We talk about testing and accountability, reading and math scores, how little knowledge of history and science our children have, the high cost of higher education, and how badly schoolteachers are paid. Love is seldom, if ever, mentioned. Nor, for that matter, has it been a topic of concern in recent memory.

Granted, the fact that something is not publicly discussed does not render it nonexistent. And yes, some educational practice does enact the kind of love under discussion here. Still, the importance of this love to the well-being of our children and our culture makes it imperative that we talk about it freely and evaluate it critically. Only then will love's place in education and education's place in love be discerned. Only then can differing conceptions of what constitutes this love be aired and tested. Only then can love's practice be improved and extended. Only then can we forestall the equally tempting perversions of overprotectiveness and overindulgence. Needless to say, public discussion is not a foolproof defense against distortions of love. Yet if breaking the taboo against linking love and education does nothing more than help us to distinguish the genuine article from harmful facsimiles, it will have proved its worth.

According to our education-gender system, since love is properly housed in the private home and family and education is located in the world of work, politics, and the professions, the gap in the public discourse is to be expected. But even if this system was once adequate, it no longer is. It rests on an outdated conception of home and workplace—namely that the norm is the two-parent household in which Father goes out to work and Mother stays home with the children.

I stress that in our obsolete education-gender system home was the designated provider and teacher of love[34] because one unforeseen result of those late twentieth century transformations is that a domestic vacuum now exists in many, many children's lives.[35] By this I do not simply mean that for much of the day, no adult is at home. I mean, rather, that even if at one time it could justifiably have been taken for granted that home provides children with the loving environment they need for both learning and living in the world with others[36]—which is what the education-gender system assumed—it cannot now be. Nor can it any longer be assumed—that is, if it ever should have been—that home helps children learn to enact this love as they mature.

Calling home and school partners in the education of this or any nation's young, in *The Schoolhome* I proposed that school share responsibility for home's domestic curriculum: in particular, that our schoolhouses become sites in which love constitutes both the backdrop of teaching and a goal of education. What I did not say enough about in *The Schoolhome* is that school and home are but two of society's educational agents. This needs to be acknowledged; for another by-product of our changed lives is that there is no longer a wall of separation between home and world.

Our education-gender system pictures home as a safe haven from an impersonal, combative, and frequently cruel world. Even if this portrayal was once accurate—and we know that it was not universally so—it no longer is. In many homes today domestic violence, child sexual abuse, or both are facts of life. Furthermore, the electronic media have become ensconced in the nation's homes, while at the same time children now tend to leave home each day for large chunks of time. Were the electronic media dedicated to the form of love whose object is the growth and development of the nation's young, it might make no difference that children spend hours daily in their company. Were the world outside home educative, it might not matter that children as well as adults now move freely around in it. But the truth is that the electronic media show little concern for the welfare of the children whose homes they have entered, and the world in which children now roam freely is miseducative in the extreme.

In the 1980s the all-consuming concern of public discourse about education was the West's cultural heritage. Are our schools neglecting to pass it down? Are women's studies, African-American studies, and other new areas of knowledge elbowing the great achievements of the past out of the curriculum? Is not Shakespeare far superior to Toni Morrison? Does not Beethoven's music exist on a higher plain than jazz? Participants in the "culture wars" did not mention that the western heritage—indeed, any culture's heritage—is composed of enormous quantities of stock, some of which constitute the culture's assets or wealth and some of which represent its liabilities. They failed to note that the wall between home and world that was supposed to protect children from acquiring those liabilities was collapsing. They refused to see how reckless, if not downright irresponsible, it is to take for granted that the next generation's growth and development are proceeding apace.

In *Cultural Miseducation* I substituted a democratic concept of culture for the narrow idea of "high" culture that has tended to dominate educational discourse. It is broad enough to cover the contributions of all members of society over the whole range of contexts and also to include a culture's liabilities as well as its assets. In that book I also developed a concept of educational agency that includes school and home, as well as church, neighborhood, police and fire departments, museums, historical societies, libraries, and archives; zoos, parks, playgrounds, aquariums, and arboretums; symphony orchestras, record clubs, recording companies, ballet troops, and opera houses; banks, businesses, and the stock market; newspapers, magazines, book clubs, bookstores, publishing houses; sports organizations, billboards, government agencies, the military establishment, nonprofit organizations, and environmental groups; TV, the Internet, and the media in all its multitudinous forms; and the myriad other institutions of society that pass down the culture's stock and in the process educate young and old.

Look at education from a cultural perspective in which both culture and educational agency are broadly understood and one begins to see that society's many educational agents are passing down to its children some horrendous portions of cultural stock. Racism, war, the sexual abuse of children, rape, kidnapping, murder, homelessness, gangsterism, terrorism: Even as I write, my daily newspaper carries headlines about these cultural liabilities and others, too.

The truth is that we can no longer assume—once again, perhaps we never could assume this to be true—that home is children's primary provider and teacher of love or that home all by itself is capable of blocking the inheritance of cultural liabilities that stunt the next generation's healthy development. Accordingly, just as one vital question for public discussion is "Who is going to provide and teach this form of love?" an equally important and difficult one is "How are we as a culture going to enact the love whose object is the growth and development of children so as to protect our young from the miseducative society that their elders have created?" One step in the process of stanching the flow of cultural liabilities must be to hold the whole range of the culture's educators accountable for their miseducative behavior. To do this it is necessary to acknowledge the multiple character of educational agency. How can we accuse, e.g., the various media of miseducating our young if we do not even recognize that they are educational agents?

It is also necessary to reject the tacit assumption that the kind of love whose object is the growth and development of children is a private matter. Consider love a strictly private affair—where "private" is contrasted with "public"—and all those educational agents now based in the so-called public world are by definition exempt from its demands. Instead of being guided by this love, they remain free to be as miseducative as they wish. Consider it a private affair—where "private" is taken to mean "belonging to me, not you"—and instead of all children being the objects of any given individual's love, its range of application will be limited to that person's own offspring.

Gilman's greatest contribution to educational thought may well have been her vision of a twofold distribution of the love whose object is the growth and development of children.[37] This love is to be distributed to all adults, whether or not they are biological mothers; and each adult is to direct this love to all children. As each adult in Herland dedicates herself to the welfare of all children and not just those whose biological parent she is, so must the adults of our land.

No cultural liabilities will subvert the love that Herland's adults have for children, since these do not exist in the educative utopia Gilman envisioned. The fact that stories about them are never told in Herland in turn means that Gilman did not have to take a position on the issue of censorship. In contrast, Plato, whose utopian state was also designed to exclude cultural liabilities, seemed to think that the best way to rid society of these was to censor stories about them. "Shall we then carelessly allow the children to hear any kind of stories composed by anybody?" Socrates asks in the *Republic*. Assured that they should not, he says: "Then we must first of all . . . control the story tellers. Whatever noble story they compose we shall select, but a bad one we must reject. Then we shall persuade nurses and mothers to tell their children those we have selected and . . . the majority of the stories they now tell must be thrown out."[38]

At odds with the ideals and principles of an open, democratic society, Plato's program of censorship is based on a faulty epistemology. Attributing infallibility to the rulers of Plato's Just State, Socrates takes it for granted that their decisions about which stories to eliminate and which to promote could not be mistaken. However, as Rousseau pointed out in reference to La Fontaine's fable "The Crow and the Fox," we can never be sure in advance what moral will be drawn from even the most moralistic story.[39] Moreover, as John Stuart Mill argued in *On Liberty*, no matter how rational and how well educated a human being is, every single one of us is fallible. Given this brute fact of human existence, no one can know for certain that the stories deemed harmful really are or if those deemed beneficial are not really harmful. Nor can anyone be sure that beliefs we think are true—even the ones we feel absolutely certain about—are not partly or wholly false.[40]

Actually, the misgivings about storytelling that Socrates expresses presuppose a particular conceptualization of storytelling, one that assumes a simple two-way relation between story and child: Child hears story, story injures child. However, parents and teachers regularly convert this *two-way* relation into a *three-way* relation: Child hears story *as it is mediated by an adult who has the child's growth and development at heart*. Adults have always acted as mediators between stories and children. We do it when we explain or clarify or elaborate on some aspect of a story. We do it when we allay a child's fears of the villain of the piece or draw out a story's moral or simply say to the child, "It's just pretend."

There is a certain irony here. Although Plato wanted his utopia to be educative rather than miseducative, he detached stories from their pedagogical contexts. Attributing harmful powers to stories in themselves, he called for their removal from society. Today's technological "advances" tend to confirm this view of the matter. A child sitting in front of a television screen, looking at pornography on the Internet, or playing a computer game is all too likely to be in a direct, unmediated relation with whatever scary or violent or lascivious or racist or misogynist story the electronic medium happens to be telling. Yet this two-way relation is not engraved in stone. The story–child relation can be turned into a mediated *three-way* relation that vitiates the story's power over the child.

I should say, all this can happen provided we distribute the love whose object is the growth and development of children across the whole population and join to it the skills required to mediate harmful stories. It is of course possible to mediate stories in ways that stunt children's growth and development. But if adults who are motivated by love possess the appropriate mediating skills, and if children are taught to deconstruct for themselves and their peers the stories passed down to them, our young can be protected from this perversion of the mediating role. It is a commonplace that critical thinking should be one of the goals of schooling. How seldom it is proposed that the critical thinking taught in schools should be directed at the print and electronic media! Yet what better way to dilute the power of the stories these educational agents tell than to teach adults to mediate them for children and to teach children to become their own story mediators!

One good thing to do with a hidden curriculum when you find one is to insert it into the overt curriculum or "curriculum proper."[41] My proposal that children become their own story mediators recommends just this, for the cultural liabilities that so many stories pass down to the next generation constitute a hidden curriculum in violence, racism, and the like. Turn the stories—or perhaps their harmful aspects—into a bona fide subject of study. At the same time distribute the habits of enacting and teaching this kind of love across the whole range of the culture's educational agents. Then we should be well on our way to closing the love gap not only in the educational text but in education itself.

Obviously, acts of love—be they the mediation of the stories children are told, the insertion of the harmful stories and their messages into the curriculum proper, or holding accountable the offending educational agents—will not by themselves rid society of the liabilities that threaten the growth and development of children. Obviously, no matter how many acts of love one might list, love is not enough. Yet one ironic consequence of the love gap in the education text is that we do not really know the strengths and limitations of love when it is distributed across the whole population of adults and children and also made both a precondition of teaching and an overarching aim of education. It behooves us to find out.

CHAPTER 2

Loving Teacher Education

LISA S. GOLDSTEIN

Introduction

The title of this chapter seems ambiguous. Will this chapter be about a form of teacher education that is rooted in love—LOVING teacher education? Will it be about a form of teacher education aimed at the preparation of loving teachers—LOVING TEACHER education? Will it be about a form of teacher education so rich and rewarding that preservice teachers enrolled in such programs will find themselves loving TEACHER EDUCA-TION? Will it be about a form of teacher education structured in ways that allow us teacher educators to acknowledge our feelings for our students, our work, and our field and to reveal the emotional energy that we pour into teacher education?

The answer to all of these questions is yes. In this chapter I describe a model of love-based teacher education that is grounded in scholarship on love[1] and caring.[2] This model is designed with the intent of educating pre-service students to be loving teachers and should be enacted by modeling loving teaching and by supporting preservice teachers in loving ways. Ideally this model will enable teacher educators to reconnect with the power-ful, sustaining emotions that drew us into teaching so many years ago.

Influenced by the growing obsession with student outcomes on state-wide standardized tests, teacher education has grown increasingly technocratic as accountability, standards, and measurable outcomes have replaced more hu-manistic and nuanced concerns in the preparation of professional educators.

This erosion of compassionate, responsive approaches to teacher preparation has had a direct impact on the nature of the programs we offer our preservice teachers. Arnstine writes:

> Teacher preparation programs are designed to deliver a predetermined curriculum that fulfills credential requirements in a short period of time. They use a system of competitive grading that reassures the rest of the campus that teacher education is academically respectable. Thus, prospective teachers are encouraged to obey authority and to work alone and independently. When school experiences consistently call for obedience and competition, even the most obvious possibilities for acting in a rational and caring way go unrecognized.[3]

Interestingly, as these rigid mandates and trends have been reshaping the lives of children in U.S. public schools and of preservice teachers in our teacher education programs, there has been a growing interest in caring's role in educational contexts. Beginning around the time that *A Nation at Risk*[4] was published and intensifying as other conservative policy documents were being published through the 1990s, this emphasis on caring can be interpreted as a strategy for relieving the tension, pressure, isolation, and competition that accompany our devotion to test scores, outcomes, and measurable achievement.

Many textbooks focused on the creation of caring classroom contexts have been published for use in teacher education courses: *Teaching Children to Care*,[5] *Among Friends: Classrooms Where Caring and Learning Prevail*,[6] *Curriculum of Love*,[7] and *The Caring Teacher's Guide to Discipline*,[8] to name just a few. These texts aim to offer preservice teachers tools for establishing management procedures and classroom practices that will lead to the development of a shared sense of belonging, warmth, connection, and community in their future public school classrooms.

Despite this, there has been little attention paid to the creation of caring educational contexts within teacher education programs themselves. A handful of scholars have attempted to incorporate strategies that enhance caring attitudes in their work with preservice and practicing teachers.[9] Nel Noddings, the preeminent scholarly voice on caring, developed a theoretical model of teacher education;[10] Rogers and Webb elaborated upon that model.[11] This dearth of theorizing and research suggests that much work remains to be done in the area of caring approaches to teacher education. In this chapter I hope to begin a much-needed conversation about the creation of caring educational contexts within teacher education programs. To do so, I outline a three-part model, which draws upon the work of Nel Noddings, Robert Sternberg, and Robert Fried[12] and offers commitment, community, and passion as the cornerstones of a caring approach to teacher education.

In the educational research literature, *caring* is the term most commonly associated with the range of feelings, experiences, and relations this model brings to the field. In my work, however, I have often opted to use the word *love* rather than *caring*.[13] Love feels right to me. When I read my teaching journals from my days as an elementary school teacher, references to love abound and references to caring are few. Teachers often speak about loving their students, but scholars who write about teachers and teaching have shied away from using that term themselves.

Because my goal is to envision a form of teacher education that models and prepares preservice teachers for the emotional depth and intensity of life in classrooms with students, it seems that love is the most honest and most accurate term to use. Though this requires flying in the face of scholarly norms, offering preservice teachers anything less than love would underprepare them for their chosen careers.

Three Cornerstones of Loving Teacher Education

Psychologist Robert Sternberg has conceptualized a model of love that I believe holds great promise for the creation of a love-based teacher education program.[14] Although it was designed to depict the dimensions of adult–adult loving relationships, Sternberg's model of love is very flexible. With a few definitional modifications, I have used this model elsewhere with great success to delineate the contours of teacherly love, and I expect that Sternberg's model will be equally useful in offering a framework within which to consider the reconceptualization of teacher education.

Sternberg calls his model "the triangular theory of love" and suggests that love can be understood in terms of three components—commitment, intimacy, and passion—that form the three sides of a triangle (see Figure 2.1).

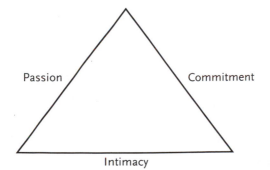

Figure 2.1

Commitment, in Sternberg's view, entails both the decision to love someone and the commitment to maintain that love; intimacy describes "the close, connected, and bonded feelings in loving relationships";[15] and passion is "the drives that lead to romance, physical attraction, sexual consummation and the like."[16]

Sternberg's three components of love—commitment, intimacy, and passion—defined in ways more relevant to our professional context form the cornerstones of loving teacher education. In this new model of teacher education, commitment is grounded in the fundamental responsibility of teacher educators and preservice teachers to enter into loving relationships with their students; intimacy is writ large and transformed into intimacy-in-community, leading to the creation of a community of learners sharing close personal connection; and passion is linked to efforts to ensure that our preservice teacher education students see the connections between love and the intellectual and curricular aspects of teaching children.

Cornerstone 1: Commitment

It is important at the outset to make a distinction between the commitment cornerstone of this model and the ways in which the word *commitment*" is generally used when talking about teachers' loving practices.[17] For example, Hargreaves synthesizes a body of literature and writes about caring, which is "interpreted as the interpersonal experience of human nurturance, connectedness, warmth, and love,"[18] as a central, pervasive commitment widely shared by elementary teachers. This commitment to the "gentle smiles and warm hugs"[19] view of caring is only a small part of what the commitment cornerstone of this model represents.

The commitment cornerstone of the model emerges directly from Nel Noddings's theories of the ethic of care. In Noddings's view, caring is not a personality trait, but a relation.[20] Noddings posits that every interaction provides us with the opportunity to enter into a caring relationship. As a result, each person stands at the same decision-making juncture many times each day and faces a choice: Will I approach this interaction as a caring encounter or will I not? Will I meet the other as one-caring? For Noddings, caring is a human obligation and the choice is clear: "One must meet the other in caring. From this requirement there is no escape for one who would be moral."[21]

Building on Noddings's ideas, then, loving teachers must make a commitment to meeting their students as one-caring, to approaching their interactions with their students as opportunities to engage in caring encounters. The central purpose of teacher education rooted in Noddings's ideas would be to develop in our preservice teachers the disposition to commit to meeting children as one-caring. Thus, commitment is a cornerstone of loving teacher education.

In order for preservice teachers to come to understand the importance of making a commitment to loving teaching, it will be necessary for teacher educators to do more than lecture about Noddings's theories: We must model those desired attitudes and behaviors. In other words, loving teacher educators must make a commitment to meeting their preservice teacher education students as one-caring, to approaching their interactions with their students as opportunities to engage in caring encounters. Because "caring is a way of being in relation, not a set of specific behaviors,"[22] there is a wide range of pedagogical strategies that would work well within this model of teacher education, including Noddings's suggestions of modeling, dialogue, practice, and confirmation (Noddings, 1986).[23]

There has been little scholarly attention focused on the nature of the caring relationships between university professors and their students or on the role of caring in teaching and learning in higher education.[24] However, I suspect that most teacher educators will acknowledge that the teacherly love we feel for our preservice teacher education candidates is very much akin to the more widely acknowledged teacherly love we felt for our young students when we were classroom teachers.[25] Teacherly love comes along with the pedagogical relationship and has little to do with the age of the students or with the material being taught.

It might seem that the commitment cornerstone is an unrealistic expectation and an unattainable goal. Is it possible to maintain a commitment to meeting all students as one-caring? What happens when teachers encounter a student they just do not like? Noddings makes a distinction between natural caring and ethical caring that eases this pressure. Central to this distinction is the foundational belief that caring is not a feeling that one either has or does not have, but that caring is a relation that one chooses to enter into or not. Even if a teacher or teacher educator does not have spontaneous personal or social attraction toward a student, she or he is still capable of making a professional decision to meet that student in a caring manner. Natural caring is "that relation in which we respond as one-caring out of love or natural inclination."[26] In cases of natural caring, "I must" is indistinguishable from "I want." This is an ethical ideal that undergirds Noddings's model.

There are many times, of course, when natural caring does not occur, times when the "I must" that accompanies the commitment to meet others as one-caring is not aligned with the "I want" rooted within the individual. Noddings acknowledges that there are many times when the "I must" whispers faintly and disappears and is then followed by the clamor of resistance.[27] In these cases, a second sentiment—"I ought"—is paired with "I must" to elicit a caring response. This "I ought" is a moral sentiment that compels the one-caring to enter a caring relation. The one-caring, in these cases, is motivated to respond not by natural caring feelings, but by her desire to be moral and her commitment to meet others with care: Responding as one-caring is an act of volition, a conscious choice stemming from a moral aspiration. Noddings refers to this type of caring as ethical caring, since it is driven by an ethical ideal.

Though it requires an effort not needed in natural caring, ethical caring is not a diminished form of caring, nor is it less authentic than natural caring. Both natural and ethical caring require engrossment, receptivity, and motivational displacement on the part of the one-caring; both natural caring and ethical caring begin with a sense of responsibility—"I must"—and with the commitment to meet others as one-caring; both natural and ethical caring encounters move the one-caring and the cared-for closer to the ethical ideal; and both are sources of great joy and satisfaction. The difference between the two is linked to issues of motive: Natural caring is driven by deep feelings for the cared-for; ethical caring is driven by the one-caring's desire to enhance her ethical ideal, her vision of herself as a moral person, or in the case of teaching, by the one-caring's professional commitment to teaching with these principles in mind.

The commitment cornerstone demands a great deal of consistency, continuity, and affiliation to these ideas throughout a program aligned with this loving model. Teacher education programs host a range of nested and overlapping relational milieus of remarkable complexity, each a site rich with possibilities for loving teaching–learning interactions: Teacher education professors care for their preservice teacher education students, who in turn care for the children in their field placement classrooms; cooperating teachers care for both the preservice teacher education students and the young students in their classrooms, and so on. If any of the links in this chain of love are weak, if any of the educators do not model a commitment to meeting their students as one-caring, the overall impact of the program will be compromised.

Cornerstone 2: Intimacy-in-Community

Applying the intimacy dimension of Sternberg's triangular theory of love to the process of teacher education requires some sleight of hand, given that intimacy generally occurs on a fairly small scale and teacher education does not. In this new model of teacher education, intimacy will still represent those "close, connected, and bonded feelings"[28] that are found in loving relationships, but the concept must be writ large enough to move from a one-on-one setting to the sort of large-scale intimacy that is impossible to imagine occurring anywhere but in a classroom. I think of this phenomenon as intimacy-in-community.

Like intimacy as it is commonly understood, intimacy-in-community embodies trust, the sharing of meaningful experiences, a degree of mutuality and reciprocity among participants, a commitment to open communication, and depth of feeling. Unlike typical intimacy, a relation that necessitates a small number of participants, intimacy-in-community requires a large group of people sharing a common experience. In recent educational literature, intimacy-in-community is most often referred to as "creating a community of learners" or "creating a caring community in the classroom." Although the term *intimacy-in-community* elegantly captures the meaning I intend, in order to keep my new model of teacher education in line with current educational parlance, I will refer to this cornerstone simply as *community*.

The term *community* has a wide range of meanings. Even within the field of education, community can mean many different things.[29] For our purposes, the community cornerstone will be defined in ways that align with the idea of a learning community. The characteristics of learning communities have been enumerated in many different contexts, and though the lists differ in detail, they are similar in overall effect.

The learning communities in the Fostering Communities of Learners (FCL) project developed and described by Ann Brown are characterized by agency, reflection, collaboration, and "a culture of learning, negotiating, sharing, and producing work that is displayed to others."[30] The communities emerging from the National Coalition for Equality in Learning (NCEL) believe in the importance of all individuals, create collective goals that are the center of school and classroom life, share responsibility for learning and teaching, and are guided by a concern for the common good of the classroom and the school community.[31] Sapon-Shevin characterizes a learning community as evidencing security, open communication, mutual liking, shared goals or objectives, and connectedness and trust.[32]

Membership in a community of learners has been determined to be an important factor in children's successful educational experiences. By extension, it would be safe to assume that membership in a community of learners would also be an important factor in preservice teachers' successful educational experiences. The benefits of membership in a learning community—being valued, supported, challenged, and encouraged and doing the same for others; having a safe place to ask questions and to take the risk of answering questions; knowing others well and being known and respected by them in turn—are as delightful to adults as to children and are likely to create classroom atmospheres conducive to learning and growth regardless of the age of the learners involved. Because of the close connections between the ideals of a learning community and the nature of caring encounters, the community cornerstone plays a key role in this new model of teacher education.

Interestingly, the role of community in preservice teacher education has been underexplored in the research literature. In their work on the impact of membership in "educative communities" on the development of reflective preservice teachers, Bullough and Gitlin discuss the importance of establishing organizational "structures which encourage more collective relations and action."[33] They advocate placing preservice teachers into cohort groups that remain together for the duration of their teacher education program and then clustering cohort members at selected school sites for their field placements in order to provide cohort members with on-going opportunity for dialogue and exploration.

However, Oja, Diller, Corcoran, and Andrew warn that "popular references to 'cohort' groups in teacher education sometimes mean no more than sharing a common date for program matriculation."[34] They argue instead for an approach to teacher education that hinges on the creation of communities of support and inquiry. These communities, Oja et al. contend, must be deliberately planned and thoughtfully integrated into the philosophy of the teacher education program in order to be effective.

It is surprising that there has been so little research focused explicitly on community in teacher education, particularly in light of the large number of textbooks available for use with preservice teachers that focus on the creation of caring learning communities with children. These texts are rooted in the belief that the preservice teachers who use the books will graduate and become teachers who will be predisposed and prepared to create caring communities with the children in their classrooms. It is easy to assume, then, that the course instructors who assign these textbooks and who have these goals for their preservice teacher education students would be likely to model these practices with the students. Perhaps they are doing so and are not researching and documenting their practices.

It is also surprising that so little attention has been paid to community in teacher education because so much attention has been paid to issues of community in teachers' working lives and in the culture of schooling. Fullan and Hargreaves decry the current state of professional community in schools and call for teachers and principals to fight for the creation of cultures of collaboration instead.[35] They argue that schools characterized by a strong sense of professional community are workplaces that "create, sustain, and motivate good teachers throughout their careers."[36]

Westheimer describes two specific types of teacher professional community—liberal and collective—and documents teachers' experiences working within each of these types of professional communities.[37] Sergiovanni, McLaughlin, Merz, and Furman and many other scholars who focus on teachers' work and teacher culture also point to the many ways that community takes shape within and offers shape to teachers' professional lives.[38]

It seems, then, that being part of a loving community of learners during preservice teacher education would not only offer our students the benefits of membership in a learning community and allow us to model the practices we want our students to be able to engage in with their students in the future; it would also prepare our students to participate in the kind of professional communities that will sustain them and offer them growth opportunities throughout their teaching careers. These are compelling arguments for the community cornerstone of this new model of teacher education.

What would community look like in a teacher education program? I suspect this might be the wrong question to ask. Community is made manifest less in the institutional arrangements of a program than in the nature of the interactions and relations among the people involved. Like many teacher educators, I have been involved in professional development school projects and other endeavors that purported to be collaborative, caring communities of one kind or another; while they may have appeared to be so on paper or on the surface, they did not feel like collaborative, caring communities to everyone involved and failed miserably as a result.

Perhaps a better question to ask would be "What would community feel like in a teacher education program?" Like caring, community is a relation. Community is enacted, community is built, and community is experienced by those involved in the process. The best that teacher educators can hope to do is to create favorable conditions for the creation of community and then work to nurture its growth.

Cornerstone 3: Passion

Sternberg defines passion, the third component of his triangular theory of love, as "the drives that lead to romance, physical attraction, sexual consummation and the like."[39] If we use this definition, passion has little place in a teacher education context. However, when viewed through a different lens, passion becomes a perfectly logical component of a teacher education program. Passion is a term frequently associated with a teacher's love for ideas, for teaching, and for students;[40] passion is what separates the great teachers from the forgettable ones.[41] This understanding of passion is the third cornerstone of this new approach to teacher education.

One of my goals in this model of teacher education is to foreground the ways in which love is connected to the curricular and instructional aspects of teaching and to the intellectual energy and expertise that teachers bring to the work they do with children. Unfortunately, the research literature on caring teaching offers little to support that goal. The empirical literature indicates that caring is generally associated with the affective and interpersonal aspects of classroom life and rarely connected to curriculum or instructional practices.[42]

There are a few notable exceptions. McCall offers a case study of a student teacher who enacted child-centered pegagogies and made specific curricular decisions that she felt would nurture and support her students.[43] Similarly, Rogers tells of a fourth-grade teacher who engaged students in carefully chosen, meaningful learning activities because of her belief that "part of caring is providing kids with interesting and challenging things to do."[44] And, as I have pointed out elsewhere, primary grade teacher Martha George's commitment to loving her students shapes her curricular decision-making.[45]

There is agreement that a view of caring teaching that emphasizes interpersonal relations and downplays curriculum, instruction, and classroom management is problematic and must be addressed and remedied. The purpose of the passion cornerstone of this new model of teacher education is to replace erroneous beliefs about loving teaching with a powerful set of understandings about the fundamental connections between love and the intellectual aspects of teachers' work. The literature on passionate teaching offers descriptions and theorizing that elegantly capture the power, the strength, and the joy the characterize the intellectual sides of loving teaching; I intend to draw on this work in developing a representation of the passion cornerstone of the new model.

The foremost expert on passion in teaching is Robert Fried.[46] An advocate of school reform strategies aimed at inspiring, engaging, and motivating students, Fried points to passionate teachers and passionate teaching as the essential elements in the equation. He writes: "To be a passionate teacher is to be someone in love with a field of knowledge, deeply stirred by issues and ideas that challenge our world, drawn to the dilemmas and potentials of the young people who come into class each day."[47] Fried asserts that "it is this quality of caring about ideas and values, this fascination with the potential for growth within people, this depth and fervor about doing things well and striving for excellence"[48] that sets the passionate teachers apart from the rest of their profession.

In describing ways that teachers can be passionate, Fried models the kind of passionate engagement he talks about:

> You can be passionate about your field of knowledge: in love with the poetry of Emily Dickinson or the prose of Marcus Garvey; dazzled by the spiral of DNA or the swirl of van Gogh's cypresses; intrigued by the origins of the Milky Way or the demise of the Soviet empire; delighted by the sound of Mozart or the sonority of French vowels; a maniac for health and fitness or wild about algebraic word problems. . . .[49]

Fried writes that *"Passion is not just a personality trait that some people have and others lack, but rather something discoverable, teachable, and reproducible."*[50] This belief about passion makes it ideal for inclusion in the new model of teacher education: We can tell students that passion is a critically important component of good teaching, and in the same breath we can assure them that passion can—and will—be discovered and learned by each of them.

Fried goes on to describe two key features of the "passionate craft of teaching." I include them in detail here because this passage captures the very heart of the passion cornerstone:

> Passionate teachers organize and focus their passionate interests *by getting to the heart to their subject* and sharing with their students some of what lies there—the beauty and power that drew them to this field in the first place and that has deepened over time as they have learned and experienced more. . . . Passionate teachers *convey their passion* to novice learners—their students—*by acting as partners in learning*, rather than as experts in the field. As partners, they invite less experienced learners to search for knowledge and insightful experiences, and they build confidence and competence among students who might otherwise choose to sit back and watch their teacher do and say interesting things.[51]

engage

Fried has linked the teacher's intellectual passion and curricular goals with his/her desire to share meaningful, pleasurable experiences with students and to bond with them in creative, productive learning partnerships; this perfectly exemplifies practices of loving teachers.

From the perspective of this new model, what I find most powerful about Fried's understanding of passion is its remarkable parallel to a key feature of Noddings' understanding of caring. Because of the unique ways in which these scholars have defined their terms, both passion and caring can be taught. This has tremendous implications for teacher education. Other definitions of caring and passion turn those terms into personality traits, attitudes, temperaments, dispositions that a student either has or lacks. In programs using definitions of that sort, teacher educators are left to stand by and watch the very caring and highly passionate students succeed and watch the less caring and less passionate students struggle and fail.

In a teacher education program rooted in Noddings' and Fried's definitions of caring and passion, students can learn to think of caring as a relation rather than a personality trait and can learn about the commitment that caring teachers make to meet their students as one-caring. Similarly, students can learn to connect with their intellectual passions and can learn to let those passions shine forth in their teaching. Because Noddings and Fried see caring and passion as teachable, all preservice teachers willing to learn should be able to succeed.

Jim Garrison argues that the cultivation of eros, or passionate desire, should be the supreme aim of teacher education.[52] Although I am hesitant to offer prescriptive guidelines as to how the new "cornerstones approach" to teacher education should be enacted, Maxine Greene offers a view of passionate teaching so magnificent that I cannot help but include it here.

Greene not only describes passionate teaching in this passage, but also embodies and depicts it:

> All we can do is speak with others as passionately and eloquently as we can; all we can do is to look into each other's eyes and urge each other on to new beginnings. Our classrooms ought to be nurturing and thoughtful and just all at once; they ought to pulsate with multiple conceptions of what it is to be human and alive. They ought to resound with the voices of articulate young people in dialogues always incomplete because there is always more to be discovered and more to be said. We must want our students to achieve friendship as each one stirs to wide-awakeness, to imaginative action, and to renewed consciousness of possibility.[53]

If we can create educational contexts for our preservice teachers that approximate the image Greene has presented, the passion cornerstone will be well modeled.

A Few Closing Thoughts

The commitment, community, and passion cornerstones of this new loving model are simply that: cornerstones. Any teacher education program wishing to apply this model in its institutional context would need to start with the cornerstones as a foundation and then build its own framework upon them.

This perspective on implementation emerges directly from Noddings' theories. Caring is a relation that is contextual, situated, and specific. The one-caring must act toward the cared-fors in ways that are governed not by rules but by the particular needs of those receiving care. Therefore, each institution with the desire to create a love-centered teacher education program must create a program that builds on these cornerstones in unique ways and meets the particular needs of the institution and its students. The cornerstones form an open-ended, flexible model that should be applied in many different ways in response to the varied needs and demands of specific teacher education programs in particular contexts; each time a teacher education program is organized around these cornerstones, an unique program will be created.

I want to mention clearly that this triangular model of loving teacher education is meant to be a tool for organizing our thoughts and not a template for limiting or constricting our thinking. Although the model is neat and orderly, with its three distinct sections, teacher education is not. For the sake of clarity, I have addressed each cornerstone in turn. But that division is artificial and arbitrary to a certain extent and fails to capture the interconnectedness and complexity of the teacher education process.

Although I would love to claim that commitment, community, and passion can be combined in a model that will work for everyone in every context, I am resisting the temptation to write a victory narrative featuring swooping angels playing trumpets and singing the praises of this approach to teacher preparation. Too many reforms have been touted as the next big thing and have vanished quickly and without a trace. However, I do believe that the principles of commitment, community, and passion, when combined in creative ways by resourceful, dedicated teacher educators, will surely offer preservice teachers a stronger and more powerful foundation than we currently provide. As loving teacher educators, we must be willing to make that effort.

CHAPTER 3

Creating Loving Relations in the Classroom

ELAINE J. O'QUINN
AND JIM GARRISON

We begin our chapter by reference to two stories. One is fictional; one is anecdotal. The first story concerns itself with the adolescent dystopic novel *The Giver* and its notion of societal "Sameness." The second centers on differences in observation that arose between one of the authors, a secondary English Education student-teacher supervisor, and another supervisor who happened to be observing the same student-teacher on the same day. The ensuing discussion invites readers to explore the difference between controlling and loving classroom relations. Our intent is to discuss three dangers inherent in the creation of loving relations, underscore the complexities of conditioning a classroom for those relations, and move on to consider the ways in which the creation of shared meaning can become a part of loving classroom relations. We conclude with a consideration of the "ethos" of love.

A futurist novel with contemporary themes, *The Giver* is about what goes wrong when a society attempts to control every element of its existence in the name of caring for its citizens. It opens as Jonas, the main character, turns twelve. Twelve is the time when children are no longer identified by age and are known instead by their appointed career assignments, something, it could be argued, that comes very close to the tracking system prevalent in our own society.

Because life in Jonas' society has always been predictable, controlled, and one of extreme obedience, that he would be "appointed" a career comes as no surprise to him. That his future should be determined in such a way is expected in a world of standardization, fixed categories, and the virtuous state of what is called "Sameness." Everything from family units, perfect weather, nutritionally correct foods, and drugs to counter any physical or emotional "stirrings" has been officially instituted by the governing body under the guise of protecting its populace from anything harmful or unexpected. Conditions are set to prevent citizens from actions or decisions that might cause upheaval or dissent. The intent is to re-produce society, not re-create it. Jonas' community is so refined in the science of "Sameness" that all disease, grief, pain, and suffering have been erased. Unfortunately, the elimination of the "problematic" imperfections of life has also eradicated meaningful pleasures. Animals, color, and sound are now nonexistent, as are feelings of joy, pleasure, contentment, and, most of all, love. Eliminating the undesirable has meant eliminating the desired as well.

In the second story, a student teacher sits with two supervisors who have just observed her tenth-grade literature class. It does not usually happen that two supervisors are present at one time, but the student teacher appears comfortable with the situation and, it is learned later, is excited to share her teaching experience with others. As one supervisor sits thinking about the least threatening way to begin the conversation, the other decides, perhaps after wondering the same thing, to just jump in. He starts by telling the student teacher how much he "hates" the desk arrangement in the classroom. Using such words as *hides* and *covers* and *undermines*, he makes a case for never having a situation where the teacher cannot see all students at all times, thereby eliminating the possibility of anyone being "off-task" or out of the teacher's authoritative "control." Configuring desks in the current manner, he says, means there will always be some students outside the teacher's scope of vision. The other supervisor mentally registers that her notes say the exact opposite thing. In fact, she has made a point of voicing her pleasure at seeing the desks moved out of traditional rows, of allowing students the opportunity to make their own decisions about how they will conduct themselves in community. Not only is the student teacher squirming a bit, so is the second supervisor.

Moving next to a list of "behavioral" problems that he has noted—one student passing around hand cream, another doodling, all of them speaking out answers instead of raising hands—the first supervisor moves in for the kill. He tells the student teacher that the lesson itself was flawed in that she was allowing for student interpretations of the text that were not informed up front by historical/contextual material. Therefore, insights students had to the text were largely "irrelevant" and allowed them to make comments that were "completely" off base and, in some cases, downright "silly." The suggestion is that future pieces of literature need to be contextualized and historicized BEFORE they are read rather than after, to avoid "meaningless" interpretations motivated by the students' limited experiences. And, he continues, did anyone else happen to notice the boy in the back holding hands with girls on both sides of him? "I know students," says the supervisor, "and that one is trouble." With that, he asks for the student teacher's signature and says he has to go.

What we would like to call to your attention in both of these stories is what happens to a community of people who are placed in controlling rather than creative relation with each other. In both stories, the very possibility of a "loving" relation is immediately defined by conditions imposed from without, insisting on a purity and perfection that are not only impossible, but inauthentic, stifling, and brutal as well. In *The Giver*, the government mandates each aspect of society under the erroneous assumption that in doing so, nothing harmful or hurtful will befall its citizens. What it fails to realize is the deadening consequence of a world focused on correctness and conformity.

In the case of the supervisor's remarks to the student teacher, any spark of originality, any flicker of spontaneity, any flare of possibility is quickly snuffed out by a top-down hierarchy that immediately assumes authority of the supervisor over the student teacher. Dialogue ceases, listening is one-way, and negotiation is not presented as an option. The primary relation among those who are different from each other quickly becomes an exclusively cognitive, knowing one, closed to the nuance of imagination and blind to the intuitions of emotional, moral, and aesthetic perception. Knowledge without imaginative perception cannot see creative possibility, while passionate perception without knowledge cannot cognize the constructs of actual contexts or execute well-conceived plans of action. In the case of the supervisor, he believes he knows the student teacher's problems, the students' problems, and the important issues of what he perceives as wrong in the teaching/learning process. While he may succeed in his authority, he fails in any desire he may have had to encourage the student teacher to develop her own ideas and insights, much less her own creative teaching style. The only "assurance" he gives is that her methods are improper and will never work and that students can only learn when they are subtly controlled and manipulated.

The kind of loving relation that declares itself solely through condition and assertion of its own will abandons all but the most repressive and controlling forms of caring, doing, and being. Driven by its fears rather than choosing to face them, this kind of relation stunts its own growth in its refusal to accept what it does not know or may not understand. Parties at both ends refuse risk, deny vulnerability, and cease to explore possibilities; in the end, a stagnating cistern of judgment and rejection caps what was once the creative flow of passionate, loving desire (eros). Anyone who has ever been locked in a relation that demands through restriction rather than encourages through openness understands the dynamic quite well. Rather than harmonizing meaning, this relation sets up false divides based on either/or interpretations. Instead of considering the needs, desires, and expressions of others, it insists on confronting them with demands for conformity. It touts an anti-democratic authority and control as means of love and care.

Because it does not allow for the spontaneous creation of meaning through dialogue and mutual inquiry, a controlling relation has no chance of being a truly loving one. It is mired in the stale notion that coming to understanding can only be accomplished through rigorous reference to that which is known, looking always backward even in its claim to be looking forward. The kind of loving relation we would like to address cannot afford to become stuck in the loop of "might and right." It sees that to claim authority, it must give up authority, a difficult but necessary move that does not erase paradox or underestimate problems. Though a loving relation recognizes the necessity for consideration of what has been experienced, is cognitively clear, and is known, it realizes too that relying exclusively or too rigidly on such thinking sometimes traps creative possibility inside predetermined concepts, categories, and standards. It concedes that we create understanding in community by inviting different values and discernments as a way of deepening that understanding. On the other hand, the controlling relation believes understanding must be dictated only by those who already have "the truth," and that acknowledging the actual is always more important than imagining the possible. In doing so, it can categorize and limit, whereas a loving relation is often able to transcend given categories and to open spaces where before none existed.

In the loving relations necessary for creative classrooms, difference is seen as an opportunity to explore rather than as an obstacle to overcome. There is no fear of an emotional or moral "wandering," if you will, for such relation believes that new meanings will certainly be revealed, even if they cannot be completely assimilated. But the controlling relation sees difference as a threat, and so privileges its needs to know "the other" by its own predetermined and inflexible standards that assign meanings rather than creatively transacting them. Once meaning, including the meaning of the ambiguous word *love* is assigned, it no longer has to be negotiated or contested. Of course, what is missing in such reasoning is that meaning is fluid. If it is not carried out in creative, reciprocal relationship, new dangers arise that, we believe, are more serious than the ones that originally needed to be overcome. As with the society Jonas inhabits, the first threat is to the possibilities of love.

After years of analysis, revision, and implementation, there remains a somewhat elusive gap in education concerning issues of otherness, difference, and diversity in race, ethnicity, sexual preference, social class, gender, and so on. The responses to this concern are often conflicted. Those who believe we must know our students well to teach them well insist that we must first know the other if we are to truly teach them. Many, especially postmodernists, counter that in one way or another it is impossible to know others who are truly different from us, leaving us then in a quandary of impossibility. Both of these estranged positions share the assumption that our primary relation to others, and perhaps to existence at large, is solely a cognitive, knowing relation. We believe this is a mistaken notion. Encountering those different from us involves emotional responses and relations, moral perception, and creative imagination as well as knowing responses. Sometimes, we believe, creating *loving* relations can overcome misunderstanding and move people from confrontation to cooperation, whereas pursuing only *cognitive* ones would fail.

At some level, we are all unique and unknowable, even to ourselves. To assume that teachers and students can have successful experiences only if they first "know" each other is to set them up for failure and disappointment. While it is important to strive to know others and ourselves as best we can, it is not solidarity contingent upon prior cognition that always serves us best, but solidarity built upon the creation of meaning and mutual understanding as a consequence of intelligent response and interaction. Recall the second story. We believe that understanding others, the world, and ourselves is a progressive process of creation best carried out in reciprocal relationship with others and not something ultimately discovered as preexisting "in" each other. Of course, there are dangers to the reciprocal creation of meaning, but then all relationships, including the knowing relationship, are dangerous. Often, though, where there is the greatest danger there, too, is the greatest hope and possibility. What we must ask is where lies the greatest danger, and what is at risk in each one?

Creative and loving relations entail complex intuitive, cognitive, and affective interactions. In our estimate, when we bring creativity and loving together, we achieve the most profound kind of relation. This relation does not grow from willful imposition or deliberate exertion of authority. Instead, it is nurtured through thoughtful conditioning rather than through the mere setting of stringent conditions. Conditioning a classroom for the possibility of loving relations requires something quite different from the imposing conditions that stem from expectation of knowing. There is a vast distance between conditioning *for* creative possibility rather than conditioning *to* perform a predetermined task. One is about taking leaps of faith, and the other is about binding ourselves to the false securities of certainty. Anyone who has ever loved or been loved in trust rather than possession will understand the difference.

Many will find the desire to create loving relations between students and teachers romantic nonsense; unnecessary distraction; or, worse, a dangerous liaison. We believe loving relationship is an ideal many teachers embrace and pursue in their daily classroom practice, even if they never name it as such. They do so because they understand that this particular relationship is every bit as fragile as any other intimate relationship that means something to them. We recognize that despite this understanding, the pursuit of loving relations is sometimes an unobtainable ideal; nonetheless, we still believe it can provide guidance to good practice, if we remain alert to its particular perils. To those who fear the dangerous terrain of love and the creation of shared meaning and mutual understanding, we acknowledge their concerns. Yet, we still contend that the tragedies of hyper-rationality lie in the excessive authoritarian ideals of conditioned "Sameness," the impossible expectations of *knowing* another in advance of relationship building, and the manipulation of risk and vulnerability to insure certainty and avoidance of conflict.

Three Dangers to Creating Loving Relations in the Classroom

Before proceeding, we wish to identify and discuss three of the many grave dangers that threaten the creation of loving relationships across differences. Each of these dangers exists in every classroom at all times, even in the most seemingly homogeneous schools, simply because of the traditional ways we have come to construct such spaces. If we add to this the fact that everyone, regardless of apparent similarities, is actually unique and different, the dangers begin to abound. However, we maintain it is possible to navigate these dangers, while using their tensions and paradoxes to create meaning and understanding that were not necessarily there in the beginning. By honoring and respecting difference rather than simply trying to know it, mindlessly control it, or change it, we can foster creative relations. By assuming that our obligation in those relations is to encourage a sense of well-being in the other, we may achieve loving purpose.

The first danger we examine often involves an insistence that love be pure and unsullied; the problem is that pure love considers all that fails to meet its prescribed criteria as dirty, disgusting, and readily discarded. Few can resist the desire to *change* those they love, hoping to make them a better version of themselves. Postmodernists speak of the violence of the reduction of "the other" to the same. Conditional love can thus become a form of violence. Because the teaching task is to *improve* their charges, this admonition makes it especially difficult for teachers to avoid conditional love. Teachers who see their role as requiring them to do something other than improve, change, or remake students may be labeled insubordinate, incompetent, or unprofessional; those who are willing to take the risk of moving beyond such a controlling belief are dangerously vulnerable. If the goal of education is to improve rather than fortify students and teachers, it reproduces an image of love rather than creating an active agent of it. If the unknown and the unknowable are seen as a weakness that needs fixing rather than a strength to build on, or, in a similar fashion, vulnerability is seen as always a weakness rather than a strength, students and teachers alike lose their capacity to evolve past unusual and different events and experiences, instead relinquishing control to the few who claim they can. In its endeavor to indoctrinate meaning and understanding to its own ends rather than encourage it for the benefit of the other, teaching and learning relationships anchored in predetermined conditions will self-destruct. Adventures into relationship are journeys into the unknown, which by their very nature should unveil ignorance and upset dogmas. Such forays exist in a nebulous realm of complexity that often waffles between awe and fear. Conformity and consistency will not insure good or meaningful relation; it is situation, not custom, that determines the best that can come of a thing.

The second danger is the subtle message of school and culture that says we must not accept what we cannot know or even understand. Sometimes we must accept in order to know. If we can accept others, we may engage in creative, even loving, relation from whence knowledge might emerge. Indeed, it is often the case that mutual creation, caring, even loving are conditions of knowledge, accompany it, or even help constitute it. Given the infinite complexity of individuals, there is bound to be some aspect of those we love that we will never know. It is part of the wisdom of love to respect and honor what we cannot understand, much less know. Further, what we do with what presents itself determines the aesthetic beauty and moral worth of our creations. The nurturing of a loving relation may reward us in ways that we will never consciously know. The result of our refusal to accept, at least in part, what we cannot know or understand is continued isolation, antagonistic behavior, hostile reaction, and a wedge driven into the gap of difference rather than the joint creation of a bridge to cross it. Surely knowing and understanding others according to the regulations of our personal or cultural "logic" limits us and allows us to avoid meaningful and transactive relationships with those different from ourselves; unfortunately, it also requires that we avoid creative possibility.

The last danger we look at involves risk and vulnerability. It is our belief that all other relational dangers grow from a desire to uniformly eliminate risk and avoid situations of vulnerability. This danger lies in a petty consistency that seeks to avoid all contradiction, paradox, and irony. When logic and knowing demand unfailing obedience to prescribed and predetermined rules of "right thinking," the demand wars with all other forms of relation and drives them away. Acts performed in the name of "love and care" may produce a violence that would eliminate the very differences we claim to embrace by reducing everything to the same familiar thing. When industry only motivates the relations we seek in the classroom, those relations will lack seriously in invention. As a result, teachers and students abandon the stories they create and live for cultural reproduction of the solitary story society wishes them to live. Those who dare step out of this box risk being vulnerable, first, to themselves and others in unpredictable ways; second, and more predictably, they are vulnerable to those who maintain power and control and who are immediately suspect of any shift in thought and action not institutionally sanctioned. It is certain that risk and vulnerability require unabashed vigilance to forces known, even when accepting the providence that comes with adventuring into the unknown. It is our belief that educational institutions currently manipulate risk and vulnerability to prevent change and preserve the status quo, thus eliminating the creative space required to realize meaning and understanding across differences. Much is lost in such exploitation, and we strongly believe that those concerned with public education must not accept the artificial restraints imposed by such manipulation.

The Complexities of Conditioning a Classroom for Loving Relation

Many teachers mistakenly believe that entirely determining the conditions for loving relation in their classrooms is the same as conditioning a classroom for the possibility of loving relation, so when events or situations arise that suggest something has gone awry, they are, understandably, frustrated and disappointed. Because these teachers frequently see themselves as caring creators of loving conditions, they then tend to think that the individual student is the source of most conflicts, "bad attitudes," or other ill moods that arise. Oftentimes caring accompanies loving; and caring, like loving, has its dangers. Conditional caring commonly accompanies conditional loving. We must guard against both. We believe that many classroom difficulties occur not because of "problematic" students, but because teachers confuse both caring and loving with controlling. Many a relationship has soured quickly in one person's attempt to demonstrate a caring attitude that is actually a controlling one. As we all know, there are some behaviors that stem from a sincere sense of caring that tends to set conditions in advance rather than cultivate and promote their emergence. These are the conducts of care that tend to be subtly manipulative, repressive, and domineering rather than creative, sustaining, and supportive. Unconsciously, they demand much more than they propose, inhibit more than they liberate, and harness more than release energies. Since many of these behaviors stem from the idea that they are "in the student's best interest," it is difficult to see them as the destructive forces they have the potential to be; when they are what drives a particular model of teaching, they diminish rather than invite learning, even though their source is well intended. In the end, what is meant to motivate learning actually blocks it, because it prohibits rather than allows for the paths of unique individuals.

When teachers care, they are sympathetic to individual students but can remain fixed in their own controlling agendas, not seeing that a cognitive response of sympathy is a limiting one that closes them to the deeper, affective response of empathy and compassion required in loving relation. The idea that we can force students to learn if our mechanisms of command and control are for the "right" reasons, that can we force particular conditions, categories, and concepts, is very near to thinking we can force someone to like or love us. We cannot *make* anyone "learn," and a loving relation recognizes why this is a good thing. Refusing to learn simply because we are told it is what we need or must do is the last bastion of a free individual. It allows one to hold out, when the stakes are higher, against the indoctrination of a totalitarian state or community, much like the millions in Hitler's Germany did when they refused to learn, or at least believe, what their schools taught them. We do not condition a classroom for learning by instilling fear of consequences; all that does is set conditions students can either choose to abide by, appear to abide by, or ignore. We condition for learning by encouraging students to debate without fear of estrangement or retribution, by allowing communication that is frank and honest, by providing a climate of comfort and trust rather than stress and distrust. Teachers desiring loving relations with their students understand that relinquishing substantial exhibitions of knowledge, ironically, may be the only way to share it. Surprisingly, a teacher's love and mastery of subject matter may inhibit the creation of loving relations with her or his students. In the classroom, as in life, it is often through risk and vulnerability that love ripens.

When teachers care, they sometimes feel compelled to put themselves in the champion role of sage leader, never recognizing that in doing so they may be jeopardizing the imaginative acts necessary for the growth and change loving relation encourages. This construct is evident from the most elusive appearances of our classrooms to the more tangible ones. Consider the teacher who spends generous amounts of time and money to get the room ready for a new class of students; every inch of the cinderblock walls is covered with posters, bulletin boards invite provocative questions, and colorful banners with catchy sayings fly across door entrances and under windowsills. All the same, in the effort to provide a welcoming environment, possibilities are inadvertently erased, because the space for student creation or ownership is already usurped. While probably appreciative of the teacher's energy, students sense very little room for their own enthusiasms; a gesture meant to solicit vigorous response may actually dull it in the end. Many teachers who believe their gestures to be caring ones often play out this example in a multitude of ways. Sadly, while such a show of attention is well intended, it can conceal an ironic violence that inflicts its wounds much like the arrow that pierces Paris of Troy; though it only grazes the surface, the poison it carries is fierce enough to kill.

Historically, students have been conditioned to repent for what they lack rather than to celebrate what they possess. They are continually ambushed by models of perfection, regardless of whether those models come from a perfectly crafted bulletin board, an impossibly pure moral exemplar, an exacting example of clear prose, or a knowing teacher's expert authority. Considered deficient in everything from knowledge to character, our students rarely expect to make much of a contribution in the classroom, nor do teachers expect them to do so, regardless of how high the official expectations may be. There is no room left to create in a perfect classroom, for any other state of affairs could only signal an intellectual, moral, or aesthetic mistake. Spontaneity and creativity are destroyed and genuine love cannot easily emerge. If students are to believe in their own and others' abilities to learn acceptance rather than mere tolerance, to not only recover from setbacks but to soar past them, and to find the strength required for commitment to a more profound self and community, then they must be allowed the generosity of their own spirit. Instead of being frequented by the stony ghost of inadequacy and shame that often accompanies what appear to be the most caring alliances but are subtly controlling ones, they must be sustained by the patience and forgiving heart that harmonizes the most loving relations. Creating loving relation demands a dynamic that is intimate and intense. It refuses to permit self-serving behaviors to masquerade as loving ones, even if on the surface those behaviors seem to be in everyone's best interest. Loving relations require the courage to let go of habit, the ability to recognize one's own humanity in order to hear others express theirs, and a belief in the largess of life.

If the otherness and individuality of students is threatening to teachers, it is only because the conditions of predetermined, stringent, and rigid "Sameness" is what they secretly desire. Conditioning a classroom, school, or community for loving relations can overcome both the reduction of the unique individual to the "Sameness" found in *The Giver* and the dogmatism of the one "right way" action described in the student teacher supervisor example related earlier. Suppressing individual differences, dissent, and upheaval also suppresses creative possibilities of all kinds, including the possibility of creating loving relations. It is a sad irony that many teachers who see themselves as givers, and are seen as such by parents and principals, are actually takers. By considering what distinguishes setting the conditions of love and care from actively conditioning for loving relations, we can understand how teachers sometimes unintentionally explode rather than build the bridges they intend. By recognizing how we often determine in advance, through externally imposed conditions, what meaning is of value, we can make the necessary changes that allow for the possibility of teachers and students creating meaning and value together inside emerging and evolving relationships. By acknowledging the anger, pain, suffering, despair, and grief, as well as the joy, wonder, pleasure, laughter, and delight of our students' experiences, we can discard the illusion that we have the ability to force their growth and can instead focus on how we might help them realize their individual potential. Teachers who care in models of love rather than in roles of power accept the risks, allow the vulnerability, and permit possibility in communion with their students without abandoning their obligation to make the classroom safe but not antiseptic. What matters most is not what teachers do in the classroom, but what they allow the students to do or not do.

The Creation of Shared Meaning

Because we all worry about the dangerous tendency to reduce all difference and diversity to the same concepts, categories, and standards that yield the authoritarian conformity we find in the *The Giver*, we have concerned ourselves with creating loving relations that preserve and cultivate the unique potential of individuals. In the first part of our paper, we recognize that knowing relations are especially inclined toward such reduction; that is one reason it seems better to us sometimes to explore other ways of relating. As mentioned, even emotional relations such as sympathy have their dangers. What does it mean to say, "I understand just how you feel" if I am a native born white male and my student is an immigrant Islamic female? Ethical relations, even, as discussed, the ethics of care, harbor similar dangers. The best of good "intentions" may result in oppressive relations. Seeking ways to have loving relations has the advantage of allowing us to continue relating to those different from ourselves even when knowing relations (epistemology) seem to fail. Striving to know the other rather than allow for the other is often not the best place to begin, because knowing assumes we are already in possession of the right categories, standards, and so on for interpreting and controlling everything.

In pursuing loving relations instead of conditional ones, others may draw us out of our already formed self, our concepts, and our intuitions, which is the reverse of reducing the other to our pre-existing selves. Understanding this allows teachers to grow both personally and professionally in very important ways and to secure the rewards of their calling. The fact that love can be possessive and threaten to devour the other is a danger of conditional caring discussed above. Though it imposes itself in the name of love for the other, it actually limits the freedom that is an important source of love. In conditioning our classrooms for loving relations, it is difficult, but important, that we tend to the excesses of such destructive caring. Possessive love and caring do not allow us to grow in the sense of living a life of expanding meaning and value. It turns on itself, imploding on its own good intent. Only relations with those who are different from us permit an expanded sense of self, because only they allow us to create novel meaning.

If we are interested in pursuing the creation of loving relations, we must come at loving through creativity. Others are different from us because they possess different meanings, values, and habits of action. Understanding them, however, does not involve a mystical union, some unmediated grasp of the meanings already in their minds. Instead, it involves sharing something. However, honest sharing cannot take place unless existing conditions are hospitable. When such conditions exist, we create mutual understanding through the co-construction of meanings. When it is not mutual, it is not understanding. In loving classrooms, students and teachers learn about each other by learning with each other through the co-creation of meaning. Only after we have made meaning together can we go on to make loving relations together.

Postmodernists and others rightly emphasize absence and decenteredness in the creation of meaning. It is a mistake to assume that meaning and mutual understanding are immediately given; we create these things together as the consequences of emergent processes rather than discovering them as antecedently existing facts. In successful dialogues across difference, participants create such meaning and understanding from what they can collect and arrange in mutually satisfying ways. Often this involves a long, sometimes unending, process of gathering what is useful and discarding what is not. Once gathered, it requires creative artistic effort to arrange things into a form that is aesthetically pleasing, morally acceptable, and cognitively comprehensible to those who have shared in its creation. A genuinely shared creation requires all who participate to negotiate about the gathering, the discarding, and the appropriate forming of what remains.

The creation of novel meaning is not effortless; sometimes it is very difficult, and often it is the sudden intuitive feeling that seizes us that guides our efforts to the most important ends. While the co-creation of a shared object does not assure agreement about what it means, sharing the creative experience builds community and provides a solid basis for further joint creation, including the creation of loving relations. All may share the joy of creating something in which all find richness of meaning, even when they do not agree about the meaning of their shared creation. They may like, even love, what they made and may like, even love, those with whom they have made it, yet not agree on the meaning of the product or process. This result is not so strange; we often love our friends and lovers not because we fully understand them, but because we enjoy what we do and make with them. By assuming our obligation in those relations, we encourage a sense of well-being in the other and may achieve loving purpose.

Creating unique meaning requires that every color in the palette be available to an artist, even if only certain colors are chosen; and everyone is an artist when trying to make meaning. Imagination as the ability to envision possibilities beyond actualities is particularly important. So too is the intuitive ability to recognize connections and perceive relations never before made. Creating meaning across differences demands emotional sensitivity and responsiveness to the requirements of the situation, including other persons as well as things. It involves discriminating emotional, intuitive, and intelligent perception. Curiously, good taste, in its dictionary definition as mental perception of quality, refined judgment, and discriminating comprehension may serve us well as a way of making meaning and eventually coming to understand others who are different from ourselves.

The shared creation of meaning commonly requires working through and living with irony, paradox, and outright contradiction. If those in charge determine the "logic" of the process of understanding in advance, they, and their "logic," will control, colonize, and even terrorize participants who think differently from them. If we are not to reduce all differences to the same preconceived categories of knowledge, thought, and action, then the genuine creation of meaning must overflow the boundaries of our already existing conceptions. We doubt there is any prescribed "logic" of creation, though there are, no doubt, intelligent methods. One intelligent method for creating novel meaning together involves an inclusive, playful, fertile, and tensed both/and logic, rather than an exclusive, serious, sterile, controlling, and unchanging logic of either/or. The logic of either/or suppresses difference; either things or people fit our predetermined categories or they do not. As differences disappear, students lose capacity to relate to what is out of the ordinary, thereby turning over power to the "authorities" who can. Meanwhile, the logic of both/and renders meanings fluid while freeing the imagination to play with possibilities; sometimes, like a good poetic metaphor, something, or someone, is both the same and different from our categories and concepts. As differences become manifest, students acquire the capacity to relate to the extraordinary, thereby acquiring power over their own learning.

Both/and logic opens up creative space in our ways of thinking; it spurs the imagination, thereby providing openings for creating and exploring novel possibilities beyond the bounds of our existing categories, concepts, and standards. Those obedient to the logic of either/or must always come to know a situation by recognizing those meanings and persons that fit their pre-existing categories. They are like the supervisor who knows immediately what is either right or wrong with the student teacher's class; either she is in control or she is not; either the students are properly arranged and on task or they are not. Such supervisors pay no attention to what the young teacher is trying to accomplish, to her purposes, or to those of the students. For them, everything is perfect and preplanned. They are like the teacher who has had fifteen years of one year of experience. Supervisors using a both/and approach would show confidence in their own knowledge while remaining open to other perceptions of the situation and its creative possibilities. For them, spontaneity and continuous planning are more important than fixed and perfect plans. They learn from their student teachers, much as creative teachers learn from their students.

Creating an Ethos of Love, Not an Economy of Results

In ancient Greek, *ethos* refers to an individual's habitual way of life, disposition, or character. It also refers to the characteristic customs, morals, and spirit of an institution or community. We believe that the way teachers create relations in a classroom is a statement of their own personal ethos as influenced by the ethos imposed by the larger society (parents, community, government, and the like). Further, we believe this imposition from outside often undermines and distorts classroom ethics; refashions care into control; and replaces love, which is personal and intimate, with desire for an abstract and detached status quo. A classroom conditioned for true loving relations approached through the creation of shared meaning results in what we would like to call an ethos of love. It is this ethos of love that, while recognizing there are no guarantees to successful relations in schools, in families, in friendship, or in work, is still able to imagine the consequences of relations blighted by technocratic "rationality" along with the economistic language of business that turns students into "customers." It can still intuit the significance of those fueled by the intimate connections that occur when the necessity for "Sameness" disappears and expectation is sustained through encouragement rather than competitiveness.

The current ethos in the institution of schooling is driven, as it has been for far too long, by the idea of accountability, an excessively cognitive knowing relation that, we believe, fails students and teachers in the most meaningful ways. Accountability depends on a standardized curriculum that is aligned to immutable standards of learning, fixed in advance of any human relationship and measured by standardized tests. Ultimately, it reduces people to numbers, relationships to ratios, and unique selves to mere ciphers. The goal of the standards movement in education seems to be to reduce students to standardized, interchangeable parts for the machine of economic production. There is little or no room for reflection or criticism, much less cooperation or creativity, on the part of either student or teacher. Instead, the emphasis is on docility; conformity; and, in its most destructive sense, rivalry. The technocratic–economistic ethos is one that reduces all uniqueness, difference, and individuality to a uniform, but false, image of caring and loving relation that has no respect for the inventions of play; prompts dishonest rather than honest relation in that it is about performance, not growth; and shrinks the boundless dimensions of loving relation to fit its own selfish needs.

The technocratic ethos is a tragedy of hyper-rationality that can only process abstract categories, concepts, and standards and lacks the imaginative vision necessary to see the possible beyond the actual; it also lacks the moral perception requisite for recognizing unique, individual differences. Such an ethos expresses a terrible irony for a putatively democratic people who pride themselves on their commitment to moral equality and unique individuality. When we talk about education in a democracy, we can never simply talk about differences in cognitive ability; how we perceive moral equality and unique individuality is of greatest concern to democratic citizens. Moral equality means everyone has an equal right to have their *unique* potential actualized, so that they might make their unique contribution to the democratic community. It eschews all classification, uniformities, and statistical averages; there are no quantitative standards common to all democratic individuals. Had a foreign power forced such a technocratic system of schooling upon us, we might well take it as an act of war.

Empathy, compassion, commitment, patience, spontaneity, and an ability to listen are all closely connected to the trust necessary for creating the conditions for loving relation in the classroom community. A teacher's simple passion for her subject matter alone will not make students learn, nor will it teach them the value of learning. An institutionalized manipulation of what it means to be "the best" will not insure that students and teachers give their best, no matter how strong the commitment to making such a thing happen. Shaming students, teachers, and schools into what a particular political agenda, moral righteousness, or work ethic believes to be the essential "truth" will not educate; it will only indoctrinate and alienate. Though that alienation may first appear as a mere trickle, it has the potential to unleash a doctrinaire and destructive flood. The tensions it incites between teachers and students leak into the larger community, pitting students against schools; schools against schools; and, finally, citizen against citizen. We believe teachers have both the capacity and the opportunity to ease the swells of this bursting dam. By determining to nurture loving recognition and response rather than instill thoughtless habits, by having the courage to take risks and exhibit their own vulnerabilities, teachers can create the loving relations in their classrooms that may convey to the larger society. We believe that is what an education can do, what a democratic education should do, and what a loving education must do.

CHAPTER 4

Tales In and Out of School

MICHAEL DALE

*The market, blind and deaf, is not fond of literature, or of risk and it
does not know how to chose. Its censorship is not ideological: it
has no ideas. It knows all about prices but nothing about values.*
—Octavia Paz

*To live is to be marked. To live is to change, to acquire the words
of a story and that is the only celebration we mortals really know.*
—Orleanna Price in Barbara Kingsolver's
The Poisonwood Bible

In Ralph Ellison's *Invisible Man,* the protagonist remembers a statue on
the campus of the college he attended (and from which the duplicitous
Dr. Bledsoe expels him). The bronze, bird-soiled statue is of the Founder
of the college, "his hands outstretched in the breathtaking gesture of lifting
a veil that flutters in the hard, metallic folds above the face of a kneeling
slave; and I am puzzled, unable to decide whether the veil is really being
lifted, or lowered more firmly in place; whether I am witnessing a rev-
elation or a more efficient blinding."[1] Recall, too, that the protagonist
throughout the novel is "invisible," as he puts it, "simply because people
refuse to see me," because of a "peculiar disposition of the eyes of those
with whom I come in contact. A matter of the construction of their *inner*
eyes, those eyes with which they look through their physical eyes upon reality."[2] I contend that schooling as most of our students experience it is
a lowering of a veil, that a prevailing conception of education evident in

schools and society constructs a particular set of "*inner* eyes" through which they see themselves and the students they teach.

A Blinding Story

Twelve plus years of being in educational institutions, nineteen plus years of living and growing up in the culture of what Finnegan in *Cold New World: Growing Up in a Harder Country* calls "liberal consumerism" leaves its mark(s) on those students who enter teacher education.[3] One of the telltale marks is the construction of an "inner eye" through which teaching and learning (including for the most part their own learning) are seen in complex and subtle ways tied to an unreflective acceptance of capitalism and economic utilitarianism. An "economic mind's eye" has been constructed. As a result, these prospective teachers and practicing teachers see education in ways strikingly similar to Bitzer, the quintessential pupil and graduate of the Gradgrind School Dickens creates in *Hard Times.* (This is the school in which Thomas Gradgrind tells us in the opening sentences of the novel, "Now what I want is Facts. Teach these boys and girls nothing but Facts. Facts alone are wanted in life. Plant nothing else, and root out everything else.")[4] In one of the concluding chapters of that novel, a chapter Dickens aptly titles "Philosophical," we read a concise description of the Gradgrind school philosophy, which Bitzer embodies to its fullest:

> It was a fundamental principle of the Gradgrind philosophy that everything was to be paid for. Nobody was ever on any account to give anybody anything, or render anybody help without purchase. Gratitude was to be abolished, and virtues springing from it were not to be. Every inch of the existence of mankind, from birth to death, was to be a bargain across the counter. And if we didn't get to Heaven that way, it was not a politico-economical place, and we had no business there.[5]

Within Gradgrind's school, knowledge and understanding have become commodities bargained for or exchanged across the teacher's desk.

I am not suggesting that students in teacher education are clones of the self-interested, calculating, and cold-hearted Bitzer. I do want to claim that their conception of education is seen in economic terms as a "bargain across the counter," that teaching and learning, the relationship between teacher and pupil, are commodity exchanges in which knowledge and understanding have become "bits of saleable value." Capitalism disposes them to consider human beings, including themselves, as little more than economic role-incumbents with narrowly defined talents and virtues to be allocated efficiently. Recent policies of narrow accountability in public schools across the country have only been additional tools for constructing inner eyes that see education, that see teaching and learning, almost exclusively in terms of economics. Jonathan Kozol in his most recent book, *Ordinary Resurrections: Children in the Years of Hope*, captures well the prevailing sentiment: "Elements of childhood that bear no possible connection to the world of enterprise and profit get no honor in the pedagogic world right now, nor in the economic universe to which it seems increasingly subservient."[6] Kozol continues by capturing the essence of the economic language that is today commonplace in the conferences at which he is invited to speak:

> The dialogue is mostly managerial and structural. It tends to be a cumbersome and technocratic dialogue, weighted down by hyphenated words such as "performance-referenced," "outcome-oriented," "competency-centered." One hears a lot of economics, many references to competition and "delivery of product" and, of course high standards and exams. . . . People rarely speak of *children* at these conferences. You hear of "cohort groups" and "standard variations." . . . The relentless emphasis at these events is on the future worth low-economic children may, or may not, have for our society. Policy discussions seem to view them less a children, than as "economic units"—pint-sized deficits or assets in blue jeans and jerseys, some of whom may prove to be a burden to society, others of whom may have some limited utility.[7]

The fundamental utilitarian and economic principles that informed Gradgrind's school are even more firmly entrenched in our language, policies, and practices in schools today. Bitzer would feel at home in many American classrooms.

Matriculating to a university is by no means an escape from this economic framing of education. Several years ago at my university's fall convocation address Cornell West said, "You come to a university not for job skills, but for wisdom." I wondered then, and even more so now, how many students and faculty agreed wholeheartedly with West's notion of a university education. "Market demand," education as a "service" turning out successful "products"—it is all too commonplace to read and hear about "clients" or "consumers" or more recently "stakeholders" in higher education. In November 2000 voters in North Carolina said "yes" to a 3-billion-dollar bond referendum to finance construction and building repair on the campuses of universities and community colleges. The public statements by politicians and academic administrators urging passage of this bond issue unfailingly appealed solely to the link between higher education and economic development in North Carolina, appealed exclusively to the need for construction and repair monies in order to enhance job preparation and maintain an "educated" workforce. And what is it that we professors do at the university? We "deliver instruction." Teaching in a classroom is an "instructional delivery system," and the latest technology simply an "alternative delivery system." Instead of reflecting upon and attempting to understand the good life and a common good, instead of inquires and conversations focused on Socrates' question "How should one live?" universities are seen as places where we are to engage (if *engagement* is even the right word here) students with the problems of "how to make a living." Or in complementary fashion, universities are to be like the anchors at some upscale mall, a Saks Fifth Avenue, not a Kmart.

From state-mandated accountability measures to the pervasive framing of education within a narrow economic perspective we find a constriction and a distortion of vision, an obtuseness in seeing the world of teaching and learning, a blindness to the lives of both students and teachers. As Martha Nussbaum puts it:

> [I]n its determination to see only what can enter into utilitarian calculations, the economic mind is blind: blind to the qualitative richness of the perceptible world; to the separateness of its people, to their inner depths, their hopes and loves and fears, blind to what it is like to live a human life and try to endow it with meaning. Blind, above all, to the fact that human life is something mysterious and extremely complicated, something that demands to be approached with faculties of mind and resources of language suited to the expression of that complexity. [8]

Utilitarian calculations construct a particular and a peculiar set of "inner eyes." Looking out on the world through these inner eyes, we do not see the full humanity of students and teachers, the complex mysteries and intimate joys and sorrows of teaching and learning. Instead, what is seen are human resources laboring in a production process.

In this state of blindness, when teaching and learning are seen as a "bargain across a counter," when knowledge and understanding are seen as commodities exchanged across that counter, when utilitarian calculations rule the day, human relations are disfigured and ultimately severed. We see clearly such a rupturing in the relationship that Gradgrind has with his daughter Louisa. From the beginning, Gradgrind, a self-described "eminently practical father," has rooted out human emotions in his relationship with his daughter as efficiently as he has rooted it (and Fancy, or imagination) out of his school. Gradgrind's insistence that even human relationships should be subject to utilitarian calculations is poignantly and pointedly revealed when he sits with Louisa and tells her of Mr. Josiah Bounderby's proposal of marriage. Gradgrind views the proposal as a simple business transaction, weighing factors such as the number of "successful" marriages between older men and younger women (Bounderby is in his fifties, Louisa in her twenties). For Gradgrind even the most personal and complex human issues and questions "were cast up, got into exact totals, and finally settled—if those concerned could only have been brought to know it."[9] Shaped both in her home and at her Father's school by this philosophy, Louisa attempts to break free at this point, but shortly resigns herself to accepting Bounderby's proposal, resigns herself to a loveless marriage:

> What does it matter? . . . "What do *I* know, Father," said Louisa in her quiet manner, "of tastes and fancies; of aspirations and affections; of all that part of my nature in which such light things might have been nourished? What escape have I from problems that could be demonstrated, and realities that could be grasped?"[10]

The consequences for Louisa of Father's schooling are not only a head stuffed full of facts, but (paradoxically) a vacuum left by the absence of imagination, love, and other emotions. As a result, Louisa achieved an acquired hopelessness.

Gradgrind is blind. Dickens tells us that "Mr. Gradgrind, in *his* Observatory (and there are many like it), had no need to cast an eye upon the teeming myriads of human beings around him, but could settle all their destinies [including his own daughter's] on a slate, and wipe out all their tears with one dirty bit of sponge."[11] Armed solely with his slate and calculating devices, Gradgrind is blind to the complexities and mysteries of human beings; he lacks the "faculties of mind and resources of language suited to the expression of that complexity." He is so blind that he suggests to Louisa, in weighing Bounderby's marriage proposal, that "love" is superfluous to her considerations, that "perhaps the expression itself—I merely suggest this to you, my dear—may be a little misplaced."[12] Increasingly the language of economic exchange in education (stay in school and get a good job, fund public schooling in order to produce a skilled workforce, invest in higher education to fuel economic growth), of educational value tied almost exclusively to economic worth, silences more humanly complex stories, conversations, and understandings of teaching and learning. In a statement ripe with implications for teacher education that I will discuss below, Louisa later in the novel confronts Father with all the harm that his system of education has done to her, but without reproaching him, "What you have never nurtured in me, you have never nurtured in yourself. . . ."[13]

As I qualified my account of Bitzer, I do not want to suggest here that prospective and practicing teachers see their own learning and teaching in quite the cold, calculating manner that Gradgrind put forward Bounderby's marriage proposal to Louisa. At the same time I do want to claim that seeing education and teaching and learning through a utilitarian "inner eye"; employing the coin-of-the-realm language of economics to describe education, students, and teachers; and calculating the worth of knowledge and understanding based on their exchange value in the job market push the teacher/student relationship in the direction we see revealed between Gradgrind and Louisa. When knowledge and understanding are seen almost exclusively as variables in an economic calculation, then they become commodities in "a bargain across the counter" between teachers and students, and the teacher/student relationship is adversely affected as a result. Anne Carson captures well the adverse relations that evolve in the contrast she makes between a "gift" and a "commodity":

> A gift has both economic and spiritual content, is personal and reciprocal, and depends on a relationship that endures over time. Money is an abstraction that passes one way and impersonally between people whose relationship stops with the transfer of cash. To use Marx's terms, a commodity is an alienable object exchanged between two transactors enjoying a state of mutual independence, while a gift is an inalienable object exchanged between two reciprocally dependent transactors. Gift and commodity represent two different notions of value, embodied in two different sets of social relations.[14]

Offering a gift to someone is not the same as conducting a business or financial transaction across a counter. Human relations and our understanding of our own "self" are seen and felt differently, depending upon whether we consider the object of exchange as a gift or as a commodity. Carson continues:

> A gift is not a piece broken off from the interior life of the giver and lost in the exchange, but rather an extension of the interior life of the giver, both in space and in time, into the interior of the receiver. Money denies such an extension, ruptures continuity and stalls objects at the borders of themselves. Abstracted from space and time as bits of saleable value, they become commodities and lose their life as objects. . . . Extinguished also is its power to connect the people who give and receive it: they become like commodities themselves, fragments of value waiting for price and sale. . . . It fragments and dehumanizes human being.[15]

Carson's point is starkly revealed in the words of Anny Gaul, a high school senior in the International Baccalaureate program at Meyers Park High School in Charlotte, NC. In an article describing the college application process she (and many other seniors) is engaged in completing, she wrote:

> The truth is that in the past few months, I've realized, I have felt like an intellectual prostitute: I've been doing nothing but promoting, pushing, and selling myself to prospective colleges and scholarship programs; and on top of it, I have to get tested all the time. . . . It seems like a microcosm of the society in which we live, which so often favors quantity over quality and regards profit or net gain as a bottom line, irrespective of ethics, scruples, or consequence. Numbers are constantly used as a measure of an individual's worth, from SATs to GPAs to how much money you earn in a year.[16]

Perhaps very few students would describe themselves with the provocative phrase Ms. Gaul uses: an "intellectual prostitute." Most students will, however, immediately recognize the sentiments she expresses, the feeling that learning is, or has become, a matter of acquiring and adorning themselves with shiny bangles and trinkets for display in an educational marketplace. The necessarily hurried pace (after all, "time is money") of acquiring information and experiences and calculating their market value leaves little time and space for love stories, for seeing and experiencing learning as the "wooing of knowledge." The voices of the marketplace, sometimes loudly, sometimes softly, repeat the words that Gradgrind spoke to Louisa that "perhaps the expression itself [love] . . . may be a little misplaced."

"Imagine a city where there is no desire [no love]."[17] So begins the concluding section of Anne Carson's delightfully insightful *Eros the Bittersweet*. Within the walls of such a city, "The art of storytelling is widely neglected. A city without desire is, in sum, a city of no imagination. Here people think only what they already know. Fiction is simply falsification."[18] Dickens, too, invites us to imagine such a place. Conceived in Gradgrind's utilitarian mind, we step into a school that is in fact Carson's desireless city. Love and imagination are rooted out, and although students under Gradgrind's and McChoakumchild's tutelage are taught to read, they are never invited into the world of imaginative fiction, into the worlds that unfold in "idle storybooks." Storybooks are rooted out of the Gradgrind school for the very reasons Carson suggests. The "unbending, utilitarian, matter-of-fact" Gradgrind and the rest of the "Hard Facts fellows" view fiction both as falsification and as nurturing the "idle imagination." Love is misplaced when storybooks and the imagination are banished from the school.

In our world and schools today, in which children are seen as "pint-sized economic units," where utilitarian considerations rule the day, and where high school seniors prostitute themselves for a chance to matriculate at institutions of higher job training, we need imagination; we need stories. We need imagination and stories to rekindle and illuminate our connections to one another—to see each other as more than bargainers across a counter. We need stories in order to create a longing for what is not and an envisioning of what is absent in our schools, in our teaching, and in our learning. The constrictions and distortions of educational vision represent an immense challenge for teacher educators. But as Martha Nussbaum has written, "Obtuseness is a moral failing; its opposite can be cultivated."[19] Reading and engaging in conversation about literature in teacher education is a powerful way of cultivating an alternative set of "inner eyes," a powerful way of beginning to lift the veil and cultivate sight that is "finely aware and richly responsible,"[20] one way in which to acquire the "faculties of mind and resources of language" necessary for seeing the richness, complexities, and mysteries of human life, and of teachers and students engaged in teaching and learning.

Literary Sight

Jo Anne Pagano has described the relationship between narrative stories and teaching in this way:

> Teaching is, among other things, a discursive and interpretive practice. . . . When we teach, we tell stories about the world. Some stories are scientific, some historical, some philosophical, some literary, and so on. Educational theories are stories about how teaching and learning work, about who does what to whom and for what purposes, and most particularly, educational theories are stories about the kind of world we want to live in and what we should do to make that world.[21]

Teaching, then, is intimately tied to the understanding and telling of stories—stories of communities, students, and the lives we all live, as well as the stories embodied in the disciplines we teach. Learning to teach involves becoming attuned to particular narratives, learning to do what teachers (should) do, learning to see, think, feel, and talk as teachers (should). Stories embody language for developing meanings and understandings, as well as the emotional and imaginative contours and content of teaching and learning. The particular stories that students hear about education (in school and out of school), the stories they live as students in schools and classrooms matter. These stories, heard and lived as learners, will shape their identities and lives as future teachers.

Students in our teacher education programs, both the undergraduate prospective teachers and those returning teachers, need an alternative to the economic story of education, an alternative to the story in which teaching and learning are a "bargain across the counter." They need a richer and more enriching story of education, including their own story of learning.

Novels and short stories contain the potential for a reflective and emotional connection to our lives and imagined lives. "Reading great works of art and reading life are different but not unrelated activities."[22] In this comparison Putnam is suggesting an intimate connection between narrative form and content and understanding human lives, our own and the lives of others. Commenting on the work of the philosopher and novelist Iris Murdoch, Putnam writes

> Murdoch emphasized that when we are actually confronted with situations requiring ethical evaluation, whether or not they also require some action on our part, the sorts of descriptions we need—descriptions of the motives and character of human beings, above all—are descriptions in the language of the "sensitive novelist," not scientistic or bureaucratic jargon.[23]

Not the language, I would add, of a calculating economic utilitarianism or the language of consumer capitalism.

Narrative forms are a means to experience and touch the world, its delights and its despairs. Imaginative engagement with literature is not to be understood as some kind of flight from reality. Murdoch argues, "In intellectual disciplines and in the enjoyment of art and nature we discover value in our ability to forget self, to be realistic, to perceive justly. We use imagination not to escape the world but to join it, and this exhilarates us because of the distance between our ordinary dulled consciousness and an apprehension of the real."[24]

Murdoch's notion strikes most of my undergraduate students and many of my colleagues in teacher education as counterintuitive. For my students, engagement with the "real" is associated with "getting out into the real world of the classrooms" in which they intend to teach; "real" is their own lives and the lives of other sentient beings whom they know and with whom they interact; "real" is "hands-on experience" in which they are actually engaged in the activities they associate with be(com)ing a teacher. Usually, although they are too polite, or timid, or docile to ask aloud, I nevertheless can see in their movements and in their eyes on that first day of class, as we go over the syllabus, the very same "terrible question" Haroun angrily shouted to his story-telling father, Rashid, in Rushdie's wonderful novel, *Haroun and the Sea of Stories:* "What's the point of it? *What's the use of stories that aren't even true?*"[25] An answer to my students' (and Haroun's) question can only truly evolve and reveal itself over the course of reading and engaging with the novels and short stories in the classes I teach. Bernard Williams addresses a similar question when he turns to Greek literature, particularly tragedy, in his book *Shame and Necessity,*

> In seeking a reflective understanding of ethical life, for instance, it [philosophy] quite often takes examples from literature. Why not take examples from life? It is a perfectly good question, and has a short answer: what philosophers will lay before themselves and their readers as an alternative to literature will not be life, but bad literature.[26]

Nussbaum deepens Williams' pithy answer in pointing out a contrast between lived experience and our engagement with literature:

> Our experience is, without fiction, too confined and too parochial. Literature extends it, making us reflect and feel about what might otherwise be too distant for feeling. . . . The point is that in the activity of literary imagining we are led to imagine and describe with greater precision, focusing our attention on each word, feeling each event more keenly—whereas much of actual life goes by with that heightened awareness, and is thus, in a certain sense, not fully or thoroughly lived. . . . too much of it is obtuse, routinized, incompletely sentient.[27]

Within the classroom, literature can become a meeting place of experience and ideas, a place where emotions and reason can come together as stories show us worlds and lives we do not know or correct our perspective on a world we "know" all too well.

Unless students in teacher education programs can come to see and know themselves and their own learning with a rich, descriptive language absent in an economic perspective on education, then they will never be able to see the mystery and complexity in the lives of the children and adolescents they (intend to) teach; they will never see and understand the ways in which their desires and aspirations and those of their students are constrained and impeded within a social context and educational institutions that view teaching and learning as a "bargain across a counter." In teacher education, novels and short stories about the complexity of human lives inside and outside of school settings give occasion for students to confront the narrowness and limitations of an economic perspective and to develop a richer conception of education, one tied to discovering truths about the human condition and our role as teachers in it. Not only do the stories confront students with how bankrupt utilitarian views of teaching and learning are, they also have the capacity to create a desire, a yearning for what has been absent in their own education. Imagination and desire are alike in being defined in terms of the absence of their objects. A yearning for what has been absent in their own learning or teaching is perhaps a necessary first step in bringing the objects of this yearning within reach.

Student Stories

In teaching both undergraduate and graduate students in teacher education, we read and engage in conversations about novels and short stories in an attempt to begin writing a story about education other than the economic one, which has played like elevator music throughout their lives, omnipresent and no less powerful because, more often than not, it is in the background, not consciously attended to. Over the years I have used a number of different pieces of literature. Just to provide you with some idea of the literature we have read in these classes, let me simply list some recent authors and titles:

1. Tillie Olsen, *Tell Me A Riddle*
2. Dorothy Allison, *Bastard Out of Carolina*
3. Ralph Ellison, *Invisible Man*
4. Charles Dickens, *Hard Times*
5. Monica Furlong, *Wise Child*
6. Anne Michaels, *Fugitive Pieces*
7. Aldous Huxley, *Brave New World*
8. Sophocles, *Antigone*
9. Kathleen Hill, "The Anointed"
10. May Sarton, *The Small Room*

I have also recently used in these classes a nonfiction work written in a narrative style, William Finnegan's *Cold New World: Growing Up in a Harder Country,* and in the past Robert Coles' *The Call of Stories: Teaching and the Moral Imagination.* The "call for stories" in education and teacher education and arguments for their worth are not new. Maxine Greene's voice has been a powerful and sustaining one for many years now. However, the assault on narrative seems particular intense and intensifying in our own "Hard Times."

It would be presumptuous to say every student leaves these classes convinced that an economic mind's eye is blind to what teaching and learning in schools ought to be. (Perhaps it is I whose "inner eyes" are peculiarly constructed.) I also cannot say with any confidence (because I do not know) that some students' reports of the consequences of reading literature has had a lasting and deep effect on their lives as teachers. With those two not insignificant qualifications, I do want to permit some of these students to "speak" to the power of literature to construct a way of seeing both themselves and others and to the power of the rich descriptions found in literature to develop the "faculties of mind and resources of language suited" needed to understand the complexity of human lives and education. I am quoting in these cases from the final reflective essays that I ask students to write. Here is what an undergraduate secondary math education student wrote:

> With all our formalized study of education, it is easy for education majors to blindly slip into the mindset that becoming a good teacher is simply dependent on utilizing and implementing the results obtained via research. We treat educational strategies like formula, trying to match the best fit one to solve whichever educational puzzle with which we are confronted at the time. I am not demeaning educational research or the beneficial implications of its use. I believe they are in fact just as important as we treat them; however, as Olsen shows us in her story "I Stand Here Ironing" there are also other facets just as important to education. Glimpsing into a lifestyle like the one Olsen presents is fascinating for me. A story like this one is the only way I have for understanding such situations. So yes Vygotsky's theories are good for learning about education, but Tillie Olsen reminds us that it also important to learn about *who* we are educating.

Another undergraduate prospective elementary grades teacher wrote:

> When I initially looked at the books we were required to read for this class I was uncertain how they would help make me a better teacher. As the class approaches termination I feel that not only the reading, but the discussion of them has caused me to undergo a self-examination of what I teach, how I teach and most importantly why I teach.

Both of these students reflect on how the novels and short stories read and discussed in class invited them to see and think about themselves as teachers, along with the students they will be teaching, in ways that they had not done so before. It seems the first student quoted is beginning to consider the possibility that good teaching is not simply a matter of inserting variables into an educational equation. She seems to be considering the idea that teaching may be as much tied up with seeing others honestly and justly as it is with pedagogical practices derived from research.

Here are the reflections of three students from a recent graduate class. One teacher writes:

> The use of literature has caused, strengthened, and intensified my understanding of the text and, most importantly, it has caused me to become passionately engaged in learning and seeking to understand myself and others. . . . As I prepare to enter the classroom again next week, I will enter this time with not only a general knowledge of the reading and learning process and with an understanding of my own personal reading and learning process, but I will also enter looking at myself and the world around me differently. Having had the opportunity this summer to look at my own life as I have looked at and tried to understand others through literature has touched my soul in ways I can't even begin to explain (an elementary grades reading teacher).

Not only does this student write of changes in her "seeing" as a consequence of the literature she read and discussed in class; in her descriptions of her "passionate engagement" and her transformed and "touched" soul we see a language foreign to the economic mind of utilitarian calculation.

A second student writes:

> After the first day of class, the day we went over the syllabus, I left Boone with a feeling that I was going to be in for a month of reading and discussing issues and topics that I rarely encounter in the Ashe County School system. I am a scientist by education and a farmer by birth. Not much shocks me and I surely could care less about the hard times faced by kids thousands of miles away. When I got home that morning my wife met me at our door and told me that we were going to have a baby, our first. As you might imagine, the rest of the day was spent calling doctors, telling family members, and making plans for the arrival of our child. Later in the evening, I retired to my study and began the reading for the next class. As I read the assignment a new feeling came over me. Suddenly, I was no longer apathetic towards the plight of the minority and lower class children I was to read about. Now, as an expectant father, apathy toward these "far away" children was replaced by concern for their well-being. I did not like this new feeling, but I could not displace it with the cold pragmatism that I used to possess. I began to see the connection, in my study on that Monday night, between the problems of these "printed" children and the child my wife and I are soon to bring into the world. . . . Many of my views have changed over the course of the last four weeks. I have had a shift from cold

pragmatism to an attitude of concern for all children (a high school biology teacher).

Literature and life seemed to have affected this practicing teacher.

A third student, a middle grades English teacher, expresses clearly the complexity of human living, the delight and the sadness, the hope and the despair that can be evoked by the novelist and short story writer and felt deeply by the reader:

> Stories without happy endings frustrate me. Does not every individual deserve happiness? This is why I spent much of the class anxious and frustrated, because no book that we read possessed a happy ending. . . . These were no fairy tales. But what began with frustration, a sense of why are you making us read these sad stories, gave way to understanding. When I stand before students in the classroom, I realize that I am not being listened to by princes and princesses who will wind up in the ivory tower safe from evil warlocks and fire-breathing dragons. . . . The literature allowed me to examine and think about the sad, suffering side of the human condition. To realize that stories do not have to be happy to be good and told.

Yet later in her essay, this same student writes:

> In our reading, two characters touched me in such ways that I am comfortable calling them "personal heroes." They touched me because not only were they caring and nurturing teachers, they also provided troubled, suffering children who had toiled on rough seas, safe harbor. They believed in the power of love to heal and they did not give up on the young people that entered their lives. Raylene in *Bastard Out of Carolina* and Athos in *Fugitive Pieces*—completely different yet united in their strength to overcome personal suffering and guide hurt children to safer, steadier waters.

And finally, near the end of her essay, she reflects:

> This paper merely scratches the surface of what I gleaned from this class. When we began class four weeks ago, I had no idea how the reading of these books and articles would affect me. Honestly, I did not quite see the point—how would the reading of these books and articles make me a better teacher? By mid-second week, I experienced a most incredible change. Something was happening to me because of my reading and experience in class. I began to view the world with a different set of eyes. It was not overt change, for bold, vibrant brush strokes were not necessary to paint for me pictures of suffering and an understanding of pain. I am compassionate and sensitive and aware that not all members of the human race have it as good as I do. The change I experienced was subtle yet potent. It was as if I had been sprinkled with a magic dust that lay on my skin, opening my mind and sharpening my senses. I felt as if I were walking the earth differently and that I was better for it. This class allowed me to envelop myself in a wonderful world of words and ideas— and what beautiful words we read.

These students attest to how reading and discussing literature can help to construct a richer and more enriching story of education than the one told by the "economic mind," how engagement with and conversation about literature can help them to see more clearly the complexities (and mysteries) of their own lives and the lives of the children and adolescents they teach. For these students and for others, I believe the opportunity to meaningfully engage with novels and short stories kindled a desire to reach beyond the bankrupt utilitarian views coloring their lives as learners and/or as teachers. Through their thoughtful engagement with literature, a kind of reconstructive surgery of their inner eyes took place, and the new eyes that looked out upon the world were imaginative ones. They could imagine themselves differently as learners and as teachers. They could imagine and begin to feel nonutilitarian connections both with what they were learning and with students and other people in their lives. And what they came to imagine they came to desire for themselves and for others.

Educational Longings

In closing let me turn to the title story from Tillie Olsen's book *Tell Me A Riddle*. In this story, Eva, a Russian Jewish immigrant to the U.S., is dying of cancer. Her children are grown and gone from home. Her life has been spent caring and sacrificing for them under harsh, materially impoverished conditions with little domestic help from her husband David. As she is dying, she returns in her memories and imagination to her equally harsh and materially impoverished childhood in Russia, to her participation in the 1905 revolution and time in prison (including solitary confinement), and to what David will at the end of story come to see as "their holiest dreams."[28] As Eva journeys imaginatively, she is also traveling literally, being taken by her husband across country to make farewell visits to the homes of her children (the fact that she has cancer and not long to live is kept from her, but at a particular point in the story a look on David's face reveals to her that she is dying). At her daughter Hannah's home she observes the ritual lighting of the menorah and reacts bitterly to what she sees in that ritual. As readers we come to know that for all that Eva sacrificed and suffered for her children, she has been silenced. Her own life is ending unfulfilled, and she has failed (not without reason) to tell her children her (and David's) stories of "their holiest dreams," the joys and the sufferings that she felt as she attempted to bring those dreams to life as a youth in Russia. (It is difficult to do justice to this story with so brief a synopsis.)

Yet even as she is dying, or perhaps because she is dying, we see the power of Eva's longings. Being transported across the country from one of her children's homes to another does not keep Eva from taking a very different journey. Through the imaginative act of remembrance we witness her longing for that earlier time in her life when she was not silenced, when those "holiest dreams" were what she (and David) reached for: "Still the springs, the springs were in her seeking. Somewhere an older power that beat for life. Somewhere coherence, transport, meaning. If they would but leave her in the air now stilled of clamor, in the reconciled solitude, to journey on."[29] Here, at least, and perhaps in the only way open to a frail and dying woman, her longings can be envisioned and satisfied in the realm of the imagination. The strength and depth of her longings are also revealed in the regrets she expresses about not telling her children her stories; these feelings are conveyed clearly in what she says to David about Hannah's lighting of the candles:

> Heritage. How we have come from our savage past, how no longer to be savages—this to teach. To look back and learn what humanizes—this to teach. To smash all ghettos that divide us—not to go back, not to go back—this to teach. Learned books in the house, will humankind live or die, and she gives to her boys—superstition. . . .
>
> Heritage! But when did I have time to teach? Of Hannah I asked only hands to help.[30]

Eva's yearning voice of regret resonates clearly and powerfully with many students in teacher education.

An economic mind's inner eyes see students as "hands" that require tooling for jobs, and "hands" for purchasing "goods" in an economy of liberal consumerism. Eva's lament "But when did I have time to teach?" is echoed by many public school teachers in a world of high stakes testing and market driven education. The economic story of education as one in which a utilitarian metric is used to judge the worth and value of teaching and learning is a pernicious story. The learned books in our house give way to marketable skills for earning a living. As Nussbaum writes, "We have to think not only about how we will earn enough to live, but also about why we live, and what makes life worth living. The humanities are essential to address these questions. If we become a population who can relate, as citizens, only on a narrow parched terrain of financial interest, we will have lost much that makes us fully human."[31] We must not fail to engage our students with these humanizing stories, stories that incite a desirable image of teaching and learning worth reaching for.

PART 2

Love, Injustice, Teaching, and Learning

It seems that a great deal of misery arises in the United States when we, as citizens, assume we have all the democratic liberty, equality, and justice we need and naively assent to the dominant cultural narratives that we are not doing nearly enough to expand the capitalistic global economy. At these moments we seem to confuse having more with being more, where being more means being in better democratic, caring, and even loving relations with one another. Walt Whitman's belief in "adhesiveness or love" as the culmination of the nation's democratic quest does not seem to be prevalent.[1] In the previous section Michael Dale, after identifying the dominant economistic discourse in American education, turned to literary narratives to tell alternative stories to teachers, students, and student teachers about intimacy-in-community. In this section, Kerry Burch seeks to "re-politicize the iconic meaning narratives of American identity" as a way of disrupting the claims of moral legitimacy circulating in the nation's public schools. He does so by using the concept of eros to provide a critical reading of "the pursuit of happiness clause" in the nation's Declaration of Independence. Burch relies on Paulo Freire's notion of "conscientization," or heightened consciousness of the contradictions and sources of oppression concealed in social reality. He argues that erotic love is implicit in the very idea of conscientization because it involves the desire to move from ignorance to knowledge as well as the desire to connect with something better in life. Nonetheless, he argues that we should augment the democratic pedagogy of love "with a well-theorized pedagogy of anger" and indignation as a way to rechannel the "negative hostile energy that grows out of injustice." With this observation, Burch broaches the conflicted emotions that arise in those who love social justice and who have the passionate desire to teach it.

Burch introduces a theme expanded on by the other contributors to this section. Following Burch, Daniel Liston and Megan Boler explore the complex, ambivalent feelings implicated when critical consciousness is approached in the classroom. Liston first looks at the kind of learning that involves "enticing beauty" or the "allure" of strange and wonderful new worlds. Such learning, he believes, is like falling in love. Unfortunately, critical theory and pedagogy often lack this erotic allure. Liston contrasts literary narratives from writers such as Annie Dillard, who describe the emotional pleasures of learning when touched by beauty and mystery, with those such as Monster Kody Scott, who write narratives of learning largely bereft of beauty and joy. Learning to be critical often involves learning about ugliness, brutality, and betrayal; it also means living with uncertainty and terrible truth. The painful emotions associated with the latter kind of learning and teaching are quite different from those in the former; they are more disruptive, unregulated, and unwieldy, though there is a kind of erotic love there, too.

Critical pedagogy strives to be engaging, uplifting, and even empowering by offering "an experience that reaches for altered identity," a recreated, critical, and creative consciousness aware of the pain of injustice and the passionate desire (eros) to overcome it. However, any time someone is undergoing identity transformation, powerful emotions arise for them and those who would change them. Liston believes it is important to listen and learn from our emotions ("if we don't listen we can't learn," he says), especially in the process of identity transformation. Here, he turns to the work of Martha Nussbaum, particularly her comments on the importance of passionate empathy when sufficiently informed by intelligent cognitive appraisal and appropriate detachment. Beyond Nussbaum, he turns to the Buddhist tradition of contemplation, mediation, and nonattachment as a source of insight into compassionate listening and learning.

Identity transformation is important to those committed to radical and critical pedagogy. When teachers attempt to transform students' identity, the students often, understandably, resist; sometimes, in repressive settings, that is a good thing. Teachers have experienced the frustration, disappointment, self-doubt, and anxiety, even anger, at a student's stout refusal to learn what we think is good for them. Megan Boler advocates what she calls a "pedagogy of discomfort," which can shatter worldviews in the pursuit of social justice. She too has recourse to the work of Freire in this regard. Predictably, results of such a pedagogy are as discomforting to the teacher as to the student. In her paper, Boler explores the struggles that ensue when a teacher and student come into direct confrontation because the student aggressively resists learning and resolutely defends his or her present identity. Like Liston, Boler seeks solace for her radical pedagogy in Buddhist teaching, which she also uses to explore the intricate emotional and cognitive dimensions of identity reconstruction.

Besides a desire to teach for critical understanding, and the identification of the multifarious emotions such teaching can cause, all three papers are committed to a kind of hope that requires affirmative and assertive action far beyond helpless and witless wishing. Burch starts his paper by stating that it "expresses an optimistic, reconstructive hope." Liston asserts that critical theory seeks to expose "the contradictions, ironies, and obfuscations of everyday living in hopes of creating a more shared and just community." And Boler attempts to distinguish naïve from critical hope. Liston and Boler both fix much of their hope on the possibility of people listening and loving, while Burch seeks to release the healing power of love. The approaches are more similar than different. Though admittedly optimistic, Burch's hope is not naïve; he has a pedagogical plan to release eros to learn. Although perhaps somewhat less optimistic, Liston also recognizes an eros to learn that allows us to remain hopeful. Boler explicitly states, "Critical hope emerges from what Paulo Freire calls our 'incompleteness.'" Incompleteness, the lack of any firm, fixed, and final identity, assures us growth is always possible. Boler also suggests that there is a passion for ignorance, a desire to ignore. Critical hope must confront the fact that if, in our incompleteness, there is a human eros to grow, there is also an equally strong, or stronger, eros to preserve our identity, grounded on a passionate desire for self-preservation. We have already encountered several paradoxical tensions in our reflections on teaching, learning, and loving; even more await us. Love in all its forms is often ambivalent.

CHAPTER 5

Eros, Pedagogy, and the Pursuit of Happiness

KERRY BURCH

Introduction: America the Beautiful?

The title of this essay expresses an optimistic, reconstructive hope: that the American formation of civic identity, as a shifting and contradictory set of ideas, values, and principles, contains a vast untapped potential for social transformation and democratic renewal.[1] Broadly conceived, the paper develops a strategy for educating this potential by applying a concept of love (eros) to a critical reading of the "pursuit of happiness" clause in the Declaration of Independence. At the center of the strategy is the claim that the pedagogic construction of democratic citizens can be deepened and extended when grounded in an explicit theory of educational eros. To better achieve "the nation," to make America more democratic, more just, and therefore more beautiful, I believe part of our task as public pedagogues must be to creatively re-politicize the iconic meaning narratives of American identity. I argue that the "inalienable right to the pursuit of happiness," as one of these narratives, has for too long been treated in classrooms as if its meaning is permanently settled. This dominant pedagogical bias against reexamining vital political ideas, such as the pursuit of happiness and the like, tames the power of the national scripture and gives the phrase a politically static, conservative cast, one that, for example, could never be expected to disturb the moral legitimacy of America's antidemocratic, oligarchic structure of public education. I want to disturb this legitimacy.

What my alternative stance implies is that iconic phrases such as "the pursuit of happiness, the right to revolution, to insure domestic tranquility, to promote the general welfare, We the People," among others, ought to be pedagogically reconceived and mined anew for their capacity to intensify our encounter with the contradictions in American culture.[2]

In the pages ahead I develop a particular construction of eros to help order a set of questions about the possible meaning(s) of these powerful yet theoretically underdeveloped phrases.[3] For instance, I argue that common sense narratives of the pursuit of happiness can be positively ruptured when evaluated in the context of the "savage inequalities" of American public education. Within such an interpretation, it can be seen that the eros of affluent citizens, their emotional and civic potential, is positively cultivated, while the eros of poor citizens, their emotional and civic potential, is institutionally suppressed. As a multifaceted symbol for human possibility, then, a sense of eros heightens our sensitivity to, and indignation about, how inequality in public education retards the developmental essence of citizenship (and thus, happiness) for citizens whose demography all too often becomes their destiny. In identifying the conceptual affinities that bind eros to the pursuit of happiness phrase, the paper draws attention to the ontological substrate that connects eros as a state of being to democracy as a state of being and defends the assumption that democratic citizenship requires a critically theorized love discourse to reach its fullest expression.[4] In the first two sections of the chapter, I establish the conceptual foundations of eros before deploying the concept in later sections as a heuristic device for measuring the depth of psychological injury inflicted on citizens by public school inequality.

A genealogical survey of eros suggests how its symbolism and vocabulary can provide educators with a strong vocational counterpoise to the cult of efficiency that dominates the current educational climate.[5] *Eros is* one of the three ancient Greek words for love, a multifaceted term used to capture an identifiable set of qualities deeply connected to any dynamic educational process, just as *philia* and *agape*, as other Greek valences of love, represent distinct yet related qualities and aims.[6] Ever associated with expansions of meaning, yet animated by a lack, eros can generally be defined as a hopeful desire for connection: to others, to an object of knowledge, to truth, and to a vision of a perceived good. On this basis Jim Garrison is right to declare that "the education of eros should be the supreme aim of education. . . . teachers desire to educate the eros of their students to passionately desire what is truly good."[7] While contesting what is "truly good to desire" within the classroom can give rise to ambiguous moral conflicts, this should not mean, as it often does, that we avoid such inquiries. On the contrary, a fully developed concept of love in relation to teaching and learning requires that we formulate inquiries that will jeopardize our student's very identities. The theme of love ought to be seen as present in a radical questioning of the values, assumptions, and truths one has learned in experience.

In this regard, recall that Paulo Freire's theory of *conscientization* is defined by a heightened awareness of the external and internal contradictions one is able to perceive.[8] Such perceptions invariably magnify a sense of inner conflict; but this tension, however unsettling initially, is creative, and crucial in generating the sufficient thrust necessary to propel consciousness toward a "higher" state of being. In the absence of such an inner conflict, the transformation of consciousness, as a structural dynamic, cannot occur. From this structuralist standpoint, therefore, love in the form of eros is implicit in the process of *conscientization*, since the "love" I am describing denotes a psychic movement of connection, from a condition of unknowing to a condition of knowing, from "submersion to emergence."[9] The desire to move toward and connect to something better, whether to a person or an idea, is not only an erotic energy, it is educable. I maintain that the ancient pedagogical motif of "educating the desires," applied to today's classroom, requires discussions in which the young learn how to ask questions about the social construction of their desire, happiness, and identity. As students begin the process of choosing themselves, and as they reflect on who it is that chooses, the realization opens up that the objects upon which their desires and identities are presently fastened may not be of their own making. When such levels of dissonance occur, new questions about the social orchestration of one's loves and desires are stimulated and developed, learned ethical activities that are best exercised when historically ripe social contradictions are freshly encountered.

Eros and the Reconstruction of Common Sense

In 1962, Raymond E. Callahan's sobering *Education and the Cult of Efficiency* appeared, a book perhaps more relevant today than when it was first published. Callahan examined why so many public school administrators during the period from 1910 to 1930 had come to adopt a business-oriented vocabulary to describe the aims of their work and their self-image as educators. He was alarmed at how deeply the values of the marketplace and Frederick Taylor's principles of scientific management had penetrated the consciousness of the schoolmen he studied.[10] These influences, Callahan showed, framed the common sense that educators used to understand and interpret the purposes of education. In today's educational climate, given the inordinate attention devoted to standardized testing and accountability, as well as on punitive regimes of discipline generally, it's safe to say that an epic sequel to the cult of efficiency is now being imposed across the nation. Among teachers, however, there is growing disenchantment with the kinds of "learning" such cults of efficiency mandate.

The introduction of bland and formulaic curriculum packets, for example, serve to de-skill teaching and restrict a teacher's intellectual creativity (loss of eros). Such practices contribute to epidemic levels of student boredom (loss of eros). The growing "method" of teaching to the test, owing to the breakneck speed with which one must cover the necessary material, forecloses both authentic dialogue (loss of eros), and spontaneously authored inquiries (loss of eros). The devaluation of democratic citizenship education within such regimes of indoctrination also means, in practice, that the nation's pedagogically fertile civic controversies will go tragically unencountered (loss of eros), an absence that can only diminish the depth of one's civic selfhood (loss of eros).

Each of the symbolic associations noted parenthetically reflects a set of qualities that capture defining strands of experiential eros. Although conceptualized in negative terms as in so many absences, these absent associations still go some distance toward justifying the deployment of eros as an organizing principle of education. Taken with the positive associations of eros in the pages ahead, these qualities comprise a sort of "conceptual handle" that can provide teachers with the theoretical clarity and intelligibility of purpose needed to educate for democracy as a mode of being, for what Dewey called "a form of moral and spiritual association."[11] A knowledge of eros, I submit, gives teachers license to rebel, license to create new space for alternative conceptions of educational meaning. The likelihood of *experiential* eros to occur within the classroom would increase if teachers first developed a *conceptual* knowledge of eros as a way of knowing—a heuristic device—for better understanding both the contradictory, creative dynamics of consciousness as well as the sources of harm that are afflicted on the psyche. The question is not so much *if* eros can provide the basis for a new common sense in education. The basis has already been laid, it rests on the erotic core of the humanist tradition, from Plato and Rousseau to Dewey and Freire, among others. Let us turn now to an exploration of some of the defining moments of this tradition.

The Erotic Foundations of Liberatory Pedagogy

Before Plato boldly reconceptualized eros as an organizing, first principle of education, the prephilosophic cosmogonies in ancient Greece had already established its divine and mythopoetic status.[12] In the prephilosophic conception, eros was considered a "god," an external deity whose force and power "happened" to one randomly and wantonly. Human beings, in this conception, exercised no agency whatsoever in terms of actually influencing the presence or absence of eros within their lives. Plato rejected this interpretation. He argued that human beings should conceive of this power as amenable to human intention and action. Plato thus educationalized eros by attaching a new ethical component to the concept. As part of bringing eros "down to earth" and humanizing the concept, Plato inaugurates the idea of *pedagogy* as a "spiritual ascent," a new theoretical vehicle required to educate desire through an ethic of questioning.[13] Without pedagogy as an "art of conversion" to help draw out the volcanic energies of eros, the concept would remain essentially prephilosophic, containing no person-centered educational and ethical component directed toward self-transformation.

The *Symposium* is Plato's testament to the capacity of eros to render human life happier and more meaningful.[14] Significantly, Plato rejects the prephilosophic assumption that "god is love" or "love is god." Rather, eros is described as a *daimon*, an intermediate third term that holds together the binary oppositions of heaven and earth, divine and human, being and becoming, appearance and reality (*Sym.* 203a). Indeed, in several crucial instances within the *Symposium*, Socrates is depicted as meditating on his internal *daimon* as a means for developing wisdom, a paradoxical condition rooted in a lack, in not knowing (*Sym.*175b, 220c).

Considering that the Greek word for happiness is *eudaimonia,* meaning to have a *good daimon,* it is reasonable to speculate that, as a virtue and as a process, *happiness is itself linked to being awake to and connected with the energies of eros.* Of this Socrates was convinced. In referring to the education of human virtue, Socrates declares there is no better friend to this process than eros: "Now, since I am persuaded, I also try to persuade others that one could not easily find a better collaborator with human nature for acquiring virtue than eros" (*Sym.* 212a).

Several speeches also make reference to the idea that eros functions as a great "builder of cities" (*Sym.* 178d), a pattern that highlights its wider social implications as an agent of community. Diotima asserts that the highest purposes of eros are concerned with the proper "ordering of cities" on the basis of justice and good sense (*Sym.* 209a). The learned capacity to imagine a common good, to think about one's social relationality, derives in large part from those qualities that have traditionally been construed as "feminine": the synergistic and intuitive and relational qualities seem to be the values upon which visions of a common good depend for their existence. Since these epistemic lenses of connection are in-*formed* by erotic undercurrents, a complete theory of eros must also include gender as a central unit of value and analysis. In developing a gender-balanced theory of eros, it would be unwise to ignore Plato's feminist-friendly conceptualization. Wendy Brown reminds us of the emotional subtext that informs

the Socratic/Platonic educational philosophy: "The myths, allegories, stories, and images in the dialogues appeal to the dimensions of Socrates'
companions that are not necessarily articulate but that feel, sense, and
yearn."[15]

The feeling, sensing, and yearning valences of eros—the emotional fuel
of the transformative moment—are described by Plato through the repeated use of feminine symbolism.[16] Diotima refers to the beautiful image
of *soul pregnancy* to approximate the expectant, about-to-give-birth buoy-
ancy of consciousness (*Sym.* 206d–209a). In the *Theatetus* Socrates calls
himself a "midwife"(149a–151d); in the *Gorgias*, Plato deliberately has
Callicles ridicule Socrates and the activity of philosophy as "effeminate"
(484d–485d); while in the *Meno*, Socrates takes care not to treat Meno
as an instance to win someone over via lecture, but as a person who is situated in history, who can inquire, and whose desires, as the stuff of identity, deserve close attention through an ethic of questioning (71d). For all
of these reasons, Wendy Brown describes Platonic pedagogy not only as
erotic but as "maternal." [17]

In a modern representation of eros, Jean Jacques Rousseau's *Emile* offers
a developmental but deeply gendered theory of how the powers of eros
should be educationally recruited to help shape a more expansive, cos-
mopolitan civic identity. The energies of love or eros are pivotal in enabling the protagonist Emile, starting in adolescence, to place himself
imaginatively in the position of others and to empathize with their suffering.[18] Rousseau wants us to educate for compassion by building up imaginative links to others and to the social realm generally by in effect using the
pedagogical relation as an erotic vehicle to transform isolated I's into a
sense of *We*. Emile's education culminates in foreign travel for the express
purpose of developing a more expansive, civic self. However, Rousseau
constructs a gendered, "zonal eros" in denying Sophie, Emile's prearranged
wife, the opportunity to also experience a civic education. In denying Sophie foreign travel and an opportunity to "do" politics and philosophy,
Rousseau restricts the civic agency of women. It is well known, of course,
that Rousseau's "thought-experiment" creates a gendered-apartheid system of education; nevertheless, the larger point here is that the powers of
eros are coded as indispensable to the full development of one's civic identity. It is important to note, for the purposes of this paper, that the restriction of Sophie's civic identity, means, in effect, that her happiness will also
be restricted.

In the twentieth century, several Frankfurt School authors have analyzed the politics of love operative within both fascist and democratic
cultures. Theodor Adorno, in his "Education After Auschwitz," describes
how an over-determined masculinity (with its gendered suppression of all

things erotic) is precisely the kind of mentality incapable of feeling or seeing from another person's perspective. "The inability to identify with others was unquestionably the most important psychological condition for the fact that something like Auschwitz could have occurred in the midst of more or less civilized and innocent people."[19] Here, the Nazi character formation reflects a severely diminished feminine relational capacity, which would permit a broader scope of human identification.

At the conclusion of their study on the authoritarian personality type, Horkheimer and Adorno introduce but do not develop the connection between love and democracy: "If fear and destructiveness are the major emotional sources of fascism, *eros belongs mainly to democracy.*"[20] Put differently, the actualization of democracy as an ethical ideal rests in large part on whether or not the erotic dimensions of human being are educated in the right way. Herbert Marcuse, author of the seminal *Eros and Civilization,* also emphasizes the cultural and political implications of eros as a symbol of liberation: "The young are in the forefront of those who live and fight for Eros against Death. . . . Today the fight for life, the fight for Eros, is the *political* fight."[21] What does Marcuse mean when he says the fight for eros is the political fight? Perhaps he is suggesting that the emotional wellsprings of eros store vast reserves of human energy and potential and that institutional structures of power and interest, public and private, function to "police" and "manage" the objects and images upon which our emotional devotions are projected. Marcuse understands why a state of cultural amnesia surrounds discursive eros—its recovery as an organizing principle could transform in unpredictable ways the aims and objects of human desire.

Eros and Lincoln's Apple of Gold; or, How to Remap the Nation

As I have tried to demonstrate, the "passion for changing things for the better" is one of the defining strands of eros. For this reason, eros can also be understood as a psychical terrain deeply implicated in any embodied *pursuit* of happiness (defined broadly as a future-directed desire and act of attention). I want to suggest on this basis, in addition to related associations, that an intimate symbiosis exists between the faculties of eros as a kind of love and the embodied fulfillment of those democratic values reflected in the Declaration of Independence. To develop this claim, we turn to a rarely discussed fragment in the writings of Abraham Lincoln (1861).[22] In it, Lincoln refers to the values and principles in the Declaration as an "apple of gold." The apple of gold, he writes, is enframed by the Constitution, by the "picture of silver." As Lincoln's musings on the relation between the two birth certificates of the nation reveal, he recognized the democratic values of the Declaration potentially exist in contradiction to the legal instrument that is the Constitution. Lincoln's reflections are relevant today because they can illuminate the tensions within a political culture whose rhetorical allegiance to equality and democracy is belied by its system of public education, which drains these principles of substantive meaning.

Before pursuing this argument, we should pause at the metaphorical level. The *apple* has generally come to symbolize "knowledge" or the "knowledge-quest," while *gold* is considered to be a metal more precious than silver. The *apple of gold* is therefore a perfectly fitting symbol for *eros*! Indeed, the Garden of Eden story illustrates Eve's attempt to acquire knowledge from the fruit of the tree of the knowledge of good and evil, a fruit that is popularly regarded today as an apple. At least according to the dominant interpretation, the "unauthorized" seizure of knowledge by Eve was deemed so dangerous that subsequent pursuits of knowledge were to be actively forbidden, a cultural construct indelibly associated with Augustine, the chief ideological architect of Western anti-eroticism.[23] The historical practice of ruling elites exercising their power to deny knowledge, particularly self-knowledge, to the powerless appears to be a universal phenomenon. In the United States, for example, before the consequences of the Civil War expanded the legal boundaries of national citizenship, laws were passed that outlawed the teaching of literacy to the slaves, an institutionalized denial of learning that gave rise to the creation of many clandestine schools.[24] Although many oppressed persons made eloquent appeals for their right to partake in the marvelous civic nutrients within the apple of gold, such appeals consistently fell on deaf ears, to which the U.S. Supreme Court decisions *Dred Scott* v. *Sanford* (1857) and *Plessey* v. *Ferguson* (1896) lucidly attest. In both the antebellum and postbellum periods, only select citizens, it seems, were permitted to eat from the apple of gold. As an erotic metaphor, then, the *apple of gold* can be seen to symbolize the incarnation or coming-to-be of a democratic civic identity. The question posed for us today is whether exposure to the apple of gold, as a form of civic literacy, is available to all citizens or whether its availability is still restricted in crucial ways.

Turning to the defining passage, Lincoln constructs a moral hierarchy in the process of comparing the two "birth certificates" of the nation.

> The assertion of that *principle*, at that time, was the word, fitly spoken which has proved an "apple of gold" to us. The Union, and the Constitution, are the *picture of silver*, subsequently framed around it. The picture was made, not to *conceal*, or *destroy* the apple; but to *adorn*, and *preserve* it. The *picture* was made *for* the apple—*not* the apple for the picture (*CW* 168–69).

When Lincoln declares "the picture was made *for* the apple, *not* the apple for the picture, he deems the substantive moral values of the Declaration paramount; they precede and trump in value the legal, procedural instrument that is the state. In applying these symbolic distinctions, as instruments of value, to the task of educating democratic citizens, an emphasis on the moral primacy of the apple of gold ordains a *developmental, embodied* model of democratic citizenship, while emphasis on the picture of silver, on abstract procedural norms, ordains a *nondevelopmental, disembodied* model of liberal citizenship. The tension between the type of civic character each instrument of value is likely to ordain—one democratic, one liberal—is demonstrated in two U.S. Supreme Court decisions that tried to define the scope of the Fourteenth Amendment's Equal Protection Clause relative to public education.[25]

Brown v. *Board of Education* 347 U.S. (1954) and *San Antonio Independent School District* v. *Rodriguez* 411 U.S. (1973) display contradictory models of citizenship. *Brown* expanded the boundaries of civic identity by taking into consideration the effects of racial segregation and unequal public education on the psyche of nascent citizens. In *Rodriguez,* however, the 5–4 majority *shrank* the boundaries of civic identity by not following *Brown's* revolutionary precedent. For the majority in *Rodriguez,* only an *absolute deprivation* of public education would have been sufficiently "unequal" to trigger the protective powers of the Equal Protection clause. In measuring instances of public school inequality according to the procedural criterion of mere physical school attendance, the majority overlooked what actually goes on inside the schools, qualitatively, as immaterial. Within this loveless, "disembodied" oligarchic universe of educational jurisprudence, the moral force of the apple of gold is repressed as a binding factor in the construction of citizenship. This repression ought to be the focus of our pedagogical activity far more than it has! Disregard for the precedent established in *Brown* therefore meant that the psyches of vulnerable young citizens would no longer be protected against the civic effects of inequality in the domain of compulsory, public education. Because *Rodriguez* sanctions the doctrine of "separate, but equal" in the realm of public education, it needs to be re-presented today as the contemporary moral equivalent of the notorious *Plessey.*

Lincoln ends the fragment on a prophetic note. "So let us act, that neither picture, or apple shall ever be blurred, or bruised or broken. That we may so act, we must study, and understand the points of danger" (*CW* 169). In the concluding section, I argue that public school inequality not only represents one of the gravest "points of danger" to the democratic spirit of American national identity, but that this danger is best studied and understood through a critical theory of erotics.

Public Education, Democratic Amplitude, and the Inalienable Right to the *Pursuit* of Happiness.

There is no need to belabor the point that the American system of public education is grounded in structural inequality. Nor is there any serious disagreement that the central funding mechanism for public education—local property tax—functions to reproduce, not reduce, inequalities in the larger society. Yet, faced with volumes of "proof" about the destructive civic consequences of public school inequality, the nation appears to be looking elsewhere and manifesting symptoms of attention deficit disorder, a civic disease evidenced in the learned passion to ignore the *Plessey*-esque structure of its "democratic" system of public education.

In *Ordinary Resurrections: Children in the Years of Hope,* Jonathan Kozol once again compels us to remember the forgotten.[26] Kozol observes the stark contrast in social climate that typically exists between high-income schools and materially impoverished ones. In comparing these social climates, Kozol mints the perfect term, "democratic amplitude," to describe the material and emotional environments necessary to foster the education of democratic personalities.

> The differences are seen not only in the size of classes and salaries of teachers but in dozens of associated matters such as the provision of attractive libraries, good exercise facilities, intensive counseling and guidance in selection of a course of study that will lead to university admissions, as well as all those other offerings, both pedagogic and aesthetic, that convey a sense of democratic amplitude and shape the ambience of opportunity and graciousness in day to day living (*OR*, 46).

The aesthetic and pedagogic offerings, the opportunity and graciousness that contribute to a sense of democratic amplitude for the affluent is "structured" not to exist for whole categories of citizen today. I would submit that for those caught in the hope-constricting consequences of public school inequality, their "inalienable right" to the *pursuit* of happiness—defined here as an equal opportunity to develop one's civic selfhood—is being violated through state-administered public education. Obviously, one of the most difficult pedagogical aspects of this problem is that common-sense understandings of the "inalienable right to the pursuit of happiness" are embedded within a privatized, utilitarian narrative of maximizing individual pleasure. Within this narrative, whatever civic meanings the phrase could reflect are erased, further relieving the public schools of their responsibility to secure for all citizens an equal right, not to happiness, but to providing the educational conditions necessary for its *pursuit*. I believe this iconic phrase contains enough interpretative fertility to accommodate such reversals of meaning. If, for example, the undertheorized "social covenant" meanings of the pursuit of happiness clause were seriously mined and, if need be, invented, the phrase could be re-scripted as the cultivation of *civic virtue*, a developmental, embodied form of citizenship that mandates that the schools have a moral and legal obligation to educate equally.[27]

This utopian, eros-informed way of thinking suggests that debates about inequality in public education need to focus greater attention on the developmental, civic strands of the psyche, on unquantifiable qualities like eros and hope and their centrality in creating the *citizenship* of the citizen. Considering also that American identity is rooted in a myth of transcendence, in a myth of re-invention, as a symbolic formation it is deeply indebted to the education of eros as a condition of its own possibility. The education of eros, in this sense, refers not only to the cultivation of qualities that would help catalyze a personal knowledge quest, but also to changing *what is desired* in relation to the very idea of a common good. The fact that access to this idea, to this specific transcendent function (the opportunity to identify oneself with a larger social purpose) is "managed" on the basis of wealth demonstrates how the oligarchic structure of American education militates against the reconstruction of a viable sense of the common good.

In speaking about one child while observing a group of youngsters in the Mott Haven district of the South Bronx, Kozol describes how the erotic dimensions of these nascent citizens are systematically suppressed.

> When I am with Elio, I am persuaded that the light within his eyes will never be extinguished. But there are many men from the South Bronx in prison in New York today—Elio's father is just one of several thousand of these men—whose mothers and grandmothers can remember the same light of goodness in their eyes as well when they were six or eight years old. The light is darkened much too soon for many children in this neighborhood and others like it to be found in cities all over the nation; and the longing of so many to reveal their light and bring their gift of goodness to our nation's table is too often stifled and obliterated long before they are fifteen years old (*OR* 42).

Based on the symbolic inventory of eros developed in previous sections, it's clear that phrases like the "light of goodness" and the "longing" to bring the "gift of goodness to our nation's table" resonate with erotic symbolism and with the feelings that would inform any pursuit of happiness understood as a civic virtue. Notice how this "light" and "goodness" are described as unselfish, civic offerings connected to a larger common good (the "nation's table"). In another poignant image, Kozol quotes a teacher who wrote to him: "There are some children who are like windows. When you look into those windows you see more than the kids themselves—more than innocence. . . . You see the deep, inextinguishable goodness at the core of creation" (*OR* 42). But this fine insight needs to be situated histori-cally in relation to the class basis of public education, for as Kozol shows, such goodness at the core of creation is routinely "dirtied, tangled and twisted."

> The natural gentility and spontaneity of many of the little ones like Elio are dirtied, tangled, twisted, and compressed too quickly. The grace and dignity of girls like Ariel are often coarsened and degraded by the time they enter junior high school, where, as teachers in the neighborhood observe repeatedly, a shell of hardness frequently is formed like a protective shield against the many injuries and disappointments that await them. Some of the children who are virtually bursting with poetic creativity when they are six years old evolve de-structive substitutes for creativity and violent channels for their disrespected energies before they even get to junior high (*OR* 42–43).

Instead of having one's human and civic potential educated, these citi-zens have their "poetic creativity," their rich endowment of human possi-bility, their eros, "disrespected" through the productive agency of the state. When we ask what, exactly, the "inalienable right" to the "pursuit of happi-ness" means in the context of our *Plessey-esque* system of public education, one is forced to the conclusion that this vital piece of national mythology is bereft of meaning for all too many citizens. For many, the pursuit of happi-ness is violated because the emotional faculties of eros intrinsic to these citizens are institutionally repressed, systematically increasing the chances that their psychological and civic character will be distorted by a tragic mix of anger and hopelessness. Although written in the early 1960s, James Baldwin's "Talk to Teachers" has never been more prophetic: ". . . if Amer-ica is going to *become* a nation, she must find a way—and this child must help her to find a way to use the tremendous potential and tremendous en-ergy which this child represents. If this country does not find a way to use that energy, it will be destroyed by that energy."[28] Let's digress briefly to ex-amine "that energy" and consider the pedagogical challenges it raises.

Part of what makes this statement remarkable is Baldwin's recognition that when human potential is so blatantly squandered, a democratic peo-ple, in order to *become* a nation and create a more democratic version of themselves, must value every person's potential. In this way a disposition of civic love finds institutional expression in the principle of equality of educational opportunity. As we consider the magnitude of the human and social loss manufactured as a result of public school inequality and observe the growing gap between America's democratic ideals and its oligarchic re-ality of public education, we are right to become angry, just as Baldwin's child is also right to be angry.

As a political virtue, few thinkers capture the positive value of anger as well as Aristotle. In an oft-noted passage, Aristotle discusses the moral legitimacy of being angry in the face of a perceived injustice, against oneself or others: "Anyone who does not get angry in the right way at the right time and with the right people, is a fool."[29] Applied to the purposes of this inquiry, Aristotle's maxim suggests, among other things, that a fully developed pedagogy of eros must also be augmented by a well-theorized pedagogy of anger. Such a pedagogy would embody the principle that it is not only necessary but possible to rechannel the destructive but no less powerful energies that grow out of conditions of injustice. But we must also cultivate, and create, in the right way, a sense of anger and indignation in privileged students about these democratic violations. But how to develop a judicious sense of educated anger? What if student anger is turned on us? The authors in this book propose to negotiate these and other ethical predicaments in strikingly divergent ways. My own thinking about the conflictual consequences of critical pedagogy is guided by the psychoanalytic perspective that love in learning means anxiety, and necessarily so, for all involved.[30] Living in a democratic society that is rhetorically, if not substantively, anchored in the principle of equality, democratic teachers are destined to inhabit zones of tension so long as social hierarchies exist. The privileged beneficiaries of such hierarchies must learn to see, however, that even they may be democratically impaired by what might seem to them like "favorable" distributions of social power.

As John Dewey repeatedly brings to our attention, the human loss associated with institutionalized inequality does not accrue only to those who occupy the lower rungs of the American educational caste; the loss penetrates to the whole of society as a constructed absence of social interchange.

> In order to have a large number of values in common, all the members of the group must have an equable opportunity to receive and to take from others. There must be a large variety of shared undertakings and experiences. Otherwise, the influences which educate some into masters, educate others into slaves. And the experience of each party loses in meaning, when the free interchange of varying modes of life-experience is arrested.[31]

Not only are individual lives "arrested" by public school inequality and the consequent lack of social capital in the affected schools, so, too, are the perspectives and life experiences of the affluent classes, whose lives cannot proceed in "ordered richness" in the context of social and spiritual isolation. In contrast to this melancholy tale of two citizens, a democratic conception of love is grounded in a love of the people, in a belief that all citizens should have an equal opportunity to develop their full human and civic potential. Proceeding on the basis of this generalized principle of love, we can begin to see more clearly how the "inalienable right to the pursuit of happiness" contains a strong yet largely untapped potential to challenge the moral legitimacy of public school inequality.

As theorists of American democracy, Cornel West and Roberto Unger offer a richly textured, democratic conception of love, one that provides philosophical justification for the project of equalizing public education.

> The soul of ordinary man and woman hides vast recesses of intensity. The sadness of much of human life lies in the disproportion between this intensity and the accidental or unworthy objects on which people so often lavish their intense commitments. That this reserve capacity for devotion and obsession can be tapped productively, for the good of the community, has always been the major tenet of the American religion of possibility. Democracy, Americans understand, depends on *demophilia*, love of the people.[32]

Again, John Dewey argued that one of the defining principles of the democratic personality formation is a "working faith in the possibilities of human nature." Nor was he satisfied with merely talking about human possibility in the abstract, since it involves ". . . a belief which brings with it the need for *providing conditions which will enable these capacities to reach fulfillment* . . . the democratic faith in human equality is belief that every human being, independent of the quantity or range of his personal endowment, has the right to equal opportunity with every other person for development of whatever gifts he has"[33] (emphasis added). When the "development of one's gifts" occurs within a "separate, but equal" structure of public education, repressive forms of social control are institutionalized for those citizens whose *citizenship* is made to atrophy: a process accurately defined as the mass production of idiocy.[34] In using the phrase "the mass production of idiocy," I want to jolt readers into a heightened awareness of the dire consequences for American democracy of producing whole categories of youth whose civic selves are systematically de-publicized, a fact that compromises their right to the pursuit of something we call happiness.

Kozol documents the vast discrepancies in yearly per-pupil expenditure that define New York's school system ($5,200 for the poorest vs. $18,000 for the richest) and situates this inequality alongside the "humanitarian ideals" of U.S. political culture and "the unforgotten dreams" of Martin Luther King.

> These are extraordinary inequalities within a metropolitan community that still lays claim to certain vestiges of the humanitarian ideals associated with the age of civil rights and with the unforgotten dreams of Dr. Martin Luther King. No matter how these differences may be obscured or understated or complexified by civilized equivocation, they do tell us something about how we value Pineapple and Elio as human beings, both in their present status as small children who rely upon our decency and in their future destinies as adult citizens (*OR*, 45).

Yes, the Pineapples and Elios of America do indeed rely upon our decency, but what does our sense of decency rely upon? In a crucial way, our *common decency* relies upon the extent to which the democratic moral values, symbolized by the apple of gold, are remembered, valued, and learned, both inside and outside the schools. If this claim has any validity, it is imperative to realize that the radical democratic potential of the Declaration of Independence lay dormant *after* 1776 for nearly a half-century, a constructed absence of public memory that was anything but innocent of power relations.[35]

During the 1830s, however, newly assertive labor and abolitionist movements suddenly revived public memory and civic meaning. Only then did the Declaration truly attain iconic status, for it was creatively repoliticized as something *democratic, future-oriented, and transcendent* to expanding numbers of people. Historian Alfred Young captures the transformation in American identity that emerged from this creative re-reading of the Declaration: "The Fourth of July, to conservatives never more than the anniversary of independence, to others had become a symbol of liberation."[36] Within a few decades, because of their daring public pedagogies—which could be described as angry yet loving—the abolitionists helped mobilize "the return of the repressed" within the negotiation of the national identity. The value of equality as a symbol of liberation was pedagogically reawakened as a force in the contest to shape the meaning of the national identity. In this way, the abolitionist and working-class recovery of the apple of gold was directly responsible for the democratic expansion of civic identity after the Civil War.

How to similarly recover and reintegrate into the American identity the public memory of its repressed democratic values? There are many paths to this destination—opportunities abound throughout the disciplines and at every level of instruction. Equipped with a theory of eros to enliven our educational visions and pedagogical interventions, teachers can enhance their power to make the schools "instruments in the active and constant suppression of the war spirit," as Dewey had so wisely envisioned.[37] Just as the "war spirit" is today pedagogically created, so, too, must a "peace spirit" be pedagogically created. Eros matters in this interminable struggle.

A sense of eros permits us to think and feel and envision images of beauty, happiness, and justice as no other first principle of education. In view of today's social climate, dominated by intensifying levels of surplus aggression and fear spliced with consumer escapism, some may justifiably ask if it is even possible to fundamentally rescript the pursuit of happiness clause and link its new civic meaning to the abolition of state-administered inequality in public education. It may be said in reply that our horizons of political possibility—our capacity and willingness to revise, and to imagine a common good, for example—have themselves been diminished by the forgetting of eros as an organizing principle of education. For these reasons, in a post-9/11 permanent war environment, the potentially subversive portals of historical memory identified in this inquiry have never been more important to open up and relearn: Only as these values and principles are remembered and enacted can America as a political body achieve the beautiful.

CHAPTER 6

The Allure of Beauty and the Pain of Injustice in Learning and Teaching

DANIEL LISTON

Introduction

In learning there is frequently an engaging, enveloping, and somewhat paradoxical allure. When we visit natural worlds, we see in those domains other realms that seem to exist unto themselves, wonder-filled worlds, which we can observe and explore. We seem both a part of and distinct from these places. Sometimes we are dropped into a novel and we find ourselves immersed in characters and settings that have come to life. When they become "real," these fictional characters accompany us through our day. When we search for algebraic patterns, we come upon regularities that entice and amaze. These patterns seem both God-given and man-made. And when we learn another language, we behold a system of expression that seems much larger than a collection of words, larger in some ways than our selves. It seems we have to submit in order to master it. When we teach, we invite our students to take part in these domains, these other worlds, these engagements, to embrace what we have found so alluring. We ask others to fall in love with what we, and others, have uncovered and found alluring. At least sometimes that's what we try to do.

But not always. Those of us who have taught within the radical tradition seem to have our sights set on a somewhat different target. Radical pedagogy and critical theories seem to lack the enticing beauty and the paradoxical allure of these "other" worlds. Beauty in this world is not what is so fetching in radical analyses. Instead, radical pedagogy and critiques promise to uncover the causes, means and, processes; the contradictions, ironies, obfuscations, and unalluring ugliness of everyday living in hopes of creating a more shared and just community. Illumination, a certain critical and telling perspective, is desired, along with paths to a more humane and just world. Alienation, injustice, harm, and hate are experienced daily by many groups and individuals. Radical pedagogy and theory aim at illuminating and alleviating those harms and affirming the shared and the distinct features of our lives. It is a promise that is engaging, uplifting, and, many would say, empowering. It is an experience that reaches for an altered identity, one that is no longer pounded down by the weight of a world that tells us we are insufficient and inept, a world that is the source of the ills that make us sick and of the ugliness that leads us to avert our eyes. Instead, we are offered a view that tells us that our pain is not so much self-inflicted as structurally induced. When we teach to empower, we examine, reflect on, and attempt to transform the pain of injustice. To do so we must know that pain and have taken part in its transformation. To do so we must desire other, more just and more beautiful worlds than those that exist today.

But all too often these promises of learning and teaching are not kept. We teach numbers to students rather than intriguing patterns to children, and we ask students to memorize phylum and genus rather than to explore water-filled worlds. We identify character, plot, and literary terms with the AP exam in mind, or we underscore the seven steps in assertive discipline so that our future teachers can pass the state exit exam. Through the newly revised terms of accountability, the power of the state exerts its force on young minds and bodies. The world is no longer a magical place but rather an achievement course filled with obstacles. For those of us who inhabit a more critical stance, our attempt to understand the exploits and harm in our worlds can also become foiled. In its stead a bald and rather naked power entrances. Rather than grounding our critical work in the struggles of those harmed, critical theory becomes a kind of detached analysis that probes the ills of this world, the ironies, and the unending deceptions.[1] The allure is more for the beauty of the theory and the desire for justice than the hideousness they disclose. Hubris is in the air that is exuded, and all too often disdain and arrogance become the coins of the realm. It is a lure that seduces the individual and one that doesn't serve the community. Regulated by state power, we can no longer be subject to, or subjects of, the mysteries that surround us. And all too often in our attempts to uncover power we become seduced by the tinsel of institutional status.

In what follows I wish to describe some of these allures of learning and teaching; note their contortions and absences; and, subsequently, claim that in teaching (and learning to teach) we need to revisit, sit with, and re-engage the experience of learning. It is an experience that is filled with emotions. The experience of teaching and learning is beset with the scratch and satin of emotional engagement. We need to recall the emotions, the feel, the sense of what was so engaging and alluring about our learning. Unfortunately, we don't handle emotions well in the academy. Affect and emotions tend to be viewed as personal and private belongings and some-times as dark forces that are best kept under cover and controlled. They are not viewed (but should be) as paths to further understanding. This is un-fortunate and disfiguring. Without attending to learning's emotions, we distort and underestimate the activity that defines many of our lives. With-out underlining the emotions of learning in our teaching, we pass on a her-itage that will certainly disfigure the souls of many others to come. Sadly, we've been doing that for much too long. I can see no reason to continue. In what follows I will touch on some of the emotions entailed in learning, underscore how those lures become distorted, and call for a return to the experience of learning in teaching.

The Allure in Learning (and Teaching)

So what is the nature of this allure in learning? In many, but not all, cases I believe it's like falling in love. It's a very romantic endeavor. When we are engaged in a topic that attracts us, when we pursue an issue that engages us, or when we become immersed in a subject that intrigues us, we tran-scend ourselves—we reach beyond ourselves for something that is greater than any of us. Elsewhere I've written at length about this.[2] Let me try and capture some of that here.

Libraries, Ponds, and Streams

Annie Dillard illuminates this allure of coming to know.[3] She conveys how our love of learning connects us to the world, how it engages our minds and emotions, and how it illuminates the sensual and sacred. In *An Ameri-can Childhood*, Dillard accomplishes this by recounting her earlier experi-ences. Growing up in Pittsburgh in the 1950s, Annie Dillard was one of four lively children in a family that did not appear to want for money or resources. Annie loved to read, and the closest library was the branch in Homewood. This branch was located in one of the black sections of town. Because it was some distance from her house, Annie's mother would drive her there. Entering the Homewood Library (which had FREE TO THE PEOPLE engraved on its facade), a twelve-year-old child with an adult card, Dillard recalls the large, vaulted rooms; the high leaded windows; and the quiet, cool floors. One day, during a visit in the adult room "in the cool dark-ness of a bottom shelf," she happened upon *The Field Book of Ponds and*

Streams. It turned out to be a truly wonderful find, for in Chapter 3 of the book, Annie Dillard found what she had not known she was looking for. In this chapter the essential tools of the naturalist's trade were explained, field procedures elaborated, and the multiple worlds of water and insect life unveiled. This marvelous little book opened whole new worlds for young Annie. In this treasure trove, the author explained how to make all sorts of nets (sweep, plankton, and head nets) and how to construct unheard of containers including glass-bottomed buckets and "killing" jars. The author also offered instructions on how to set up freshwater aquariums, mount slides, and label insects on their pins. This book outlined the accoutrements of the naturalist trade, and in doing so, fitted Annie Dillard for one of her most beloved adventures. She learned that when a naturalist went out into the "field" she wore "hip boots and perhaps a head net for mosquitoes. One carried in a 'rucksack' half a dozen corked test tubes, a smattering of screw-type baby-food jars, a white enamel tray, assorted pipettes and eye droppers, an artillery of cheesecloth, . . . and [of course] *The Field Book of Ponds and Streams*" (*AC*, p. 81). In ponds and streams, the reader was assured of finding, and distinguishing among, dragonfly nymphs, planaria, daphniae, water pennies, and salamander and stone fly larvae. With the tools of her newly discovered trade, she was assured of not only locating these marvels but also capturing them and entering into their worlds. With these tools she could immerse herself in ponds and streams.

At her young age Dillard was astonished that anyone had actually lived the "fine life described in Chapter 3" and that such life-filled ponds existed. She wanted to write to the author . . .

> and assure him that someone had found his book, in the dark near the marble floor at the Homewood Library. I would, in the same letter or in a subsequent one, ask him a question outside the scope of his book, which was where I personally might find a pond or a stream. But I did not know how to address such a letter . . . or how to learn if he was still alive. . . . I was afraid, too, that my letter would disappoint him by betraying my ignorance. . . . What, for example, was this noisome-sounding substance called cheese cloth, and what do scientists do with it? What, when you really got down to it, was enamel? If candy could, notoriously, "eat through enamel," why would anyone make trays out of it? (*AC*, p.82)

The *Field Book of Ponds and Streams* bowled Annie Dillard over. It was, as she recalls, a "shocker from beginning to end." And, she adds, the "greatest shock came at the end." On the last page of each library book was the book's card, with the past borrowers' numbers inscribed and the due date sheet. Upon checking her beloved book out for a second time, she noticed that the book's card was almost full, with numbers on both sides.

My hearty author and I were not alone in the world after all. With us, and sharing our enthusiasm for dragonfly larvae and single celled plants, were, apparently many Negro adults. . . . Who were these people? Had they, in Pittsburgh's Homewood section, found ponds? Had they found streams? At home I read the book again; I studied the drawings; I reread Chapter 3; then I settled in to study the due-date slip. People read this book in every season. Seven or eight people were reading this book every year, even during the war. . . . Often when I was in the library, I simply visited it. I sat on the marble floor and studied the book's card. There we all were. There was my number. There was the number of someone else who had checked it out more than once (*AC*, 82–83).

I've never fallen in love with a field book, but, thankfully, Annie Dillard has. She conveys her beloved book's appeal along with her library's special feel. Having lingered in midwestern and northeastern Carnegie neighborhood libraries, those minor monumental edifices built during the early 1900s, it seems Dillard captures much of the experience. One can almost smell the books' mustiness, peer into the dimly lit stacks, feel the coolness of the marble and stone floors. These sensual features seemed to enhance the library's intellectual and emotional allure. After one or two successful visits, the library's particular promise becomes apparent. Libraries open worlds, worlds otherwise not easily accessible, and in doing so they allow us all sorts of unimaginable pleasures. A library's holdings offer the possibility of immersion into other worlds, immersion into natural, unnatural, and human landscapes. These landscapes take us beyond ourselves into alluring realms that seem to beckon our imagination and beg for further exploration. Dillard's discovery of *The Field Book of Ponds and Streams* did all this. It outfitted her in naturalist's gear and took her into the microscopic world of water insects. To the naked and untrained eye, water is water; but with a field book in hand, hip boots secure, and collection jars ready, we can begin to plumb the depths of a pond. Once we have glimpsed the water pennies, dragonfly nymphs, and salamander larvae, other worlds exist beside(s) ours. The library's field book opened up attractive worlds of water and, in doing so, illuminated unseen connections within that natural world. When we explore these worlds, we create webs of connection with and within those worlds. And having been introduced to these worlds, Annie Dillard craved to know more.

Dillard wanted to take her understanding further, fill in the gaps and holes, and hopefully, correct those troublesome conceptions that didn't fit with her ways of seeing the world. This seems to be a common experience. Coming upon new material, we "check" it against what we already know and understand. We try to fit it into our current ways of understanding the world and ourselves, but all too often it just doesn't fit. If we are going to grow, and if we feel somewhat secure, we explore further these gaps and misconceptions. But if we are insecure and defensive, we may try to hide or ignore the poor fit of the new material. Coming to know seems to inevitably entail, at some point, a sense of insufficiency. As Anne Carson notes, the "activities of knowing and desiring . . . have at their core the same delight, that of reaching, and entail the same pain, that of falling short or being deficient . . ."[4] Noisome cheesecloth and enamel trays don't quite fit. Is it a problem with me or the world? Dare I speak up and find out?

Dillard wanted to write to the author in order to acknowledge the book's gift and to connect with the author. Acknowledging these gifts is never a simple or easy task. With books I love, I generally have many purposes in mind, some I'm unaware of. I want the author to know how special the experience was, that it touched me. Frequently, I want to respond to the author, to connect, commune, and communicate with "him." I have questions to ask. I also want to hear this powerful, creative, or keenly analytic voice; I want to be in her/his presence. I don't regularly acknowledge the gift but usually end up seeking out others who have delighted in the book's treasures. When I find others, I am pleased to know that they too have enjoyed the book's pleasures. I share with my fellow readers, and they with me, some of what I would have shared with the author. Annie Dillard did not write to her author. She imagined the questions she might pose, but did not address, to the author. Instead, she sought out other readers. Inscribed on the book's card were other patrons' numbers. Card-carrying Homewood residents had glimpsed these dew-filled worlds, still ponds and swirling streams wet with life. Others had imagined building the naturalist's tools and had toyed with the possibility of exploring these wet lands. Her excursions into the field book were not alone; her journeys were shared with others, and sitting alone on the stone floor she felt comforted by their presence.

With her heart and mind she had explored the world. Doing so she found, to her amazement, that there were many treasures in the world. She writes:

> I had been chipping at the world idly, and had by accident uncovered vast and labyrinthine further worlds within it. I peered in one day and stepped in the next, and soon wandered in deep over my head. Month after month, year after year, the true and brilliant light, of the actual, historical, waking world invigorated me. Its vastness extended everywhere I looked, and precisely where I looked. . . . Everything in the world, every baby, city, tetanus shot, tennis ball, and pebble was an outcrop of some vast and hitherto unconcealed vein of knowledge, apparently, that had compelled people's emotions and engaged their minds in the minutest detail without anyone's having done with it. There must be enthusiasts for everything on earth—fanatics who shared a vocabulary, a batch of technical skills and equipment, and perhaps, a vision of some single slice of the beauty and mystery of things, of their complexity, fascination and unexpectedness (*AC*, pp.157–59).

Attracted by the many worlds around her, Dillard was touched by a singular beauty and mystery that they somehow all shared. When exploring the water-filled and rock-strewn worlds, she also encountered, within herself, an emotional terrain that pushed and pulled her forward. When we learn, we are frequently pushed and pulled by our emotions. Dillard's natural worlds engaged her in wonder and awe. They pulled a curious mind along further into the natural eddies and crevices to experience the beauty, complexity, and mystery therein and pushed her to explore further. These are worlds that fuel our enthusiasm and imagination.

Getting Critical

Not all learning and teaching entice us through existing beauty and mystery. Sometimes our engagements are activated by a sense of outrage and harm, propelled by a passionate desire (eros) to understand these hurts further, and motivated by a yearning to curb repulsive injustice while creating better and hopefully more beautiful worlds. For some individuals these injustices are discerned empathetically, whereas for others they are felt directly. Many of those who know oppression, whether it is grounded in race, gender, class, or some other social force, feel great pain. Some search for ways to understand it. They try to come to terms with it, know its sources, understand its dynamics, and they look for ways to change their and others' circumstances. The lure is not beauty in our existing worlds but rather the beauty and potential in a more just world; it is not the attraction of being drawn into another world and seeing it on its own terms. Instead, the lures are critical examinations of the world in which we live; depictions of derangement that are more telling than the renditions normally offered; understandings that affirm pain, outrage, and humanity and perhaps offer some way of changing the terrain of that pain. Paulo Freire writes of the peasant who, after experiencing the literacy program, said: "I can't say that I've understood everything you've said just now, but I can say one thing—when I began this course I was *naive*, and when I found out how naive I was, I started to get *critical*."[5] Understanding a bit of what it feels like to *get critical*, the lures that accompany the movement from naivete to critique can and ought to be discerned. The emotional attractions are rarely discussed in professional circles. Discerning a few of the emotional facets that accompany getting critical allows us to understand further the lures in our learning and the potential in our teaching. Detailing those lures also provides a window through which we can look at our current and, I believe, truncated and hyper-rationalized version of "critical learning."

If you grow up brown, poor, or female in the U.S. you're inevitably bound to encounter obstacles that others seem to miss. The structural conditions of poverty, patriarchy, and racism make it difficult for some to flourish or achieve in this system. If you're poor, chances are that you will be offered an education that is resource thin and institutionally harsh. If your skin tone is dark, you may become the shadowy other, the other that those who are paler fear or despise. And if you grow up female, in hetero-sexual situations you will likely be viewed as a sexual object. Growing up brown, female, and/or poor, individuals encounter these obstacles and at times begin to internalize the dominant portrayals. If my school is barren and cold, it must be what I merit. If people don't see this darker self, don't seem to regard me, then maybe this is what I deserve. If my body con-stitutes me, then maybe my mind has little to offer. Feeling pain and heartache in the world around them, some individuals begin to think they are the cause of that pain. Becoming critical provides an alternative stance toward this world of oppression. It offers a perspective that questions the dominant, and frequently self-incriminatory, master narrative.

In *Monster: The Autobiography of an L.A. Gang Member,* Sanyika Shakur (also known as Monster Kody Scott) chronicles his life as a gang member in south central Los Angeles in the 1980s.[6] It was a gang life that included a strong sense of membership as well as extreme brutality and violence. End-ing up in jail, incarcerated for his gang misdeeds, he began to look at him-self and the world around him. He began a process of critical education, what some call consciousness raising. He read, sought out other inmates and advisors, and attended the Black Muslim prayer services. At the prayer services he received a pamphlet entitled *Message to the Oppressed,* a text heavily influenced by Malcolm X. Shakur writes:

> In my cell on the Rock, I reread for the hundredth time *Message to the Op-pressed.* Malcolm came on strong: "We declare our right on this earth to be a man, to be a human being, to be given the rights of a human being in this soci-ety, on this earth, in this day, which we intend to bring into existence by any means necessary." As I read on I felt the world seeping deeper into me, their power coursing through my body, giving me strength to push on. I was chang-ing, I felt it. For once I didn't challenge it or see it as being a threat to the estab-lished more of the 'hood, though of course, it was (*M,* p. 223).

He adds:

> here I was totally absorbed in the . . . written word of Malcolm X. Each emo-tional lash was tantamount to the resounding echo of gunfire. But unlike gun-fire, no one was killed. This was my first encounter with brothers who could kill with words. Their words were not mere talk, either. Action followed in the wake of their theories, and their presence demanded respect long before their words were spoken (*M,* pp.228–29).

Later, after prison officials replaced the Black Muslim minister with a Christian preacher, Shakur writes:

My consciousness about the larger enemy was being raised bit by bit. Why wouldn't someone want us to learn about who we really are? Is our knowledge of self so threatening that such measures as sending a Christian preacher into an air conduit are necessary to hinder its attainment? (*M*, p. 232)

In the end, the Muslim formulation of a New Afrikan Independence Movement offered the critical perspective Shakur was seeking.

I received the New Afrikan ideological formulation material and it redeemed me. It gave me answers to all the questions I had about myself in relation to this society. I learned about how our situation in this country was that of an oppressed nation, colonized by capitalist-imperialists. The science was strong and precise (*M*, p. 351).

In Shakur's terms he grew from resisting blindly as a gang member to becoming conscious and politically resistant as an incarcerated New Afrikan man. Getting critical meant dispelling a gangbanger's gangster mentality and focusing on larger political and ideological structures. It meant coming to terms with the brown on brown violence perpetrated in south central L.A., which was painful enough; it was even more painful to realize and come to accept his complicity in that violence. It meant giving up an identity that had pleased, and imprisoned, him for one that was uncertain but felt right and seemed accurate. And it meant seeing his former activities as part of his people's plight and problems and believing that a better, more beautiful and just world was possible. It was a big psychological change, cognitively and emotionally. The world looked different and his place in the world had been altered substantially.

Twenty years earlier George Jackson, in his *Soledad Brother: The Prison Letters of George Jackson*, conveyed a similar transformation.[7] Writing angrily to his father, who had sent an "Uncle Tom" letter that was intercepted and subsequently read by prison officials, Jackson expressed his outrage at his father's deed and noted his changing understanding of black folks' travails. He wrote:

I have always respected and loved you people, and hated myself, cried bitter tears of remorse, when, because of circumstances and conditions which I didn't understand, I let you down. Even after I discovered the true cause of my ills, when I found that this social order had created, through its inadequacies and its abandonment of our interests, the basis for my frustrations, I forgave you for not preparing me; for not warning me, for pretending that this was the best of all possible worlds. . . . I've read extensively in the fields of social-economic and political theory and development, all of this done against serious resistance from all sides. But because I knew one day I would find what I'm after, and answer some of the questions that beset my mind with confusion and unrest and fear, I pushed ahead in spite of the foolish conformity that I saw in you people. Now I have arrived at a state of awareness that because of the education system few Negroes reach in the U.S. (*SB*, pp. 59–60).

And his understandings were not naive; they were quite critical. In a letter to one of his legal advisors, Fay Stender, he outlines the modern system of chattel slavery. He wrote:

> The new slavery . . . places the victim in a factory or in the case of most blacks in support roles inside and around the factory system (service trades) working for a wage. . . . The sense and meaning of slavery comes through as a result of our times to the wage. You must have it, without it you would starve or expose yourself to the elements. One's entire day centers around the acquisition of the wage. The control of your eight to ten hours on the job is determined by others. . . . Neoslavery is an economic condition, a small knot of men exercising the property rights of their established economic order, organizing and controlling the life style of the slave as if he were in fact property. Succinctly: an economic condition which manifests itself in the total loss or absence of self-determination. Only after this is understood and accepted can we go on to the dialectic that will help us in a remedy (*SB*, pp.190–91).

George Jackson and Sanyika Shakur delineate some of the personal features of this process of getting critical, of coming to know the world in a way that illuminates some of the sources for their pain and, as a result, becoming quietly outraged and soundly affirmed. It was for them and is for many others a process of consciousness raising and the desire to create a more just and hopefully more beautiful world.

Consciousness raising, when it arises from populist or grass roots yearnings, is understood as intimately infused with feelings, mixed and strong, and with perceptions of ourselves and others. Consciousness raising is the process whereby those who are oppressed and disenfranchised examine together the contours of that oppression. We locate in the world, not simply in ourselves, the sources of our pain and heartache. We reflect on our pain, we examine our world, and we begin to grow in our understandings. Shakur and Jackson experienced this, and so did many women in the women's movement of the 60s and 70s. Catherine MacKinnon captures a bit of the process when she writes that the feminist consciousness raising:

> redefines women's feelings of discontent as indigenous to their situation rather than to themselves as crazy, maladusted, hormonally imbalanced, bitchy, or ungrateful. It is validating to comprehend oneself as devalidated rather than as invalid. Women's feelings are interpreted as appropriate responses to their conditions. . . . It [consciousness raising] is collective and critical. It embodies shared feelings, comprehensions, and experiences of women as products of their conditions, through being critical of their condition together. In so doing, it builds a community frame of reference which recasts the perceived content of social life as it alters the relation between the "I," the "other," and the "we."[8]

In consciousness raising we begin to think and feel in concert. Getting critical is not a singularly rational or intellectual endeavor, but rather a social activity grounded in individuals' common thinking and feeling. It arises out of obstacles encountered, frustration felt, anger experienced, and alienation acknowledged and understood. Emotions are an integral part of this learning, a feature of understanding ourselves and our worlds. Whether we are engaged in the hurt and pain caused by structures that disfigure, or immersed in the attractions of beauty and wonder of the worlds around us, our learning is fueled and motivated by our emotional attachments.

Experience and Emotions Ignored

But we find little of this emotional terrain discussed, evoked, treasured, or analyzed in the professional literature on teaching, learning, and schooling; and only infrequently is it explored in school settings.[9] Mystery and beauty are rarely summoned, and consciousness raising, when it is formally approached, tends to be examined by the privileged in their university contexts, not pursued with the oppressed in our society of plenty. Certainly some academics broach the topic of emotions, but for the most part scholarly discourse seems to repress or suppress teachers' and students' emotional experiences. And there are those outside the educational establishment who, with others, pierce through the pain and deception of the proffered master narratives.[10] But in academic and scholarly realms emotions seem excised from our accounts of learning. As a result, the richer layers of learning are diminished, and thus our understanding of teaching is diminished. In an era in which the forces of accountability dominate, with state test scores determining more and more the formal curriculum, public schools are driven to produce higher and higher test results. In these settings learning and teaching offer thin and shallow depictions of our worlds. Students' actual experiences are neither valued nor explored. Teachers' and students' experiences become ignored as primitive life materials. The content of our learning becomes impoverished and small.

But is this depiction accurate? I've asserted that we ignore emotions in our discourse on and practice of education. I believe it is a relatively accurate claim. But I have neither substantiated that this is the case nor explored why it may be so. I can't do that here. That would require a separate and distinct line of reasoning. However, I'd like to suggest a possible account for why we ignore emotions and then move on to discuss ways we could integrate rather than ignore the emotional facets of our experience.

Many of us seem to live lives in which a preoccupation with narrow ego concerns predominates, concerns with achievement proliferate, and the desire to control and have power over the seemingly chaotic and fractured features of our lives takes precedence. Concerns with ego, power, achievement, and control seem to dominate the landscape of our personal and professional lives. In these lives we tend to diminish the importance of emotions, and try to excise them out of our lives. Emotions tend to be viewed as volatile, eruptive forces, remnants of a more primitive stage. Reason is viewed as our tool to control these inner, dark forces.

This predicament is not new to our age. It is a human tendency and one that Simone Weil captures in her "The Illiad, Or Poem of Force."[11] There she portrays a view of human interactions in which power and force prevail. She points to an extreme case, that of war, but for her the lessons extend beyond this outermost example. In war, Weil observes, both victim and victor believe that the exercise of force is the only option and *the* heroic route. She believed both to be deluded. For Weil, the *Illiad*'s central character is not the warrior but force itself. In the *Illiad,* as in life, force, power, and the drive for achievement seduce, diminish, destroy, and prevail; and war represents the extreme, not the exception, in human interactions. Concerning Weil's *Illiad* commentary Eric Springsted writes:

> The relations between the inner person and force are not essentially different in other spheres of life [i.e., spheres other than war]. Because we fear death and nothingness, we seek to gain more and more power to fend off the threat. Then two things happen to us. First, because we can never truly be possessors of force, we become possessed by it, and because one force tends to increase indefinitely until checked by another, we rarely exercise any self-limitation in the struggle for power. . . . The race for power . . . [is present] . . . as we seek to increase our wealth, security, and prestige. The second consequence of our blind quest for prestige, then, is our coming to identify true human life with what is ultimately only an exercise of power. At this point we begin to see ourselves as essentially the sum of what we possess and wield, and our longing for anything beyond what we can gain by force starts to degenerate.[12]

Consumed by a desire for security, prestige, and power, we tend to identify ourselves and others with what we have and can control and not with who we are or what we experience. We not only lead our lives in this manner but we also initiate others into this way of seeing and being in the world. Schooling becomes a means to acquire prestige, power, and control, not a path through which to explore and extend our worlds. When we are focused on acquiring emblems of status and power, we tend not to experience the richness, the fullness of life. We become blind to the beauty and numb to the pain of our own and others' existence. For Weil, the only way to escape the predicament of force is through the gift of grace. "It is only by the gift of one beyond the play of forces that we can ever escape the illusions of force."[13] And for Simone Weil, this gift of grace is attained, in part, through attending lovingly to our own and others' experience, and (I would emphasize) the emotional contours of those experiences.

But how do we attend to our emotions when they are viewed as disruptive, unregulated, unwieldy forces that happen to us? I think there are at least two viable and perhaps not unrelated paths: one grounded in a basically western conception of the knowing self and emotions, and the other rooted in an eastern, contemplative tradition. I outline those below.

Listening To and Learning From Our Emotions

Over the last two decades Martha Nussbaum, classics professor and literary and legal philosopher, has elaborated a cognitive/evaluative view of human emotions. In contrast to the understanding of emotions as necessarily disruptive, irrational, blind forces that cause eruptions in our lives and thinking, Nussbaum construes emotions as entailing cognitive appraisals of things that matter. In her most recent and lengthy elaboration, *Upheavals of Thought,* she writes that emotions "are appraisals or value judgements, which ascribe to things and persons outside the person's own control great importance for that person's own flourishing."[14] In her view of emotions there are three salient features: Emotions entail a cognitive appraisal; they pertain to the individual's concern for his or her own flourishing; and they generally revolve around the importance of "external" features in an individual's life. When we are angry, we are frequently cognitively engaged in appraising the danger that some force holds over someone dear to us, our wishes, or our future. When we are attracted by beauty, we are responding cognitively to some feature of the world that promises to offer something alluring. And when we are sad, we have deemed some person or thing as obstructing some wish or desire we have for ourselves or for others.

For Nussbaum particular emotions have a distinct and important place in public rationality, in a reading of literature, and in an understanding of our lives. And in her account empathy is central. Empathy allows the reader of novels and the citizens of democratic communities to see others' situations, to come to view others' plights as if they were our own, and thereby enlarging our understanding of others' and our own lives. But empathy alone can't create the desired basis for understanding others. Nussbaum explains that:

> Novel-readers have both empathy with the plight of the characters, experiencing what happens to them as if from their point of view, and also pity, which goes beyond empathy in that it involves a spectatorial judgment that the characters' misfortunes are indeed serious and have indeed arisen not through their fault. Such judgments are not always available within the empathetic viewpoint, so the novel-reader, like the tragic spectator, must alternate between identification and a more external sort of sympathy.[15]

This spectatorial outlook is key in Nussbaum's approach. It allows a measure of detachment and distance from an event's perceived onslaughts. For Nussbaum, not all emotions are good guides in our understanding and assessment of situations. To be a good guide, an emotion must "be informed by a true view of what is going on—of the facts of the case, of their significance for the actors in the situation."[16] It must be the emotion of a spectator, not a participant. She writes that the device of the judicious "spectator is aimed above all at filtering out that portion of anger, fear, and so on that focuses on the self. If my friend suffers an injustice, I become angry on his behalf; but . . . that anger lacks the special vindictive intensity of much anger at wrongs done to oneself."[17] According to Nussbaum, one needs to see others' situations both internally with empathy and externally with a measure of detachment.

In learning, and in teaching, we can gain a great deal from seeing the world empathetically and with a measure of detachment. In fact, for Nussbaum, it ought to be one of the results of learning that we come to see the world empathetically and with some detachment. For Nussbaum it is through an engagement with literature that we come to terms with the interplay of emotions, events, and sustained narrative structures. Through reading about the lives of others we both understand the world from their point of view and from a larger, more detached perspective. Others, such as Annie Dillard and Oliver Sacks, might claim that their naturalist explorations taught them a great deal about the allure, complexity and beauty of their worlds along with a certain detachment from, an understanding of their "otherness."[18] Their explorations were fueled and accompanied by a wealth of emotional engagements. When they recount their early scientific forays, one sees them both walk into, become immersed with, and yet also recognize the irreducible distance between themselves and the objects of their explorations. There probably are many disciplinary paths, but if we continue to ignore the emotional contents of our learning we will be hard pressed to learn from them. If we don't listen, we can't learn.

Another somewhat distinct path of listening to and learning from our emotions comes from the Buddhist contemplative tradition. Grounded in a Tibetan Buddhist nonsectarian approach to contemplation and meditation, Richard Brown describes the process of meditation as a practice of "noticing and then letting go," which has the effect of softening our "sense of ownership and the accompanying rigidity."[19] He writes:

> Plans and inspirations that may arise for us as teachers are transformed by this practice of acceptance and spaciousness. "My" plan, "my" feeling, "my" opinion, "my" theory, are experienced less as possessions of truth than as open transitory, participatory creations. Often this radical acceptance of and simultaneous

non-attachment to our inner experience, can be a painful, disconcerting, and humbling process, but it is the Buddhist path to compassion.

Because meditation invites our emotional lives to be included in our practice, we gradually become familiar, relaxed, and trusting of our feelings. By learning to experience emotions clearly, spaciously and without attachment, meditation seems to enhance our natural, compassionate, empathetic and intuitive qualities.[20]

For Brown it is through meditation that one learns to view emotional experiences from a more detached perspective. One learns to notice the various qualities, energies, and timings of distinct emotions. The emotion grabs less and we are able to observe more. As Brown says, "Rather than having an emotional experience we participate in an energetic experience."[21]

There are distinctions between Nussbaum's spectatorial approach to experience and emotions and the Buddhist contemplative stance. But those distinctions don't matter much for my present purposes. I have claimed that we lack attention to the emotional undertones of our learning experiences of beauty and pain and that by ignoring them we diminish both our learning and our teaching. So as to illuminate further our understanding of the worlds in which we live, and in order to enrich our teaching, we need to revalue and reconnect with the experience and emotions that are there. We have to learn to listen to the emotions engaged, and once we listen, we will hopefully learn a great deal more.

Conclusion

When I invite others to pay greater attention to the emotional contours of learning and teaching, my invitation is not always well received. When I ask others to look at the romantic yearning of coming to know that is a part of learning and teaching or to understand the anger and desires that fuel getting critical, I am frequently confronted with a look of disbelief. Some of my listeners seem disturbed by the fact that I am requesting that they attend to the emotional contours of their experience. They seem perturbed that I have not learned that emotions are volatile elements in our lives. According to this view, our emotions obstruct, distort, and create upheavals in our thought. Construing learning and teaching as inextricably emotional endeavors unduly complicates the tasks of teaching, they argue. All sorts of problems arise. For example, if we view teaching as an invitation to others to come share in the worlds and activities we love, we become vulnerable and as a result could grow to be disenchanted. If we explore anger and disenchantment, who's to say that it won't ensnare us? Why talk of teaching and learning in such ways? It seems to me that we have no choice but to recognize the emotional contours of teaching and learning. Ignoring those dimensions won't make them go away. In learning and teaching, emotions are ever present. Ignoring or suppressing those emotions harms students and teachers alike. It's time we found some other avenues. Martha Nussbaum and Richard Brown provide us with two avenues. There are probably more.

CHAPTER 7

Teaching For Hope
The Ethics of Shattering World Views

MEGAN BOLER

Out beyond ideas of wrongdoing and right doing, there is a field. I'll meet you there.
When the soul lies down in that grass, the world is too full to talk about. Ideas, language,
even the phrase 'each other' doesn't make sense.
—Rumi

Every semester while teaching a required course in social foundations of education, I engage three categories of students. There are those willing to walk down the path of critical thinking with me, who find their world-views shattered, but simultaneously engage in creatively rebuilding a sense of meaning and coherence in the face of ambiguity. Secondly, there are those who angrily and vocally resist my attempts to suggest that the world might possibly be other than they have comfortably experienced it. Third, there are those who appear disaffected, already sufficiently numb so that my attempts to ask them to rethink the world encounter only vacant and dull stares. While I should probably be most concerned about those with blank and vacant faces, I am given the hope and inspiration to go on by those who embrace the opportunity to rethink the dominant propaganda that has constituted the majority of their education thus far. However, it is often the case that the most intense emotions of suffering are experienced by both myself and the students who loudly resist having their worldviews challenged. How can educator and student make productive use out of this suffering and discomfort? What role does compassion play in helping negotiate the minefields of ambiguity and contradiction encountered when asked to rethink worldviews?

Those of us who teach any course that emphasizes critical thinking, especially if the content has to do with issues of race, class, gender, sexual orientation, or other cultural histories, will often find ourselves teaching students who may prefer to avoid thinking about social inequalities and institutionalized oppressions. Most public schools will have exposed students to partisan histories well documented by such books as James Loewen's *Lies My Teacher Told Me.*[1] Steeped in these nationalist myths, students may cling to the myth of the American Dream, to individualism, and to a faith in meritocracy as the arbiter of privilege. Attachment to these myths is not merely cognitive but deeply emotional: The American Dream may be a dream that offers students hope—for their own family; for themselves; or a naïve hope that others, less privileged than themselves, may improve their lot in life if they would only work hard enough.

Because the educational system does not systematically teach U.S. citizens about the histories of disenfranchised groups, students encountering social justice curricula—reading, for example, Jonathan Kozol's scathing indictment of unequal education in *Savage Inequalities*—may well experience a shocking cognitive dissonance: Can it be that the world is not as I was taught to perceive and believe? For some students, such curricula do not threaten but rather validate a worldview that may have been missing from their official schooling. Students who are hungry for untold histories indeed do not find social justice curricula threatening, but rather find resources in the readings and discussions that help shape their sense of self in positive ways. On the other hand, there are many students who, as mentioned in the opening, vocally resist attempts to suggest that the world might possibly be other than they have comfortably experienced it.

An angry, defensive response to social justice and analyses of power and oppression signals someone who is struggling to maintain his or her identity in what feels like a threat of annihilation. On an emotional level, social justice courses can make some people feel like they are the bad guy, that they have no place of belonging. And those who respond in this manner are not only white males. Every semester I encounter as well a woman and sometimes, though more rarely, a person of color who is angry and defensive, who is clinging tightly to a belief that sexism (or racism) does not exist, that everyone should stop whining because there is equal opportunity for all. To shatter worldviews—specifically, to suggest that some unfairly benefit from (white, or male, or heterosexual) privilege—can be emotionally translated into feeling one has no place of belonging. Are not angry protestations the cries of someone trying to save his- or herself from annihilation?

suffering & comparison

To develop compassion for those suffering from "dominant cultural withdrawal," as this might be termed, is a slippery slope: I do not feel that my responsibility as a social justice educator is to pamper those who have experienced a life of privilege, nor to validate desires to cling to privilege and not to recognize injustice. However, education is not effective if it is combative and alienating. The story I tell in this essay reveals to me that compassion and offering hope are important complements to a pedagogy of discomfort.

In this essay, I examine how a "pedagogy of discomfort" engages critical inquiry regarding the emotional investments that shape both educators' and students' attachments to particular worldviews. Secondly, I define and explore what I call "inscribed habits of emotional inattention," which are revealed when a pedagogy of discomfort challenges one's usual beliefs and views. The focus of my chapter is to better understand the vocal and loud resistance to rethinking one's worldview and the suffering caused to student and to the educator in this process of renegotiating understandings of how power defines social stratification. In relation to this edited collection, my focus on suffering and compassion suggests one model for understanding the dynamic relationships between educator and student. If education is a commitment to growth and change, then that change will require facing up to our investments and experiencing the discomfort of new thinking. I will discuss the kinds of compassion that are necessary to complement a pedagogy of discomfort.

Before defining a pedagogy of discomfort and its emotional vicissitudes, I wish to foreground the comments of Buddhist psychologist Mark Epstein. In a book that analyzes the overlap of Freudian psychology and Buddhist philosophies, Epstein offers important insights into the contradictory and ambiguous terrain of emotions. His comments quoted here emphasize the necessity of moving beyond binaries and instead recognizing the ambiguities of experience and meaning.

In Buddhist psychology emotions are classified as "skillful" or "unskillful." The "afflicted" ones of anger, envy, pride, worry, agitation, and greed are opposed by their counterparts of love, compassion, humility, patience, tranquillity, and generosity. The model is a simple one: Two opposites cannot occupy the same psychic space. Anger impedes and occludes love and vice versa. Turn one down by cultivating the other. But there is another way of understanding this model, one that is more attuned to the ambiguities of contemporary psychoanalysis. In this view, these skillful and unskillful emotions are opposite because they are part of a single dialectic. Anger is a perversion of love, transformed in the crucible of frustration. Anxiety is restricted excitement. Envy is a contracted form of apathy, since both spring from the capacity to know another's experience.[2]

The dialectic model understands, then, that the angry resistance of those who feel threatened in our classrooms is also a complex cry for recognition and care. This highlights to me that suffering and compassion are not mutually exclusive. Specifically, in teaching, by "following the affect" rather than the words people actually utter, one can begin to see how emotional investments reflect both individuals' willingness to grow as well as the embedded quality of dominant cultural values. Epstein emphasizes the value of becoming conscious of what I call "inscribed habits of emotional inattention" as a means for creating "space" where once there was rigid habit:

> [I]n our desire for freedom, we imagine that we have to eliminate unwanted aspects of ourselves. My understanding does not support such an approach. Change will happen naturally as we open to the truth. The more we bring our attachments into awareness, the freer we become, not because we eliminate the attachments, but because we learn to identify more with awareness than with desire. Using our capacity for consciousness, we can change perspective on ourselves, giving a sense of space where once there was only habit. Discipline means restraining the habitual movement of the mind, so that instead of blind impulse there can be clear comprehension.[3]

Epstein's insight underscores a pedagogy of discomfort's key aim—to disrupt emotional habits and equilibrium in search of reevaluating attachments to rigid notions of self and world. However, to engage in dissecting the comfort of a familiar worldview can involve a kind of "shattering" emotional experience. Compassion may be called for as a crucial element of a pedagogy of discomfort so that students are able to move from fear and anger to what Epstein described as "clear comprehension"— comprehension of the historical and cultural reasons for the attachments that one has to particular worldviews.

A Pedagogy of Discomfort

I now turn to define a pedagogy of discomfort that offers context for the story of conflict between myself and Sam, which shall follow. As its name suggests, a pedagogy of discomfort emphasizes the need for both the educator and student to move outside of their comfort zones. In the final chapter of *Feeling Power: Emotions and Education*,[4] I introduce a "pedagogy of discomfort" to describe how I engage students in a process of critically analyzing cherished beliefs and assumptions such as that of the American dream and pervasive individualism. In that work, I contrast "spectating" vs. "witnessing" to outline how students can engage critical reflection and take social responsibility in the act of reading texts and films and, more generally, in looking at the world.

The "comfort zones" we inhabit are inscribed cultural and emotional terrains that we occupy less by choice and more by virtue of dominant cultural values, which we internalize as unconsciously as the air we breathe: "Hegemony refers to the maintenance of domination not by the sheer exercise of force but primarily through consensual social practices, social forms, and social structures produced in specific sites such as the church, the state, the school, the mass media, the political system, and the family."[5] The comfort zone reflects emotional investments that by and large remain unexamined, because they have been woven into the everyday fabric of what is considered common sense.

hege mony

A pedagogy of discomfort recognizes and problematizes the deeply embedded emotional dimensions that frame and shape daily habits, routines, and unconscious complicity with hegemony. The purpose of attending to emotional habits as part of radical education is to draw attention to the ways in which we enact and embody dominant values and assumptions in our daily habits and routines. By closely examining emotional reactions and responses—what we call emotional stances—one begins to identify unconscious privileges as well as invisible ways in which one complies with dominant ideology.

One should not make the mistake of assuming that a pedagogy of discomfort seeks only to destabilize members of the dominant group. A pedagogy of discomfort invites not only members of the dominant culture but also members of marginalized cultures to reexamine the hegemonic values inevitably internalized in the process of being exposed to curricula and media that serve the interests of the ruling class. No one escapes hegemony. Those born in the United States as well as those who immigrate to this nation absorb, consciously or not, common sense beliefs about what it means to be an "American." Of course, every individual will have their own idiosyncratic experiences of discomfort. Heterosexuals, for example, may as a group tend to experience discomfort when asked to think carefully about their views toward lesbian and gay people. White people may be more "uncomfortable" discussing racism than are people of color. However, there are moments in which it is uncomfortable for a gay person to consider his or her own internalized homophobia or for a person of color to reflect on his or her own internalized racism. In short, no one escapes internalizing dominant cultural values despite the fact that these values take different forms in different individuals.

To engage students in sophisticated critiques of difference requires unlearning the myth of neutral education. As Donald Macedo writes in the Introduction to *Chomsky on MisEducation,*

> Given the tendency for humans to construct "satisfying" and often self deceptive stories, stories that often damage themselves and their groups, particularly

when these deceptive stories are rewarded by the dominant social order, the development of a critical comprehension between the meaning of words and a more coherent understanding of the meaning of the world is prerequisite to achieving clarity of reality. As Freire suggests, it is only "through political practice that the less coherent sensibility of the world begins to be surpassed and the more rigorous intellectual pursuits give rise to a more coherent comprehension of the world."[6]

To gain a "clarity of reality" requires particularly close attention to those stories that naturalize themselves through common sense or familiar cultural myth. The story I share below illustrates how a pedagogy of discomfort reveals what I am calling inscribed habits of emotional inattention. I believe that critical pedagogy benefits from attending to these emotional habits as a means to excavate the internalized effects of hegemony.

I propose *inscribed habits of emotional inattention* as a way to describe the embedded, cultural habits of seeing and not seeing. These habits come to feel like one's chosen self and identity, but are in fact as much social and cultural as they are personal. Habits of emotional inattention offer an explanatory concept that integrates the difficult notion of the "unconscious" with the notion of hegemony. Such habits of belief—for example, a belief that each person is individually responsible for his or her own destiny—usually reflect dominant cultural ideology but are internalized by individuals and in turn become part of a person's sense of self. This process describes hegemony: Dominant ideology enforces itself, not necessarily through violent means, but through people's agreement to abide by and value a status quo that benefits institutionalized powers.

This emotional selectivity some philosophers call "patterns of moral salience." Like Aristotle, John Dewey analyzed "selective emphasis" and argued for the ethical importance of seeing the "whole context."[7] To attend carefully to the relationships we create with our students as we each engage the painful process of recognizing habits is a process of encountering suffering and developing compassion we may not have known we had.

The emotional fallout of hegemony for those who do social justice education is that we encounter individuals who are so deeply invested in the dominant cultural values that these values have defined their sense of identity, and to question these values feels emotionally like an annihilation of self. Thus one faces loud and vocal resistance to rethinking the world as it is hegemonically constructed: "But the American Dream does come true for some people, so it is not a myth!" "If those children just worked harder, or if their parents made an effort to help them more with their homework, they could get to college!" And sometimes the resistance is more than ideological: Students denounce our courses, write bad evaluations, refuse to engage written work as assigned, become generally unhappy and angry in our presence—thus posing genuine challenges about how a pedagogy of discomfort requires compassion in order to recognize the suffering of some students and often of the educator, as I shall describe in what follows.

Impasse: Resistance and Suffering

One result of this pedagogy is that I frequently have the opportunity to witness students' intense emotional reactions and resistances to rethinking cherished assumptions and worldviews. Lately, I have also been forced to reevaluate the costs and benefits of my own emotional investments in students' willingness to change. I am learning to accept that *people will not go where they don't want to go.* For understandable reasons, students may not welcome the invitation to rethink their worldviews in ways that disrupt and shatter their comfortable status quo. Inevitably, each semester, I find myself encountering my own emotional investments and reactions to students who dig in their heels and blatantly refuse to engage in critical thinking. For example, my own serenity was "shattered" by one particular student who, as a result of his vociferous resistance and the large amount of space he inhabited in our classroom expressing his anger, was, as they say, living rent-free in my head far too much of the time.

My irritation and obsession began during the fifth week of that semester when, at the end of a class in which we were discussing white privilege, the said student ended the class nearly shouting, and visibly shaking, proclaiming "My name is Sam [pseudonym]! I am a human being! I am an American! None of this history, race, or anything else has anything to do with my identity. The fact is the world is divided—someone has to clean the toilets!" I took a deep breath and asked, as calmly as possible, why it was that brown and black people are primarily the ones cleaning toilets? His face reddened as his body tensed with great physical agitation and anger, while the other fifteen students squirmed uncomfortably in their seats in part because of their own discomfort with his emotion. He retorted in loud and harsh tone, in clear defiance of the previous five weeks of readings and discussions, "They *choose* to clean toilets! That is their *choice!*" These words shocked me. Somehow, despite the fact that I know that individualism and choice are perhaps the hardest discourses to critically challenge, to hear this explicit rationalization of social injustice took me aback. We had spent five weeks dissecting the myths of the American dream, and most had been willing to engage and accept some of that critical thinking. The clock signaled the end of class, and I was left with a shattered sense of my own investments and vision of "transformational educational process."

Following his highly emotional—and in many ways vulnerable and courageous expression of his visceral feeling that he does not possess white

privilege, a sentiment no doubt shared albeit not voiced by some of his colleagues—I struggled with whether or not I should say something to him.
What was the ethical response as an educator? Should I say, "Thank you for
being so bold and courageous, I appreciate your courage in expressing
these views"? My worry was that if I said anything, I would be simply affirming and condoning his right to refuse to rethink his position of privilege. I did not want to say something that would give him the impression
that his refusal to be open-minded is an acceptable educational stance.
Nonetheless, from a "caring" place, I was aware that he had made himself
vulnerable, and that his expressions had, no doubt, reflected feelings and
thoughts that others in the class likely shared.

After much internal deliberation, my lingering discomfort regarding
the fact of his emotional outburst and secondly, my concern to reiterate
how white privilege is embedded in our society pushed me to change the
agenda slightly the next week. I began the subsequent class by acknowledging the courage it had taken to share such strong feelings. I reiterated that,
while members of the class held very different opinions, I hoped that we
could each listen with an open mind and that we would each make an effort to reevaluate our views.

However, despite my best intentions, I actually believe that my having
publicly acknowledged him in this way simply fueled his fire. To address his
insistence that we should all just be "Americans," I screened a 15-minute excerpt of a video called *The Color of Fear*. The 90-minute video documents a
highly emotional weekend workshop of discussion among nine men of different ethnic backgrounds regarding the effects of racism. *The Color of Fear*
documents a group of nine men of Anglo, Asian, Black, and Hispanic de-
scent who, during a facilitated weekend retreat, confront issues of racism
through an ongoing dialogue. The film portrays an unusually intimate and
politically charged scenario, in which the viewer has the opportunity to witness emotionally harrowing and poignant conversations. The video has
some very heated moments; in particular, one in which the most articulate
man in the film, Victor, who is African American, confronts David, the
quintessential White Liberal. The heated exchange reveals David's privileged denial of racism. In effect, David's position as a privileged white male
can be characterized as follows:

> I am not racist. I employ Mexicans. I am very friendly to them. I do not know
> why you colored people are so angry. You should not be angry. The white man
> does not want to stand in your way. If you are having trouble making progress
> in the world, you are standing in your own way.

This video clip that I selected for class directly illustrates why it is difficult for persons of non-European or non-Anglo heritage to claim the iden-

tity "American" in any simple way. The men of color in the video explain to a "resistant" white man that because the dominant cultural norm of identity in North American culture is that of a white Anglo-Saxon middle-class male, and because being an "American" in a melting pot requires assimilation, to identify oneself simply as "American" is in many ways to "pretend to be white." In the video, the men of color express the profound frustration and anger they feel living in a racist society and the anger and frustration they experience precisely because white persons in this society can afford to be ignorant about the cost of assimilation for people of color.

During the discussion following this video excerpt, Sam proceeded to railroad the conversation with assertions that entirely missed the points voiced by the men of color in the video. When he began angrily demanding "evidence" that he has "white privilege," I responded by shifting the class discussion to examine statistics I had prepared for our discussion about gender issues and education. The statistics detail degrees conferred nationwide and illustrate the radical gender disparities between fields such as engineering, which is predominantly male, and those such as education, nursing, and social work, in which women are over-represented. My hope was that he would be able to translate this evidence of "systemic inequality" of male privilege to understand white privilege as an interlocking system. It did not seem to work. Apparently, no amount of statistical evidence or rational persuasion is effective in the face of this particular kind of defensive and angry investment and the fear of allowing one's worldview to be shifted.

I regret to report that my suffering regarding this student's anger continued throughout the term to take up far too much space in my own emotional world. I found myself describing the experience to friends and colleagues, clearly encountering my own experience of discomfort. The day after the just described class I attended a remarkable lecture by a leading African-American female scholar. My students are required to attend cultural events during Black History month and Women's History month. The auditorium was packed full of students, as well as community members, an unusual occurrence at this campus. During the first 45 minutes of the lecture, I found myself distracted, picturing whether or not my belligerent student might be convinced by this charismatic speaker. As she echoed what I had been teaching in my class—namely, that racism is alive and well and secondly that we all need to take responsibility for the contemporary privileges and costs of racism—I found myself obsessively wishing that the student could be hearing these words from someone other than myself, who might possibly push him to change his intransigent position. Ironically, 45 minutes after her talk had begun, I happened to see him walking into the auditorium. My heart leapt: I was at first thrilled to see him arrive. But then, I spent the last 15 minutes of her talk furious that he had disrespectfully missed the majority of her lecture and therefore missed the opportunity to be transformed. My obsession continued: I found myself thinking, when he turns in his two-page synopsis of the cultural event to receive his five points, why should I give him five points when he didn't hear the whole talk? (And indeed, lo and behold, he turned in a most bizarre response in which he said, "I have heard her speak before so I won't summarize. Let me just say how irritated I was during the talk that 50 students were going in and out of the lecture, being disrespectful and distracting and not attending the whole event even though they will write up a report for credit."!!!)

Suffice to say, my form of caring about his emotional and educational growth was not particularly effective. I began to think that it was not effective because I was the one who was suffering. And the suffering, while valuable for my growth, was showing me my own sites of attachment to another's change, which in fact is, quote, beyond my control. It is only months after this experience, as I reflect back on what occurred next between Sam and myself, that I also see that there is a need for compassion as part of the pedagogy of discomfort. A particular compassion might be required for those who feel their "self" is being annihilated and who are angrily protesting, not necessarily because they cannot see how power operates but because they need something to replace what I am threatening to take away from them.

An Unexpected Shifting

Toward the end of the semester, I happened to present an early version of this paper at the American Educational Research Association Annual Conference. During the discussion following our session, someone asked if I thought Sam would change. I answered unequivocally, "I have no hopes that we will ever reconcile our differences nor that he will ever love me!"

One can imagine my surprise when, two days later having returned to campus, after our class he asked to meet me during office hours. I found myself quite fearful and left my office door open when he entered—even asking a colleague to keep an eye out, as I feared a belligerent exchange. Sam perched on a chair, clearly nervous and fearful. I began to invoke my compassion: I smiled and consciously breathed in and out, recognizing his discomfort and mindfully making myself present. He then blurted out an apology for his behavior throughout this semester. He had come to realize, he confided, that he was acting out his frustrations with "this system of oppression" on me, but that he realized his anger needn't be directed at me. I took in this information still smiling, trying to breathe deeply in the face of both of our discomfort.

Rather struck by what seemed a significant change of heart on his part, I asked him if there was anything about the class or my conduct that I might change to make students like him feel more engaged and less resistant to my curriculum. He told me that the material "felt cold." He said that he had also been upset because I didn't seem to state in class that all these screwed up things in the world could possibly change. He said he wished I had told the class that "just by virtue of you sitting in this class, things can get better."

I responded by thanking him for the feedback. I replied that perhaps I hadn't said that because I don't necessarily believe that things will get better simply by people sitting in my classroom. I did reply that I would try to be more encouraging of the fact that I do believe people can choose to advocate for social change and can thereby make a difference.

Finally, he told me that the other action that had significantly changed his feelings was that when he came into my office, I had smiled at him. "You don't smile a lot in class," he reported.

In the ensuing months, I feel I have learned quite a lot from Sam's two comments, the significance of which have taken time to settle into my consciousness. His first comment was that he wished I had told him that there was "hope"—even though the world is so screwed up.

For those who do not feel threatened by the course content, reading about social inequality itself can offer a kind of hope or validation: Their perceptions are perhaps being validated in many cases for the first time. But for people like Sam, who had held so desperately to an identity carved through illusions of "we are the same" meritocracy, course content may well need to include clear delineation of what will replace the sense of self lost. I detail some ideas on this replacement in the discussion of critical hope below.

Sam's second comment, that the simple act of my smiling when he came into my office enabled him to reevaluate the appropriate object for his anger, makes me think about how compassion facilitates change. As discussed in this essay, for those who feel significantly threatened by course content, something needs to be offered to replace what feels like loss or annihilation. Smiling is in part a way of recognizing the other as he or she is, of communicating a compassionate acceptance. I do not think this act need mean "You can go ahead and refuse to rethink the world and maintain your privilege." Rather, it means that compassion is especially crucial for those who feel they are out on limb.

It is worth noting, considering issues of gendered emotional labor, that for a man to ask a woman to smile more is also a complicated request. In my office I recall smiling at him quite intentionally, practicing what Buddhists call tonglen and maitri, or lovingkindness. I have, during the ensuing months following his comment, made an effort to smile more during engagements with students. I confess I feel torn about the implied admonition to "smile more," because I have no doubt that part of the demand for this smile is a demand for a form of gendered labor. I am positioned by this young man as distinctly female, and his request for my smile is in part a request for a nurturing mother. Is it the educator's duty to smile as part of the emotional work of seducing students into social change? Political analyses can indeed come into conflict with simple calls for compassion.

To return, however, to Sam's request that I tell him there is "hope" when I am simultaneously asking him to recognize the rather overwhelming inequities of our society: Rather uncannily, his comment about hope reflects something I had previously written about—critical hope versus naïve hope. It is only in the process of writing this essay that I saw the connection between Sam's request for hope and my own previous intellectual analyses of critical hope.

Beyond Discomfort: Critical Hope

As one recognizes inscribed habits of emotional inattention and disrupts these tenacious habits, one may cry out for something new to hold on to. Between utter despair, which may come about with the dismantling of worldviews, and the denial that typifies hegemonic mystification is a middle ground. While "shattering" may occur with a pedagogy of discomfort, one lifeline is to build "critical hope." Here I will describe first a framing of critical hope, drawing on concepts from Maxine Greene and Paulo Freire. I will then briefly suggest some specific curricular directions that might offer critical hope to someone like Sam.

What does Sam want when he asks me to tell him that "even thought the world is screwed up, your being here in this classroom, Sam, will make a difference?" What I don't want to offer to this request is naïve hope, which stands in stark contrast to how I shall define critical hope. Naive hope may be defined as those platitudes that directly serve the hegemonic interest of maintaining the status quo, particularly by espousing humanist rhetoric. These platitudes include the rhetoric of individualism; beliefs in equal opportunity; the puritanical faith that hard work inevitably leads to success; that everyone is the same underneath the skin.

In contrast to naive hope, critical hope recognizes that we live within systems of inequality, in which privilege, such as white and male privilege, comes at the expense of the freedom of others. A willingness to engage in in-depth critical inquiry regarding systems of domination needs to be accompanied by a parallel of emotional willingness to engage in the difficult work of possibly allowing one's worldviews to be shattered.

Critical hope entails a responsibility—a willingness to be fully alive in the process of constant change and becoming. Maxine Greene emphasizes this throughout her writings. "When habit swathes everything," she writes, "one day follows another identical day and predictability swallows any hint of an opening possibility."[8] In an astute description of the interrelationship between habit, sense of self, and what we do and do not wish to see or feel, John Dewey writes

> Habit reaches . . . down into the very structure of the self; it signifies a building up and solidifying of certain desires; an increased sensitiveness and responsiveness . . . or an impaired capacity to attend to and think about certain things. Habit covers . . . the very makeup of desire, intent, choice, disposition which gives an act its voluntary quality.[9]

Critical hope directly challenges inscribed habits of emotional attention and signifies a willingness to exist within ambiguity and uncertainty. One knows, for example, that there is no assurance of justice, but one is yet willing to fight for justice. As Greene notes, "There are always vacancies: there are always roads not taken, vistas not acknowledged. The search must be ongoing; the end can never be quite known."[10] Similarly, Freire writes: "What makes me hopeful is not so much the certainty of the *find,* but my movement in search."[11]

Freire's emphasis on process resonates with the Buddhist emphasis on the difficult process of change. One can see the distinct resonance between the two in this previously quoted excerpt from Epstein:

> Change will happen naturally as we open to the truth. The more we bring our attachments into awareness, the freer we become, not because we eliminate the attachments, but because we learn to identify more with awareness than with desire. Using our capacity for consciousness, we can change perspective on ourselves, giving a sense of space where once there was only habit.[12]

The cliché that "change is hard" is explained when one acknowledges that critical hope can only emerge from what Paulo Freire calls our "incompleteness." Rather than being absorbed by the myth that our world is static, unchanging, and complete, we recognize that our selves and our world are in a constant state of dynamic change. In recognizing the dynamic present, we also recognize that our relations to others and the form of reality itself can be other than they are. What Freire describes in terms of love and humility as central to dialogue, I have emphasized here as compassion. Sam asked me to tell him he can make a difference. My response is to outline critical hope: There is hope if we are willing to step beyond our known selves. The educator has a compassionate responsibility to show students others who have walked down this path.

Making Up for the Loss

If I am asking students in some sense to annihilate the self as they have known it, I must be able to meet their discomfort with compassion—and with resources to help them replace the lost sense of self. Most importantly,

Sam's request for hope makes me think that critical hope requires a clear explication of what is lost and what might be gained through this suffering of loss. If a pedagogy of discomfort takes away someone's worldview, in compassion it needs to replace the vacuum with something else.

Productive "replacements" for the loss might be found in the following focus of course content. First, one might engage discussions of how the construction of masculinity or white privilege, for example, also bears a cost to those who benefit (Sut Jhally's video *Tough Guise* addresses Jackson Katz's analyses of how violent representations of masculinity are damaging to men, for example). A second approach is to make use of first-person accounts, such as Minnie Bruce Pratt's essay "Identity: Skin/Blood/Heart"[13] in which she describes her shift from not recognizing her complicity in white supremacy to becoming an anti-racist activist. A third approach is historical, emphasizing social movement history in more detail, including histories of white Northerners who came to the South during the 1950s to help do such work as enlist black people to vote.

Critical hope requires seeing one's self within historical context, reevaluating the relationship of one's privilege to others in the world. It entails as well seeing how these relations of power shift and change over time and in one's lifetime. This pedagogical relation is a negotiation of hegemonically constructed habits, internalized as attachments to particular beliefs and corresponding emotional reactions to change. But I wish to stress that this inquiry is a collective, not an individualized, process. Searching for freedom, as Greene notes,

> never occurs in a vacuum. Freedom cannot be conceived apart from a matrix of social, economic, cultural, and psychological conditions. It is within the matrix that selves take shape or are created through choice of action in the changing situations of life. The degree and quality of whatever freedom is achieved are functions of the perspectives available, and the reflectiveness on the choices made.[14]

This process of searching for freedom takes place as a collective process. Second, this process depends on learning to notice how our selves and perspectives are shifting and contingent. This collective process depends most centrally on the interpersonal relationships between educator and student and between students, interpersonal relationships shaped in a political context—in a sense, on teaching as a form of lovingkindness. To unravel the complex emotional fabric of relationships, often fraught with heated differences of perspective, entails, as I have described, a particular compassion or lovingkindness for the suffering that may be involved in this rethinking of oneself and the world.

In *Pedagogy of the Oppressed*,[15] Freire writes that dialogue requires love, faith, and humility. Humility is in part the ability to listen to others as we forge connections and the courage to recognize that our perspectives and vision are partial and striving and must remain open to change.

Conclusion

I have explored how a pedagogy of discomfort reveals one's inscribed habits of emotional inattention, a process that may well cause suffering for educator and student alike. By introducing critical hope, I have tried to outline how educators may take seriously the ethical implications of shattering someone's familiar and comfortable worldview. What can we offer to replace the sense of self and values that may be threatened and displaced through a pedagogy of discomfort?

I have suggested critical hope as an approach that takes the cry for help seriously and that recognizes with compassion the need for something to hold on to as the world is made to seem ambiguous and chaotic when learning to see differently. By recognizing the other's suffering with compassion, one is pushed to smile, even in the midst of conflict. One is pushed to offer blueprints for roads that lead to hope, "even though the world is screwed up."

Struggling for social justice is rarely easy work. Unlearning one's habits of being and thinking, and one's inscribed habits of emotional attention, can be painful labor as well. In the midst of this discomfort, compassion suggests an attitude of lovingkindness. Compassion means developing a patience for my own shortcomings. It means developing patience and respect in the face of the other's suffering, no matter how painful it may feel to be the object of another's anger.

Rumi's words offer a description of the space of dynamic interaction that exceeds our words and thoughts in educational encounters: "Out beyond ideas of wrongdoing and great doing, there is a field. I'll meet you there. When the soul lies down in that grass, the world is too full to talk about." To meet the other in this field beyond ideas of right and wrong asks us to open ways of understanding that do not rely only on words. Compassion is one bridge between those suffering a pedagogy of discomfort and those who have invited new ways of being fully alive into a world replete with imperfections.

PART 3

Love's Losses and Love Regained

When we love anything, whether it be persons, places, things, or ideas, we reach out and strive to hold on, but no love lasts forever. Because loss is integral to human destiny, learning to let go is part of love's wisdom. The first two papers (by Rachel Kessler and Ursula Kelly, respectively) in this section deal with grief and reparations. They teach us how love may bring order out of the emotional chaos that follows profound loss of love. From them we learn a great deal about reconciling ourselves to, and recovering from, loss by repairing the damage done so we may learn to love again. The third paper (by Ann Diller) explores the necessity of overcoming "attachments" to beliefs, images, standpoints, perspectives, and even other persons. Kahlil Gibran writes of love, "Even as he is for your growth so is he for your pruning."[1] We cannot grow without loss, without giving up our attachments; but learning what to give up, when, and why requires discerning wisdom. Such wisdom lies beyond knowledge alone, though it cannot be without knowledge. These three essays contain a good deal of such remarkable insight.

These papers do not just show us how to cope with life's inevitable losses, but how to learn and grow from them. Only those who have suffered and grown wise from such painful experiences have the moral perception and empathetic compassion to comfort others. Those who have learned to nurture and protect themselves against loss while reaching out to others for help can offer the preservative love we all need in times of trouble. In this way, they pass on the gift of love they have received. As teachers, they are the ones who celebrate the last day of every school year in sadness, tears, joy, and laughter.

Modern society is remarkably transient; friends and classmates depart frequently, immigration remains steady, and the divorce rate is high. Then, too, there are the inevitable losses of loved ones arising from the normal cycle of life commonly experienced by most students. There are other losses such as family pets, favorite toys, and innocence, which we should not belittle. And there are the illnesses and departures of those we love. There is nothing in the contemporary instrumentalist educational rhetoric that even acknowledges the existence of such problems. Students, nonetheless, bring these and many other losses to school every day. Teachers, who teach students and not just subject matter, must somehow cope with them.

Teachers like Rachael Kessler, who have learned to make friends with grief, are able to help their students make friends with theirs. Kessler expresses the concern that our culture provides little preparation for dealing with the grief that loss brings. Often there are no safe places for children to grieve within schools. Students who cannot learn to assuage their sadness readily fall into numbness and depression. Refusing care, connection, and love from others as they grow into adults (even teachers), these individuals are unable to help others deal with their grief and loss. Kessler takes us through the cycle of grief with concern, kindness, and insight. Helping us understand the losses we may still grieve, she better prepares us to help our students in their time of need.

Ursula A. Kelly shows how coming to terms with love's losses enhances our teaching, since it enhances our lives. She begins by discussing the connections among grief, mourning, and identity that emerge out of the emotional chaos that accompanies profound loss. Her theme is one of reparations, of making amends, of repairing damaged relationships with one's self as well as others in our present as well as our past. By exposing the reparative sources of her own desire (eros) to teach, she invites us to examine our teaching eros in thoughtful ways. Probing deeper, she realizes that reparation has a place as well as a purpose. From these insights, she begins to outline a pedagogy of reparation. Kelly is particularly interested in teaching across social and cultural differences. Understanding how reparation works allows teachers to avoid unfortunate unintended consequences such as perpetuating inequality through neo-colonial arrogance about what values schooling should bestow. With Kessler, Kelly recognizes that coming to terms with grief need not be lonely work; she also shows that the same holds for making appropriate reparations. Comprehending love's losses, making friends with grief, and properly proportioning reparations have profound consequences for any relational activity such as teaching.

While love in the West breaks many boundaries, Ann Diller's paper transports us beyond the bounds of western thought. Although, as Kelly indicates, we must remain wary when working across cultural difference, still, what Diller writes conveys something of great worth even if our understanding is partial and imperfect. Diller looks at the four Buddhist Brahmaviharas to see what we can learn from them. It is a search for "wise love," and she finds a good deal of it.

The four Brahmaviharas are "lovingkindness," compassion, sympathetic joy, and equanimity. Every Brahmavihara should infuse and flow through the others, and each has near and far enemies that inhibit the flow of love. The near enemies are deceitful because they mimic the Brahmaviharas they obstruct. The far enemy of lovingkindness is hatred; its near enemies are fixed and immutable attachments along with the desire to control. Compassion's far enemy is cruelty, while its near enemies are pity and self-righteous anger. Sympathetic joy's far enemy is envy and its near enemies are affectation and hypocrisy. The far enemies of equanimity are anxiety and restlessness; its near enemy is indifference.

Let us look briefly at lovingkindness, since beginning to comprehend it helps us better understand the border defining the difference between East and West concerning the discourse of love. Diller indicates that most

Buddhist teachers choose the term *lovingkindness* to avoid entangling the meaning of the word *metta* with western notions of romanticism, sentimentality, sexuality, pious religiosity, and superficial emotionalism. Diller, though, follows that minority of Buddhist teachers who find *love* too beautiful a word to abandon. The word *metta* has its roots in the Buddhist word for *friend,* denoting friendship. Ideally, it is friendship free of inhibiting attachment and the desire to control. Clearly, it is a view of friendship devoid of the conditions imposed by Aristotle. Many interpret lovingkindness freed of attachment and control as an impersonal form of love, but Diller believes it has more than personal meaning. It is love seen in the larger, uninhibited, free-flowing context of the remaining three Brahmaviharas. It is an expansive, all-embracing love.

CHAPTER 8

Grief as a Gateway to Love in Teaching

RACHAEL KESSLER

To heal the world, we must feel the world . . .
—Jewish prayer

Introduction

Richard was a school psychologist who told this story in a sharing circle about teachers who inspired us by positive or negative example to become the educators we are today:

> I was in first grade. I can see her face, but I can't seem to remember her name. My brother had just died before I started school. She had a rocking chair in the classroom and on the first day of school, she picked me up on her lap in the rocker and began to rock me. She rocked, and I sobbed. And sobbed and sobbed. It was something I couldn't do at home—not the way my family handled these things. And you know, she did that for months, every day for minutes or sometimes what seemed like hours. She took me into the chair and rocked me for about five months, when my crying was done.

While he experienced the "American way of grief" at home, Richard had a rare encounter with an educator who was willing to help this little boy make friends with his grief.

My colleague John McCluskey was not so fortunate. After crying much of the way through his first encounter with a workshop on grief, John recalled:

I was the youngest of eight children living with a single mother. I was thirteen when my mom died. Suddenly I had to move in with my dad and his wife—I hadn't had much contact with these people before.

When I think back, I realize that not a single one of my teachers that year ever asked me about how I was doing with my mother's death, or with all the changes in my life. Not a single one. I didn't even realize that was strange.

In just these two stories, we begin to see the powerful impact of educators' responses to loss in their students. Adults in traditional American culture have little preparation for dealing with grief. "Like many people in our society, teachers often feel uncomfortable discussing death and loss. This reluctance can adversely affect the children in their charge, who look to their teachers for truth, knowledge and support."[1]

Many parents and teachers are so uncomfortable with discussing loss that students feel they have no safe place to go with these feelings. Children have a keen sense of this discomfort in the adults in their lives. They see it, smell it, hear it in its most subtle forms and protect their parents and teachers from their own feelings of loss. And when they don't, when they are so desperately needing care in their grief, they are often turned away. For children, the suppression of grief often results in numbing or depression, which in turn leads to shutting down of their capacity to care, to connect, and to love. In its most extreme forms, numbed grief becomes a ground for violence to the self and others. For teachers who have had these experiences in an American childhood, unexpressed grief can cut off their capacity to bring love into teaching—to be open and authentic with students, to have passion for a subject, and to care deeply about students. Lacking the guidance to make friends with our own grief, teachers often continue this cycle of discomfort and denial. We become the adults who convey by our very presence a wall that keeps most students from expressing any feelings of loss.

In this chapter, I will share what inspires me as an educator to strengthen my ability to deal with grief and then present a model that has been useful in doing so. My primary emphasis throughout this essay is to describe a series of experiences that might enable educators to deal more adequately with this challenging emotion in ourselves and others and move on to the terrain of love and hope.

Why Should Educators Deal with Grief?

Most of our students have a storehouse of unexpressed grief. Traumatic losses from death, divorce, geographic relocation, and dislocation are common experiences for children and youth. Some students also experience the traumatic premature loss of childhood through experiences such as abuse or teen pregnancy. In addition, all students encounter the ordinary losses of growing up—saying good-bye at the end of each school year; leaving elementary school for middle school; middle for high school; and leaving high school, home, and community. Leaving college—especially when it has provided meaningful community—is also a time of enormous loss for many young people. These experiences of ordinary loss not only trigger feelings of grief for what is happening in the present but often bring up significant unhealed losses from earlier in childhood.

The cycle of grief can be triggered by significant change of any kind, including "positive" changes such as a promotion, the completion of a project, or the retirement of a colleague. All of these experiences provide the challenge and the opportunity of learning to say good-bye to an old self— a relationship to self, to others, and to the world as we have known it.

Today, as the immigrant population once again swells in our schools, we are working with children who have been wrenched from place and family, language and culture. Some of these children, in addition to all of these losses, are struggling with the grief of having watched the death and destruction of people and places in war-torn homelands. Newcomers, both children and parents, need educators who can hold an awareness of this grief even when it is unspoken. And, whenever possible, they need the opportunity to express the range of feelings that, bottled up inside, may be another impediment to learning.

When we consider the broad range of experiences that trigger grief in our students, we realize how vital our ability to respond with love may be. Writing not about grief, but about the need for social and emotional learning in the classroom, a teacher from a small town in Washington gives us a litany of loss:

> In my classroom of twenty-four children ages 6–9, I have:
> Two children going back and forth between divorced parents. Their homework, permission slips, and after-school needs are often left at one or the other house.
> Two children going through messy and cruel divorces. One child has become a hypochondriac and has low reading scores. The other holds all her emotions in check. She's hard to read.
> One child's father is battling an aggressive form of cancer.
> Two children live without any contact from their fathers. One mother tries desperately to make up for the loss by giving her child everything asked for and blaming all failures on the child's loss. The other mother is too consumed with her own life to consistently help her son. This child at 7 is obese and has trouble focusing.

As a classroom teacher, how can I overlook their inner lives? While there are many skills and resources a teacher can develop to respond to students with care, compassion, and guidance, one of the most critical is an understanding of, and comfort with, the cycle of grief.

Searching for a Model

I was first introduced to the well-known "stages" of grief in the 80s. A workshop I attended on children and stress asserted that all change—negative and positive, ordinary and traumatic—produces feelings of loss, which arouse in the human heart the same cycle of emotions associated with the grief that follows a death of a loved one. The degree and persistence of the emotion might be less, but the cycle is basically the same.

As I reflected on the "stages" of grieving presented, I was not satisfied.[2] I had lost a husband after seven years of marriage when I was only 26 years old. My own experience of grieving was not embraced by the Kubler-Ross model. I realized she had meant those stages for the dying, not for the living left behind.

A few years later, I was deeply moved by some mimeographed materials on grief developed by a native Eskimo teacher, Liz Sunnyboy. She believed that all of the psychological and social problems of her people came from unexpressed, unhealed grief. The model I offer in my workshops, and which I will provide here, is an adaptation of her framework.

A journey through the territory of grief:

First, let's look at the map.
  I. *Protection*
      Shock
      Denial
  II. *Feeling*
      Anger
      Guilt/Shame
      Fear
      Sadness
  III. *Healing*
      Acceptance
      Hope

Knowing some basic contours of this landscape prepares us to navigate this terrain:

- Time alone will not heal grief.
- The grieving process can actually transform grief into personal growth.
- There are two keys to healing through grieving:
    1. Become conscious about the process and the range of feelings.
    2. Find opportunities to safely EXPRESS the *whole* range of feelings.
- Grief is not only the feeling of sadness. ("I never felt grief," said one parent. "I would just call it an acceptance process.")

- Not everyone goes through all of these stages or through these stages in this particular order. People grieve differently from other people who are suffering the same loss; they also grieve differently from ways they grieved another loss in the past.
- You do not necessarily complete the stages of grief and then feel finished with the process.

The Wheel of Grief

Protection

The first phase of mourning involves a variety of strategies built into the psyche, mind, and body designed to protect us from overwhelming pain: shock and denial. If we have had ample time to prepare for a death, this phase may be softer and shorter. But with a sudden death, especially the death of a person not yet elderly, we need protection. If we were to think the unthinkable and feel the unfeelable, the horror would destroy us. The wisdom of our ancient neurobiological systems takes care of us by ensuring that we cannot think, feel, or even talk about this pain.

Shock

"Our whole being becomes numb, or stunned," writes Liz Sunnyboy. "One can't think, cry, talk, laugh, or feel. Shock is a temporary escape from reality."[3] Shock is the dimension of grieving that I have found to be least understood or recognized. The consequences of this ignorance can lead to isolation of the bereaved. Even worse, misunderstanding shock can lead to judgments and condemnation that create ongoing damage.

When I suffered the loss of my first love, I was blessed with an almost immediate instruction on shock that changed everything—for me and for the people I teach. My husband, Carl, was a young doctor when he died of a lethal interaction between a glass of Scotch and one or two sleeping pills. Like everyone around him, I was totally unprepared for his sudden death.

In the years before this tragic loss, I had suffered from the persistent pain of a slipped disk. Nothing seemed to help. Weeks before his death, Carl learned that a neurologist at Yale was opening one of the first pain clinics in the nation for dealing with chronic pain. He scheduled an appointment for me. That appointment came two days after his death. I chose to go, feeling utterly desperate. "How will I deal with this physical pain," I wondered, "when I know I will have more emotional pain than I could ever imagine?" I knew I needed any help I could get.

The doctor greeted me with so much warmth and empathy that I felt immediately at ease. "I'm surprised you are here, but I am so glad. Now I can show you what shock really means. So few people actually understand."

He took out tools that looked like they were meant for torture, not healing. Rolling devices with pins and needles, they were designed to discover where the body could detect sensation and where the nerves were dead or asleep. As he poked through skin on my limbs, I was startled to feel absolutely no pain. "That is shock," he explained. "That's your body protecting you against feeling. Because if it didn't, if you could actually feel in a normal way, the pain you would feel right now in your heart could destroy you. . . . It's not just the nerve endings in your body that have gone numb; you won't feel much emotion over these next weeks and months. It may be disorienting. The good news is that your back will probably heal. You will get a break from the pain and fear, so you can start to move actively again, which is the best thing for you at this point. You will also probably not have a period for many months. Your whole system is on hold."

He was right. Right about my back pain and about my menstrual cycle going on hold. And knowing about the mechanisms of shock, I could begin to understand some of the other strange experiences I was having—like difficulty driving and making ordinary conversation.

I didn't cry much. I didn't laugh. The only emotion I felt with strength in those first few months was fear. It would come to me only at night—as crippling terror, screaming nightmares as I looked into the jaws of my own death. I could not sleep in a house without others. Except for my fear, shock had wrapped me in a cocoon of protection. Years later, this allowed me to support my students through the mysteries of shock.

Cindy was on a freshman retreat at our high school when she learned that her father had dropped dead on the tennis court. When she returned to school after a week at home, her best friends were deeply troubled and angry. "What's wrong with Cindy?" they asked their life skills teacher. "How can she be so cold? She's just acting like nothing has happened. She never cries and she doesn't even look sad. We can't look at her without thinking about what just happened. We're feeling so sad—and she's not. Doesn't she have a heart?" These deeply emotional 14-year-olds wanted to shower their friend with the love and compassion they knew they would want in this situation. Cindy's loss awakened them to the fear that their own parents might not be invincible. They were quick to judge Cindy because of her stony demeanor and would have backed away, leaving her with a double loss. Fortunately, their teacher explained to them that, with their distance from this loss, they could afford to feel the depths of their grief and that Cindy could not survive this level of feeling right now. Shock is what gets us through at first.

Americans often isolate the bereaved because we don't know what to say or do around grief. Then isolation hits a second time because of our ignorance about shock: By the time the numbing has begun to melt and the strong emotions begin to erupt, many friends have "moved on." We have moved quickly through our milder grief and assume that the mourners should have completed their process as well. We are caught in a wild impatience about grief. Three or four months, we assume, should be enough to heal. If people take longer, we assume they are morbid, depressed, self-indulgent. The grieving process can, and often does, take years. It doesn't really begin to move toward healing until the shock subsides and the deep feeling begins. But before we move ahead to that feeling, let's explore denial—another form of protection.

Denial

Denial, says Sunnyboy, is about disbelief. "No, it is just not true," says the mind. And, like shock, in the early stages of grief, it is beyond our control. I have often heard the phrase "she's in denial" as a form of put down—a judgment that so-and-so should wake up and come to terms with reality. In the protection phase of mourning, we can't afford to wake up. Denial is a necessary, healthy defense mechanism. Denial of grief can often be sustained for a long time after a first encounter with traumatic loss. A second loss usually opens the door. Unfortunately, when this occurs, there is a huge legacy of unexpressed grief that burdens the grieving process for the current situation.

Alan lost his father when he was in eighth grade. Denial was his only comfort. He began to build his personality around the refusal to feel. His main comfort after his father died was a relationship with his grandfather that grew stronger and stronger. I first met Alan at the beginning of tenth grade when his grandfather died. I could almost feel the scraping of the lid off his denial. He was still trying to hold it back and hold himself together. Unfortunately for Alan, Samantha was also in this human development class. Samantha had lost her dad in ninth grade. Unlike Alan, her coping style was to express, celebrate her dad, talk about her healing process, and share her grief. Alan despised Samantha. They had been childhood friends. But ever since she lost her dad, Alan could not bear to be around her. She was a trigger to Alan's loaded gun. And now that his denial was being ripped off by his grandpa's death, Alan needed more than ever to control the pace of his grief. He couldn't do that with Samantha present.

As a teacher, I was too new and inexperienced to recognize that Alan needed to be moved out of that section. Eventually, after too much disruption from Alan doing his best to make our class unsafe for the expression of any authentic feeling, I got it. Meeting with Alan, his mother, and the dean, I decided to grant him a waiver so he was not surrounded by students talking about feelings. He needed the respect that allowed him to move at his own pace. I learned how important it is for me as a teacher not to take on what is not mine to handle, not to put "inclusion" above the actual needs of the child.

Denial may be unavoidable in the early months of a shocking loss. But at some point, there is more choice. There is a critical time when we either begin to go through the feeling stages of grief or shut down. Denial is the primary mechanism for this shutting down. Shutting down the grief also seems to shut down the capacity for deep feelings of any kind. Denial may be a necessary form of protection, a healthy defense mechanism at a time when too much feeling is dangerous. And it may become an unhealthy dam, blocking the flow of feelings that will promote healing only when they are felt and expressed.

Moving into Feeling

Now comes the fork in the road. Do we find the support and the inner strength to move into our feelings or do we lock into protection, shutting down our capacity to feel deeply and stunting or delaying the healing process? The latter will often bring on a depression—which is not necessarily a phase of grief so much as it is an avoidance of grief. Grieving may include sadness, deep sadness. But the depression that comes from avoiding feelings is a flat, exhausted, isolated, hopeless, and helpless place that settles in and is very difficult to lift.

If we choose the road of feeling, here are some of the emotions that may surface: sadness, anger, fear, or guilt. For each person, for each loss, a different set of feelings emerges, a different sequence. We all heal in different ways. And these differences can add another challenging dimension to grief. People who are grieving are often intolerant of those who are grieving the same loss in a different way. Husbands and wives often feel unsupported, misunderstood, or riddled with judgment and anger because their spouse doesn't seem to be "really grieving," or seems to be "unwilling to move on." Perhaps this is one of the reasons that couples who lose a child often lose their marriage as well.

Anger

When anger erupts in the cycle of grief, it finds many targets. Some people are angry at God for taking their loved one or requiring this unwanted move or change. With suicide or divorce, anger is commonly felt and expressed toward the lost loved one. Even when the person did not choose to die or had very legitimate reasons for moving across the world or leaving this job, we may feel anger toward him or her for lurching us into primal feelings of abandonment. When we are the ones required to leave, we may feel rage against life for making us lose a community or person or place that we love. That same anger can be directed against the very people from whom we have been separated.

Anger after loss may find its target in yet another place. It may turn inward, a rage against the self we call guilt—which we will explore shortly as another phase of grief. And often, anger is simply an energy in the system, simmering, boiling, spilling, erupting with no particular target in mind— not anyone or anything. An assistant superintendent, Duneen Debruhl, shared a story about an extremely angry middle school student from her days as a principal.

> I was the one in charge of discipline for the school, so I saw this boy again and again. He was angry all the time, and it took little for him to erupt and cause trouble wherever he was. Grace allowed me to love that boy. Each time he came back expecting punishment and anger, I greeted him with love. One day, he just melted in my office. That poor boy had just lost his mother, his home, his place in the world.

He was in foster care now, and behind that firewall of anger was a blaze of grief. Anger, unlike denial, is a strong emotion. But anger can also be a bridge, an intermediary step between denial and grief. It can be a protection against the sadness that is the most vulnerable place on the wheel of grief. While such protection may be necessary, like shock, in the early months after or preceding a loss, it can become dangerous when we become stuck there because we are too afraid to move into vulnerability. Such refusal to move through the stages of grief can lead to a personality change—a person for whom anger is a way of life, a lens through which all of life is experienced and expressed. But like the story above, deep caring and love for the angry mourner can melt that anger to expose the sadness underneath. And once the sadness is felt and expressed, healing and hope are possible.

Anger is a common emotional strategy among families who are preparing to lose a high school senior to the larger world. Unconsciously, someone in the family—student, parent, or sibling—"decides" that it will be easier to say goodbye and move on if there is distance, not closeness.

Guilt

Guilt is said to be a form of anger—turned inward against the self. Like anger, its pain can feel more bearable than the abject vulnerability of sadness or fear that lies on the other side of the protection phase. For in anger and guilt, human beings maintain some sense of control over life and death. Blame—whether it is against another or ourselves —presumes control. Without blame, we can feel ourselves at the mercy of a totally unpredictable world—an experience that is too vulnerable to be tolerated at some stages in life. But while it provides protection to the unconscious, guilt can be a torment for a mourner if it takes hold and prevent the flow into healing.

The curse of guilt is a well-known response of children to loss and grief. Developmentally, children are all too likely to see themselves at the causal center of all that happens in their lives. One of the most damaging effects of divorce is the guilt children take on because they believe they must have caused the animosity between their parents.

Guilt can seize parents as an expression of grief when their child is born with a disability. Parents blame themselves for the genes they passed on, the diet or other substances they imbibed that may have caused the mysterious afflictions their child is born with. Through acts of omission or commission, they believe they have harmed their child. Or they are riddled with guilt for any moment of failure to accept the differences in their child, to accept everything that goes with the role of being a parent to a child with special needs. As I have listened to such parents, I discovered that redemption was deeply connected to an experience of forgiveness. Only when we can discover the strength to forgive ourselves, our lost or damaged loved one, God or fate, can we move back out of the inlets of anger and guilt and into the river of grief that will allow us to heal.

Fear

In 1972, when I saw my husband's dead body, I felt for the first time the reality of death. For weeks and months after, I awoke screaming in the night from nightmares of my own death. A decade later, I watched my mother confront this same specter in a dream as we tried to sleep in the waiting room of the hospital the night after the surgery that killed my father.

When my friend Ken's daughter Jenna died overseas, I worked to support a dozen of her sorority sisters. Virtually all were afraid to sleep alone. I assured them that this was a common reaction in the early weeks to the fear that arises after an unexpected death. I told them my own story and stories of three families I knew with independent adolescent sons or daughters who had each moved into their parents' bedrooms for months after a sibling died.

Fear can take many forms in grieving. And the source is often not conscious or clear. We can be afraid of our own mortality. We can be afraid of ghosts, of guilt, of punishment, of succumbing to sadness or to the terrible vulnerability of helplessness and loss of control. We can be afraid that grief will drive us to madness or will drive away everyone who loves or cares for us.

This very last fear is so unnecessary and yet so true in a culture where we are averse to grief. People often do lose friends, family, and colleagues because of grief. The best antidote I have found to this very real fear is truth. Acknowledging the reality of avoidance that can greet mourners seems to ease some of the fear. Internal or transpersonal resources may come into play when we realize the rejection or abandonment from our community is not personal, not about us so much as it is about a person and a culture afraid to sit with the feelings of loss. Compassionate truth-telling is especially important for children and youth who may use this rejection to fuel their guilt, which we have seen can stop or stall the healing process.

Sadness

When we feel safe enough to be vulnerable, we can feel and express the sadness that is almost inevitable at some point in the journey toward healing from loss. Tears, hurt, loneliness—all of these may flow. Liz Sunnyboy suggests what she calls seven natural healing processes that allow us to move into this vulnerability that will ultimately allow the feelings to move through and out of us. Talking, crying, sweating, shaking, laughing, yelling, yawning or sighing—this unlikely family of actions can release and express deep grief.

A fourth-grade teacher, Brian Geraghty, found a strong current of sadness flowing in himself and his students as his first year of teaching came to an end.

> It was my first year of teaching and the learning curve was extremely high. I had this great group of kids and we grew closer than I ever expected. It was the year of the Columbine tragedy, so we had to do a lot of talking. They were able to see a lot of my feelings. Just seeing your teacher cry and realizing it was okay for a teacher to show feelings in the classroom—it brought us so much closer.
>
> They gave me so much. And when the end was coming, I felt such gratitude, I wanted to give something back. I had so much feeling. I didn't know how I was going to say goodbye.
>
> I wanted to write a song for them. We were talking about stars, about constellations. And I was talking about that light—how the star could have died in the time of the dinosaurs, but we can still see the light. And then the words just came. "You're all stars, shining so bright. Keep shining on, so people can still see your light after you're gone." I played and sang to them a few days before the end. I bought a package of glow-in-the-dark stars and gave each one a star to remember our class. There were two big stars in the package, which I gave to the two kids moving out of state. "You need to burn brighter," I said, "because you'll be farther away."
>
> I still get choked up thinking about it. I put one star on the end of my guitar—I keep it there as a reminder.
>
> On the last day of school, the parents came, too, and we had a fun day. The parents asked me to sing the song—the kids had told them. I sang it and then everyone was crying. I was crying, the kids were crying, the parents were crying. Lots of hugs going around. It was my first year, so I didn't know if I'd ever see them again.
>
> You know, it was definitely the most spiritually rewarding experience I've had in teaching so far. It was so fulfilling to be in that role and to touch their

lives that way. I broke down when I was talking to them in April about Columbine—"I can't even imagine what would happen if something like this happened to you. I love all of you guys so much."

And I reminded them on the last day of school. I'm not afraid to tell my students that I love them. And sometimes I don't have to tell them; it just shows. I never thought I'd be telling my kids I loved them. None of my teachers would ever have said that.

I opened myself up so much to these kids. It was such a profound loss, such sadness when it was over. When you open yourself up for that, you're opening yourself up for everything. Then I was so surprised at the end—whoah, I didn't want it to end.[4]

The willingness of this teacher to share his sadness—both in response to the traumatic losses in Littleton and the ordinary loss of ending the school year—opened wide the gateways to love in himself and his students. He brought an intention and creativity to goodbye that was an essential lesson for his students in the possibilities for real completion and commemoration when it's time to leave. How often can we bring such an undefended heart to our students? How sweet the communion and learning when we can.

Healing

Once the challenging feelings have had the opportunity to flow—at whatever pace they may need—healing becomes possible. Acceptance comes, and with it, hope. Liz Sunnyboy offers the voices of acceptance: "I am alright, I had a loss and I went through it and I'm not alone. I can make choices about how to care for myself. I have a new appreciation of life and my own life."[5]

Acceptance can come after a long period of sorrow and anger or can come in a flash. Two of the sorority girls were experiencing ecstatic joy when I met with their group just a few weeks after their loss. They had been blessed with the opportunity to fly to the memorial service and to share in a communal expression of profound grief and love. Returning home was a journey fraught with challenges graced by strangers providing solutions. They began to feel their friend was watching over them. They felt her ongoing presence in their lives and with that loving presence, an explosion of mystery and joy. While their sorority sisters were angry, accusing them of denial, I felt they had been catapulted through the stages of grief in an intense and rapid way that graced them with the acceptance and hope that usually come much later.

In my friends who lost children, I watched the first signs of acceptance come only after many years filled with turmoil and anguish. In each of these parents, I saw that their own capacity to accept their loss was deeply entwined with their ability to provide service to others in a way that grows out of the strength they have discovered in navigating this perilous journey of grief.

In these acts of service to others who are grieving, or who need to respond to someone in grief, or to young people with the same interests or illnesses as their deceased child, I see them rediscover hope. I cannot separate acceptance from hope in neat, clean categories. They flow together. "A ray of light after darkness of loss," says Sunnyboy, describing this stage of hope:

- I got help and others can be helped. I survived a loss and I can be supportive to others.
- I have new energy to look forward, to plan new things.
- I can *feel* again and I can accept reality.
- I am stronger now and I may have a better understanding of my purpose or of life's meaning.
- I can live, love, and laugh again!
- And I am not thinking so much about this loss.

[handwritten margin note: spiritual not religious]

Perhaps the greatest gift of fully experiencing the process of grief is this emergence into a stage of character in which we can feel more deeply, love more fully, serve more generously, and have a new clarity about why we are here and what matters deeply in life. The hope that can break through when one has fully lived the grief is not the pollyanna-ish hope of innocence and naivete. It is an attitude toward life and the living that includes an awareness of limits, of the inevitability of endings, of the depth of human suffering and the possibilities of human strength.

Endings and Returns: Using this Model

I experienced melancholy beginning in September of every year for about ten years after Carl died. Often it was not until October, when I would begin to see all the signs of Halloween coming in the stores, that I would realize I was having an anniversary reaction. Once I knew what was going on, I was less frightened that depression was about to take hold. I was better able to manage the return of grief and find ways to express it and honor it so it could move through me.

"Like adults, children don't work through their grief on a particular timetable," writes Naomi Naierman in *Educational Leadership.* ". . . Young people may grieve intensely, but sporadically. A major loss in early childhood can reverberate through the years as the person progresses through life's milestones—first date, graduation, marriage and parenthood."[6]

As educators, we must be sensitive to these anniversary reactions if we want to respond to our students with compassion and care. The child who lost his or her mother at four or twelve or sixteen may become moody and depressed or angry as he or she approaches these milestones without having any idea what is causing this suffering. Buried in the unconscious are feelings of immense regret that this parent can not be there, witness and support them as they navigate these joyful or challenging events. And of course, it can be useful to know this about ourselves and our colleagues as well.

I wrote this chapter primarily to support educators in making friends with their own grief so it does not block the door to the full flow of love possible with their students. I don't offer this model to be employed in a didactic way in response to a loss. People who are grieving do not feel loved when their feelings are put in a box, a construct, a generalization. When you are working in a classroom with an immediate loss—be it personal or what might be called tribal losses such as Columbine or September 11 that can touch an entire community or nation—you can choose from a number of ways to support the students deeply affected by grief. Let's look at some options.

Accommodation

"Accommodate these students" is a core piece of guidance to teachers from Ken Druck, executive director of the Jenna Druck Foundation. "You might liken it to accommodations in the workplace or for children with special needs. Invite the child to sit in the front of the room; allow her to reorient certain work projects to themes more in accord with the powerful experience that is commanding all of her attention."[7] Ken speaks with gratitude about the high school teachers who were willing to "relax their standards" to accommodate the grief and disorientation of his younger daughter following the sudden death of her sister. He urges teachers to see such times as a "transient state of special need" and asks them to be willing to adjust their expectations for "a work product to a level she's capable of. Provide take-home tests. Understand that she's not going to be able to function at a certain level. And realize that students who have just sustained a traumatic loss will have a rough edge socially—they're not going to be able to engage in ordinary conversations."

Commemorate

"Schools have an ability to commemorate and honor the loss of a child in a way that helps everyone cope with the grief with love and grace." He describes the cooperation between a school and his "Families Helping Families" program to provide this kind of conscious grieving for a child who died and all the mourners left behind.

> One of our parents lost a seven-year-old daughter. It went from "I have a headache, Mommy," to seeing her child dead in three hours. Our facilitators went in to the classroom and did a debriefing with all of the kids. We explored the idea

of leaving her desk intact for the rest of the school year. The children decorated it —it was a way they could express their grief.

Instead of "let's cover this over and remove the desk quickly," this teacher and her students created a sacred place in the classroom, where they could hold a place for her in their hearts, a physical place where she could be remembered and loved. The parents picked up all the notes—they loved reading them.

Now we've created a program for helping teachers deal with the grief of the other kids when there's a death—it's called "Jenelle's Chair."

The Jenna Druck Foundation also offers teachers the tools for helping students sort out what to say, and what not to say, to children returning to class immersed in grief.[8] "The object is not to make someone feel better; it's about being a loving presence. In the presence of someone who's loving and free of judgement—we at least don't feel alone. Alone is one of the most devastating social aspects of grief. We not only lost the person, we lost our world. And for children that world is their classroom."[9]

Expression

When our entire classroom is dealing with grief because of an experience like Columbine or when a student or teacher in the class or school has just died, we can create a safe structure for all the feelings to be shared. Alone, or with the support of a colleague or trained professional from the school or community, you can work with your students to set the ground rules that make such disclosure feel safe and appropriate. You can offer a sharing circle or council in which each person has the opportunity to speak without interruption for a brief period or to listen respectfully in silence.[10] The option to pass is essential. At the end, you may find a gentle, respectful, and personal way to weave some information for your students about the way that each of us may find ourselves at different places on the wheel of grief at any particular moment and that they are all legitimate.

If you do choose to offer such a circle, your willingness to speak first, from your heart, about your own feelings is a powerful foundation for the safety of your students. Your own tears and heartfelt sadness can help students feel safe. Uncontrollable hysteria will do the opposite.

So ultimately we come back around to the question of whether or not you have made friends with your own grief. If you are terrified of grief— your own and that of others—you may convey a stone-cold feeling that disallows the free flow of your students' feeling. Or you may feel your grief erupt like a volcano that is completely beyond your control. If you have worked with your own grief—past and current—in the privacy of your own world or with colleagues outside the classroom, you can bring yourself to the grief of your students with the capacity for authentic and appropriate expression.

Conclusion: On to Hope and Love

When we know how to let ourselves grieve, we can lose a loved one or end a relationship, a class, or a phase of life with a sense of completion and fullness that allows us to love again next time. When we are willing to feel the sadness of grief, we can afford to care deeply for those whom we must eventually let go of. When we have never had the support and guidance to grieve in a healthy way, endings of all kinds can feel like a vital piece of ourselves is being ripped away. Why would we want to be that close, care that much ever again? When we are so afraid of grief that we close our hearts to sadness, the doorways to love, to beauty, to joy are closed as well.

Educators can make the difference in the lives of students and colleagues who are struggling with challenges or reaping the harvests of meaning that come with grief. If we can make friends with all the feelings that may come, we can offer comfort and companionship when others are running and shunning in fear. We can learn to help ourselves, our students, and our colleagues to roll on the whole wheel of grief through the landscape of change and trauma and the ordinary goodbyes of moving from one stage of life to the next.

There is no "right" way to grieve. Everyone grieves in his or her own time and sequence of feelings. "To heal the world, we must feel the world," counsels a Jewish prayer. Whether it is our own personal world or the larger communities in which we participate, allowing ourselves and others to feel our grief is an act of courage that can transform wounds into gateways to love.

CHAPTER 9

The Place of Reparation
Love, Loss, Ambivalence, and Teaching

URSULA A. KELLY

Beginning Places

What brings one to teaching? What does one bring to teaching? Why do these questions present themselves now? Despite their resonance in various workday contexts, from interviews with candidates for teacher education programs to discussions in teacher education classrooms, for me, now, these questions have renewed meaning within the changed circumstances of my (work) life—where I am and what has brought me here. It is the manner in which these changed circumstances have come to bear on these questions that I wish to explore here. The ordinary and mundane form of the subtext of any curriculum vitae, the context of any course of life. Between the lines of my vitae, for example, is a series of movements, one of which may be described in this rudimentary manner: The work of teaching took me away from my familial, geographic, and spiritual home; during my years away from home, both parents died, my mother more recently; and, two years following my mother's death, I returned home. From this very ordinary story of movement/migration, loss, and return arises a series of questions about the interrelationships of love, loss, and teaching. It is to the exploration of these questions, which attempt to probe the emotional and psychic life of (my) teaching, that this paper is directed.

In her psychoanalytic inquiry into teaching and learning, Deborah Britzman focuses on the intricacies, difficulties, and possibilities of a theory of education that "can tolerate the vicissitudes of love and hate in learning [and] that can begin with a generous curiosity toward the subject's passionate capacity to attach to the world."[1] Reiterated in her prolonged argument for a theory of education that centers education as psychic event is the importance of reckoning not just with the struggles of the student with/in learning but also with those of the teacher. At stake is how we understand what can be accomplished through education—or what education should attempt to accomplish—and in what ways, for it is at the intersection of the psychic and the social that the parameters for any educational project are constructed. In this respect, an underscoring of the importance of teacher self-analysis constitutes more than a theoretical point; it becomes an ethical challenge to grapple with one's investments in, passions for, and refusals of teaching and learning. Yet, this challenge comes undirected, even if not directionless. As Britzman acknowledges, "[s]elf-analysis must be subjective and oddly singular, just like the vicissitudes of learning. There are no directions to follow, no grand plan to ensure consistency, no guarantees."[2] And the project is an interminable, ever-confounding one, a continual confronting of the surprise moves that are the emotional work of teaching and learning.

Several rich examples of such self-reflective work to which Britzman alludes already exist.[3] When pursuing an investigation, however limited, of one's investments in teaching and learning, immediate struggles that might suggest a haunting pattern of stubborn preoccupations and ongoing contradictions are an obvious place to begin. Thus, in an effort to begin to articulate the basis of some of my own educational attachments, this paper investigates the seemingly banal nexus of biography, geography, and pedagogy as psychic passions, as constituted (and constitutive) sites of ambivalence in teaching and learning. Specifically, I strive to establish a series of connections among telltale passions with a beginning investigation of what might lie beneath a lifelong set of loyalties, beliefs, and practices.

In pursuing this series of connections, I focus, first, on the psychoanalytic notion of reparation, as developed by Melanie Klein, and its usefulness in an analysis of autobiography and teaching—and teaching in general. My purpose here is to unsettle taken-for-granted expressions of a desire to teach by asking, in my case, on what impulses is such a desire based and what (reparative) urges might constitute a love of teaching? Secondly, I explore the relationship of love, a love of place, and a love of teaching in relation to reparation and teaching. Finally, I discuss a notion of teaching as reparative and address some aspects of a pedagogy of reparation. In so doing, I focus explicitly on the relationship of reparation and teaching within a teaching rendered overtly political, the desires of which reach toward justice and education across social and cultural difference.

While each of these discussions is decidedly autobiographical, each also posits a series of theoretical questions that reach outward beyond the singular, but the answers to which reside in the autobiographies of others.

Making Reparation

Every story is a story about death. But perhaps, if we are lucky, our story about death is also a story about love.
Helen Humphreys[4]

I began to revisit the work of Melanie Klein while investigating the relationship of grief, mourning, and identity, a pursuit impelled by the emotional chaos following the death of my mother, a chaos that registered on many sites and, as profoundly disruptive, on the site of professional identity, that is, around a particular notion of teaching and my self/selves as teacher. The profundity of grief is well known, yet its effects feel always oddly singular—as are its manner(s) of disruption. Richard Johnson writes of specific forms of grief's disruptions as they relate to challenges to regressive sexual identities. He argues that mourning, as a reflective process, is productive and can provide the basis for the reconstitution of identities and a renewed understanding of one's life work. In writing of his mourning following the death of his wife, he comments:

> [I]t seems to me that death is another kind of "border" and that grieving and its accompanying activities are another kind of "patrol." Like all "border patrols," grieving rituals and practices are there to police the boundaries. . . . [M]ourning is a work of reassurance and boundary—maintenance against the shock of death and loss. But the reassurance is necessary—even though it may not succeed—because the death of someone close to us produces a "madness": overwhelming emotions that throw into giddy, vulnerable, high relief *all* our own identities.[5]

In what Johnson calls these "grievous recognitions" that accompany reflective mourning are new questions, new directions, and/or renewed commitments to one's lifework. I want to argue that such recognitions are or can be *radically reparative,* that is, constituted by a particular politics for which the urge toward reparation is part of what it means to teach with social conscience and for social justice. Such a notion of reparation and its relationship to love, loss, and (my choices in) teaching now form some of my own grievous insights, a tentative exploration of which I begin here.

Revisiting Klein's work, following Johnson, provided an opportunity to engage her explanations of key aspects of the issues with which I struggle.[6] Klein contended that any situation of mourning reactivates early psychic/developmental processes, in particular, what she called the infantile depressive position, coincident with weaning, in which the child mourns the loss of loved objects (the mother's breast) and all that these objects have come to symbolize (love, comfort, security, satisfaction). According to Klein, at this stage in its development, in its unconscious mind the child develops feelings of concern for the loved object born out of feeling responsible for its harm or loss because of persecutory feelings / phantasies of aggression and hatred toward it when the loved object was not available or able to satisfy the needs of the child. In this depressive position, love and hate coexist and ambivalence develops as a safeguard against hate. As the child contends with its own felt aggression and these destructive impulses toward the loved object, guilt ensues. From these feelings of guilt comes the desire *to make reparation,* to repair, to make good on the injuries done to the loved objects. Through reparation, largely accomplished through having and creating experiences of love in the world, the (internal) loved object is restored and a foundation for security, trust, and a belief in goodness and love in the external world is established. With the internal and external worlds so interconnected, the ability *to make reparation* becomes an essential quality in the health of both worlds, as it is in making reparation that integration is accomplished. In this explanation, reparation is recognized as an essential character of all expressions of love as the conflicts out of which it arises, and its expressions are transferred to new relationships as the child's world expands and grows. That is, residues of these early dramas accompany us throughout our lives as part of the struggle to contend with the conflicts defined in the early stages of development and to secure for ourselves a loving place in the world.

Klein argued that, when mourning an *actual* loss of a loved one in death, the need for reparation is intensified as the psychic world of the mourner is imperilled, thrown back, as it were, to these early stages of development; and the good object, lost in death, is, once again, jeopardized by the bad, thereby renewing the threat of dominance of the bad object. Ambivalence and mistrust are again heightened in mourning as the psyche struggles to contend with the guilt aroused by the reliving of fears and anxieties associated with the loss of the loved object. In this state, relationships (with friends, partners, colleagues, oneself, and so on) are thrown into question as the ability to trust and to feel understood is jeopardized. Normal mourning, Klein argues, is the process of reparation, through which the inner world is once again repaired and rebuilt, a belief and trust in the existence of good objects is reinstated, and peace is achieved. In these senses of (living in) love and loss, then, reparation may be understood as (re)constitutive, productive, and structuring.

My relationship with my mother had always been deeply and consciously implicated in my teaching. Teaching was something we had in common; mothering was not. Following her death, I did experience the psychic imperilment described by Klein through a deep disorientation and dishevelment around my (teaching) work; a questioning of my confidence and faith in teaching; and a growing distrust of the intentions, possibilities, and effects of teaching for social change. Yet, why was so much of grief's disruption located within my work? What was I to do with this gnawing loss of faith? As the complexity of this implication, its nuances and intricacies, continue to unfold as grievous insights and to reshape my teaching, I have begun to (re)discover teaching as a practice of love and reparation. In this way, in attempting to understand the profound impact of the (life and) death of my mother on my life, I began to explore and come to terms with the profundity of grief; its relationship to love; and, for me, the relationship of love (and grief) to (my) teaching. Understanding my own practices of reparation is a crucial aspect of these realizations and reconciliations.

The work of teaching and learning has (pre)occupied my life. As I reconstruct my story of teaching and learning, as post mortem, its thematic gist seems so obviously reparative. At some level, I have always known that school achievement secured my place with my mother. A busy, overworked mother raising a family alone, with a husband away at work, our intimate moments were those times carved out to attend to my schoolwork, a mutually purposeful space in which I held her attention and she held on to her waylaid dreams. Her decision to leave teaching upon marriage was her interminable regret, solace for which I sought for her in my own work of study and teaching. Literally, I would go on "to profess" what she had been denied. In so doing, I also saw myself negotiating my own independence and separation, as I simultaneously solidified our connection. But achievement was also how I convinced myself I was worthy of love. My achievement could mean that I was not a(nother) burden, but a reward. Attachments to admired teachers were likewise secured through achievement, as I became the "good student", in part as a reward for their "good mothering." But achievement garners resentment as well as respect. I managed the resentment of others through self-effacement and diminishment of the very achievements on which I relied for approval, thus learning to never fully realize, accept, feel comfortable in, or celebrate them—to self-deprecate in the name of love. Along the way, I learned to regard achievement with great ambivalence, as asset and as liability, as something that met some needs but threatened others.

Clearly, my struggle for love and approval existed in an educational nest. Within, I (as, in varying ways, do all teachers) unwittingly (re)created elements of the most challenging and informing psychic dramas of familial relationships. Teaching is a place where one can be heard, attended to, adored even. But it is also a place where one feels and confronts intense dislike. In this sense, it is a fitting place to stage and restage psychic dramas of

love, hate, and ambivalence—reenacting the drama in the hope of changing it. As well, teaching is an endless rehearsal of separation. At all levels,
teaching is structured in strictly defined temporal arrangements. Along
with love, the lure of teaching is loss and necessary leavings.

This story (of mine) is not uncommon. That teaching is fraught with
the perils of object-relations, as elaborated by Klein, has been well established. *In loco parentis,* as a metaphor of teaching, can trap us all, and not
surprisingly, given that students come to us—and we go to them—not far
removed, temporally, from our own parental/familial relations.[7] The elaborate psychic processes of idealization, splitting, persecution, projection,
and negative and positive transferences confound constitute the work of
teaching and learning. There is no altruistic position. Insisting otherwise
reenacts a negation that preempts a grappling with the complex ways in
which our psychic dramas (and those of others) are implicated in our
teaching (and learning). But what seems most significant about the recognition of the psychic dimensions of teaching and learning is expressed by
Sharon Todd when she notes that "affect[ive dimensions are] not simply an
individual or idiosyncratic feature of pedagogical life but [are] structurally
operational in what gets learned, by whom, and how."[8] As such, the shift to
"implication rather than application"[9] heralds a radical self-reflexivity in
teaching and learning.

Britzman notes that transference, understood as these (re)new(ed) edi-
tions of old conflicts, is inherently "ambivalent, invoking both unresolved
conflicts and profound desires for love."[10] But, as a site on which to recon-
stitute and to replay psychic (and familial) dramas, teaching, for me, may
now be a site of impossible love, even an impossible site of love, one which
offers oscillating and extreme forms of acceptance / love and resentment /
rejection. Herein, it seems, ambivalence is double-edged: It is the lens
through which one views and is viewed. Ambivalence not only manages
one's impulses to hate; it also manages trust, the extent to which one will
love and (believe oneself to) be loved. As I go to teaching, always, in the
name of an other, yet never quite separate from this other, my conflicts and
my ambivalences frame who and how I am as a teacher. My feelings about
teaching, grounded as they are in this mother–daughter relationship, resonate on other (related, I now realize) sites: Teaching is something that
carries with it both joy and dread; it is something I cannot abandon, yet
never stop wanting to leave; it is something I love but do not want to do.
My feelings toward it are, in a phrase, highly ambivalent—a two-step waltz
in which the dance partners are separation and connection. The loss of my
mother brought these ambivalences (and their psychic sources) into high
relief, but their fuller confrontation—and the longed-for rest from them—

would require a change of setting, a confronting of another ambivalence, that of return.

The Place of Reparation

> *Home is where you are loved.*
> Lawrence O'Toole[11]

A map representation of the island of Newfoundland recalls the shape of a closed hand, a fist, on which the index finger points slightly northeastward. In many ways, this image is a fitting one. On the most easterly edge of Canada, lodged defiantly in the North Atlantic Ocean, its dramatic shoreline of sharp cliffs and jagged rock suggests the harsh severance from the main that was its creation as an island. A cultural mythology of struggle, attachment, protection, and survival is at one with this geography. The grip of the place on its people is as the grip of the sea in it: fierce, passionate, unrelenting, haunting. It is a place that does not let you go; it is a place that does not let you forget. In a novel brimming with vivid, sensual, poetic evocations of this place, E. Annie Proulx captures, in a simple, exact(ing) phrase, what many describe as a central character of Newfoundland: "a strong place."[12] It is also a place that elicits strong emotions (of love and hate), a place of great paradox and contradiction, at once somewhat insular and stubbornly separate, yet also inviting, open, caring—a condition born, in part, of a history of political struggles, with various forms of separation / connection.

My relationship to this place has always felt somewhat primordial, certainly spiritual, and much less about family and community (although threads of these relationships are part of my relationship to this place) and much more about the drama and power of the geography itself. In many ways, it *is* the geography of the psyche. Newfoundland is a place I have called home. But what does it mean to call a place 'home'? If social relations take root in place, what sets of relations are conjured in calling Newfoundland home? Philip Sheldrake remarks that "place is always a contested rather than a simple reality [and] the human engagement with place is a political issue . . . because the way it is constructed means that it is occupied by some people's stories and not others.' "[13] In this sense, the description provided in the opening paragraph of this section is both connotational and relational. What might an exploration of these issues of the politics of engagement and attachment reveal about the relationship of teaching and place? As many cultural producers —writers, visual artists, filmmakers, and so on—have demonstrated, Newfoundland is not without its social anxieties and repressions as well as and along with the communal capacity to offer redemptive opportunities. *Sense of place,* when constructed on a series of denials posing as pride, loyalty, nostalgia, defensiveness, and introversion, can smother efforts to name what has been denied and repressed. Such psychic maneuvres foster a protectionism that can stunt growth and discourage any substantial change.

In his insightful work on the social psychoanalysis of place in relation to the American South, William Pinar points to the presence of the past in the social subjects of the South; the inhibiting effect of presentism; and the need, culturally and personally, for Southerners to re-experience suppressed pasts in order to enable growth and renewal. Pinar's point is that places and cultures are rendered psychoanalytically, as are individual subjects.[14] Similarly, in his Newfoundland memoir, Lawrence O'Toole writes of the impact of the history of Newfoundland on the constitution of its people, noting that the history of a place like Newfoundland is an "*emotional* history [which] becomes . . . encoded in our behaviors."[15] Teaching infused by a sense of place, then, necessitates a radicalism that preempts such conservative impulses born of acritical pride and defensive regionalism. It asks of its subjects how such an emotional history is constituted; how its attendant loyalties betray repressions and denials, as well as love; and how our attachments to and struggles with place reiterate other psychic relations.

Much has been written about disabling, nostalgic notions of home as enduring (unchanging) presence. Klein herself wrote of relationships with homeland as part of her discussion of *displacement,* the process by which love is externalized to objects other than the mother but that, simultaneously, stand in for her. Klein's arguments point to the psychic depth of these attachments and provide insight into their persistence—and importance:

> The process by which we displace love from the first people we cherish to other people is extended from earliest childhood onwards to things. In this way we develop interests and activities into which we put some of the love that originally belonged to people. . . . By a gradual process, anything that is felt to give out goodness and beauty, and that calls forth pleasure and satisfaction, in the physical or the wider sense, can in the unconscious mind take the place of this ever-bountiful beast, and of the whole mother. Thus we speak of country as the "motherland" because in the unconscious mind our country may come to stand for our mother, and then it can be loved with feelings which borrow their nature from the relation to her.[16]

Interestingly, several of Klein's examples of love displacement included in this essay allude to place. Klein argues that the explorer, in the work of charting new territory, reenacts early psychic patterns of an escape from and simultaneously—through new places—a rediscovery, preservation, and renewal of the relationship to the mother. Similarly, she explains stubborn loyalty to places that are harsh and destructive as enacting comparable patterns of preservation (of place as mother). In such reparative instances, staying (in a place), despite its unforgiving, ungiving nature, can be equated with preserving and maintaining closeness to the mother, while leaving (to explore) can be equated with a quest to find a new, more (for)giving mother. In my own case, struggles with separation from place had the emotional layering, intensity, and resonance of other, earlier struggles. But struggle is also a state of ambivalence. In light of the ambivalence of struggle, what, then, might returning to this home/place mean?

Migration is generally understood as movement of people from one *place* to another and, in so doing, a moving from/through one set of social and cultural relations to another occurs. Herein, place is definitional, constitutive. The twentieth century brought more migration than at any other time in world history. As a new century begins, we grapple with the implications of movement, temporality, in-betweenness, fluidity, transition, and time–space compression. Metaphors of hybridity, creolization, and improvisation capture theoretically the mark of movement on/in identity as diasporic peoples (intra-, inter-, and transnationals) negotiate displacement. Against this backdrop of movement, strong attachments to place, often articulated in terms of region, nation, province, and state, have stubbornly remained—even as some of these same places, in name, anyway, have "disappeared." In part, I would argue, unrelenting attachment to place remains as a sign of the repressions and longings that form the basis of these attachments that, when left unconfronted, cannot easily be redefined. Separation is conflicted—as it is in child/parent relationships—because of the complex nature of (projected) feelings of guilt, ambivalence, and longing around such places.

At present, part of what marks the evolution of Newfoundland within a global economy is massive out-migration, in the last decade that of nearly 60,000 people of a total population of only one-half million, a trend not expected to reverse in any near future. Often accompanying the difficulties of leaving a place one has, for generations, called home and reestablishing oneself elsewhere is the hope and/or longing for a later return. How do psychic dramas infuse this hope of return (often expressed as a right of return)? Gayatri Chakravorty Spivak reminds us of the mythic (and biblical) dimensions of diaspora, the root, in sin and guilt, of such "scattering." What Spivak calls this "ancient diasporic thematic of responsibility and reparation"[17] resonates in (some) contemporary forms of ambivalence toward homeplace/land by those who have migrated or left. In this sense, reparative impulses born of migration echo ancient mythic and psychic movements. Part of the effect of diaspora is written in the grammar of the psyche. The powerful unsettling of migration finds its register in the psyche. It is the struggle for separation, the ambivalence born of a love–hate relationship: the migrant as child of the mother(land).

In writing about alterations in the mother–child relationship at various points in the child's development, Klein mentions the "store of love" that, in full identification with the good mother of her own, the mother holds prepared for her (adult) children for whenever they may need it, a safe sanctuary to which they may return.[18] Part of the intensity of grief I felt on my mother's death was this loss of sanctuary. I could not believe it gone. In grief, life without it was incomprehensible. My return to Newfoundland two years *following* her death I suspected would confirm this loss I could not fathom or realize. Instead—and as well—my return affirmed *the place of reparation,* a place in which I could begin the larger project of mourning, of staring down my illusions and, in so doing, beginning the larger project of remaking the loves that had, for a lifetime, stood in for love. It is, then, an ironic twist that I now realize that a partial result of my return to this place is enabling me to love and to feel love(d), to fear and to find solace, to (be) hurt and to forgive and to be forgiving, in short, to make reparation, to shore up the existence of a world that can be good and just so that I might (re)commit to the imperfect work of educating toward this vision. Being here helps me remember what, in grief, I had come to forget as a deliberate refusal of pain: To educate is to reach toward goodness, to encourage meaningfulness—through and in all its difficult detours. In this sense, teaching *in this place* has become a deliberate practice of reparation.

Doreen Massey rightfully points to the potentially regressive nature of attachments to homeland, of "views of place as Woman, as Mother—as what has been left behind and is (supposedly) unchanging." She comments that such a view "is comforting but it is to be rejected. Places change; they go on without you. Just as Mother has a life of her own."[19] Yet, rejection of constitutive ideologies and/as attachments is neither easy nor simple, any more than is separating from parents. The psychic complexity of attachments of any sort must be understood before they can be dismantled and one might conceive of possibilities for progressive separation-as-attachment. In the axiom, *you can't go home again,* both the traveller and her home are fluid, changing elements. Yet, it is more readily acknowledged in the longing to go home that it is the traveller who has changed and who can no longer fit (back) into the set of relations which (once) were 'self at home'. But *you can go home again* if one's goal is to live within a new set of relational dynamics, one that refuses the *myth* of oneness, security, and belonging for a committed *ethic* of responsibility, change, and interconnection.[20] This return—to confront rather than to recover a past and to participate in building a new future home—requires a mourning of old, regressive relationships (be)for(e) the adoption of new progressive ones—here or elsewhere.

But return is not a common part of the migrant journey and, when it is possible, the choice to return is often (and usually) yet further cause for displacement. Actual and nostalgized relations intersect upon return. The actual cannot live up to the highly edited, flawed creation of the intersection of loss, longing and memory that is nostalgia. But these nostalgized images are also not entirely false. In mourning, I found myself searching for the very reassurance Klein identifies—the existence of good objects through a community of remembrance of the one lost. I could not find this community where I was so, in this sense, return held an imperative, prompted by a need to rediscover and (now) more adequately respond to a source of love that has cradled me at various points in my life: a reparative (re)turn. My own return to Newfoundland has prompted a coming to terms with (some of) the conditions of self-change following years of focus, through teaching (elsewhere), of encouraging change in others, my students. In teaching, now, as always, love and place (re)configure social and psychic designs for learning. But, in the name of love, home can no longer compel me to stay or to go. The pulls and pushes of this place are multiple, complex, like the place itself, like me. And my ambivalences are now creative wellsprings, sources of critical posturing and agenic lea(r)nings.

As presence and absence, Newfoundland had always been strongly implicated in my teaching. My early understanding of education as political was in my work as a high school teacher committed to teaching as a vehicle for cultural esteem and celebration and as a means to enact history to build resistance and encourage change. This commitment continued in my work as an academic away from this place. It seems less odd to me now that my identity as a Newfoundlander was disrupted more by my return than my departure. Being away, I clung to that which I had left / abandoned, as I also reinvented it. My return was a watershed of grief, a mourning that shored up my separateness from family, from place, and from the ways of knowing, the epistemologies, on which old connections to these were founded. The reparative (re)turn to Newfoundland created the space for a sea-change, a healthier perspective on (the possibilities of) reparation.

Teaching as Reparative

> *Wounds need to be taught to heal themselves.*
> Jeanette Winterson[21]

What are the implications of understanding the work of teaching as reparative? How might an understanding of Klein's notion of reparation as the development of particular forms of consciousness, as *conscience*, be useful in teaching? In my own work, an ongoing dedication to education across social and cultural difference is problematized herein. In retrospect, my reparative urge, to contribute to social change through education, was fueled, in part, by the urge to contribute to changing the conditions of the lives of others, particularly women, because, as a child, it was not possible through any efforts or achievements for me to change the conditions of my mother's life. And while I was able to change the conditions of my life, I could not live them freely, without ambivalence and guilt. If loss-as-regret is bequeathed, its inheritor accepts it guilt-wrapped, inviting reparation. But it is what is done with such a legacy of loss that is important—what is made of it and what it makes of us—for such bequeathals are not deterministic; we are always both inheritors and creators. Even if not clear-sighted, reparative urges, as Klein points out, are creative and dominated by love, and they are greater than ourselves, connecting us to others in caring ways.

In my own work in teaching across social and cultural difference, understanding how reparation works now strikes me as essential if one is to avoid, in contemporary struggles for change, a new edition of the colonial missionary position. Noting the sources of the reparative tendencies of those of us who do this kind of work is one issue worth exploration beyond the confines of any autobiographical analysis. Jen Gilbert, in her discussion of colorblindness and anti-racist education, asks, "How will we know whether our attempts to make reparation with others are working through the dynamics of inequality, or whether our theories are getting us stuck?"[22] Reparative urges in education have often resulted in bad effects of good intentions. As a response, Deborah Britzman poses a reminder of the premise on which this discussion began: "[I]t behooves educators to engage in the making of reparation that begins in the acknowledgement of their own psychic conflict in learning and how this conflict is transferred to pedagogy."[23] The questions of "what brings one to teaching?" and "what does one bring to teaching?" are profound questions of educational implication.

As well, specifying the context of reparative teaching—what it means to teach across social and cultural difference *in this place*—raises issues about the particularity of the repressed history that has not been confronted and has not been mourned effectively, and what might constitute what Pinar calls "a curricular provocation" of such repressed history.[24] For my teaching in Newfoundland, questions about the ambivalent nature of our relationship to imperial England, on the one hand, and "the Irish diasporic family," on the other, constitute one point of analysis, and our place within the Canadian "family of provinces" another. The conflicted histories of gender, race, and social class divisions / denials, as they relate specifically to this place and its provincialism, are among others. How forms of hatred (and love) are learned, as culturally specific and systemic, is a broad-reaching question, the answers to which must be responsible to a new future for this place.

In her discussion of *idealization*. Klein points to the intensification of love / hate in relation to one's parents during adolescence and, concomitantly, the development of highly idealized and highly vilified (even demonized) figures, figures of love and figures of hate. According to Klein, idealization works to reassure one of the existence of good. Vilification, or hatred of certain others, she claims, works thus:

> The division between love and hate towards people not too close to oneself also serves the purpose of keeping loved people more secure, both actually and in one's mind. They are not only remote from one physically and thus inaccessible, but the division between the loving and hating attitude fosters the feeling that one can keep love unspoilt. The feeling of security that comes from being able to love is, in the unconscious mind, closely linked up with keeping loved people safe and undamaged.[25]

In other words, just as love is projected outward onto others, so too is hate. The intensification—galvanization, even—of social and cultural hatreds (homophobia, racism, sexism), as projections are commonly noted by the teachers who work with adolescents. An understanding of love and reparation and hatred and persecution can begin to help educators understand and address such dynamics beyond the limited educational reach of attitude adjustment. In her discussion of antiracist pedagogy, Deborah Britzman warns against the educational folly of a "reliance upon cognitive content as a corrective to affective dynamics."[26] Not only does such reliance limit our understanding of the intensity of forms of social hatred and widespread tolerance of inequities, "[n]or does this reliance on cognitive correction reach the more difficult question of how internal conflicts fashion and attach to discourses of hatred."[27] As Klein and others have established, hatred is a problem of the psychic dynamics of love and its implications; the historical markings of/on identity are far-reaching.

Reconciling the struggles and torments of identity are at the heart of a radically reparative pedagogy. Rinaldo Walcott uses Klein's notion of reparation in a discussion of creolization and what Walcott calls a creolized pedagogy, one in which the complexities, ambivalences, and (re)inventiveness of identity, in particular, Black / African identities in relation to slavery, might be recognized, analyzed, and interrogated. It is Walcott's contention that "creolization offers a way of seeing defeat as more than lost/loss. It is a practice that may impede the transformation of defeat into (our) shame."[28] Central to this work of confronting productively the presence of repeated violent trauma in relation to one's identity, Walcott argues, is the psychic process of reparation, "a way to come to terms with the rupture that produced a Black diasporic population in the Americas." That is, confronting the "love/hate relationship of the Americas . . . is [a way of] making reparation to ourselves, an acceptance of the ways in which the pain and the pleasures of history have intervened to invent us."[29]

Walcott's work is a compelling example of a pedagogy of reparation, a pedagogy of love. He emphasizes, in concert with Klein, the importance of self-love and self-acceptance (of a self-fragmented, creolized, hybridized) as a precondition of ethical relations with others. Problematic attachments no less deeply felt by being so can be negotiated and changed in the space created to offer a loving gesture to oneself. In this (loving) space is also created the opportunity to form new attachments to old sources of love, attachments that bear the mark of responsible engagement for change. But for such work to begin to be successful, the objects of our displacement must be clearly scrutinized for what they tell us about how love has both helped us *and* hindered us. Walcott writes of the diasporic Black and the haunting issue of allegiance to "Mother Africa," noting that separation demands neither guilt nor repression of the historic conditions of diaspora.[30] While it is important not to lose sight of the specificity of Walcott's arguments as they relate to diasporic Blacks and, further, to underscore that the conditions of different migrations are not the same or equal, Walcott's point is salient in relation to migrant groups other than Africans. The broader points of separation, guilt, and repression—and the subsequent role of reparation—can be more generally and as aptly applied.

New Reparations: Grievous Lea(r)nings

> *Grief moves us like love. Grief is love, I suppose. Love as a backward glance.*
> Helen Humphreys[31]

The disruption that is the (re)enactment of loss through death created the conditions through which I was able to realize some of the ways in which three sources of inspiration and love—my mother, my home/place, my teaching—were of a (psychic) piece. The complex (re)considerations that form the basis of this re/cognition are part of what it means (now) for me to explore, differently, the place of love—and its vicissitudes—in teaching. If love has been the acritical "surround sound," the heartfelt core of a story of teaching, then grief has been its deciding, decided aside, the parenthetical comment, the footnote to the story. Just beneath the surface of my own passions—my love of teaching, my love of place—and masked by competencies, achievements, and successes, was a desperate daughter, refusing separation, longing to be loved (more), and angry and heartbroken at the impossibility of it all—the limits of longing.

The best teaching and learning will reach for this ultimate achievement of love, a meaningful emotional life free(r) from the strictures of our histories through reparative gestures toward oneself and others. It is likely that, in teaching, it is only possible to approximate the level and quality of caring such education demands. Its complexity—part of a pedagogy of reparation, or understanding teaching as reparative—requires more than can be summoned by a call for (more) caring in education or a reinsertion of (regressive notions of) the maternal in teaching. Teachers who understand that the basis of a good relationship to others, for both students and teachers, is a good relationship to oneself; who understand the psychic complexities of teaching; and who bring an informed, loving presence to learning environments embody key elements of teaching as reparative. A certain *carefulness* about the emotional life that is (re)created in the relational work of teaching and learning is what is required, a carefulness that provides space for a meaningful redefinition of the habits of experience. Proceeding in teaching with such an attitude of carefulness requires a lens that might enable us to examine what our pleasures and pain, our anxieties and antagonisms, our refusals and reprisals tell us about the psychic life that constitutes us as teachers and learners—and the grief and grievances out of which they were born and, as Alice Miller reminds us, out of which only mourning can lead us.[32] Mourning as healing.

In her eloquent, courageous, and moving account of her psychotherapy following treatment for cancer, Eve Kosofsky Sedgwick writes of practising a Buddhist meditation, which involves trying to recognize in each face in a crowd a mother you may have had in another life (and the child you may have been to that mother). In so doing, she tells of learning "to find [in every face] the curve of a tenderness, however hidden. The place of a smile, or an intelligence."[33] Carrying this recognition into her classrooms and seeing that, she, too, figures in the relational dramas of her students, repositions Sedgwick in her teaching. Through such exercises we can practice seeing ourselves and others differently, more compassionately, in connection, and with love. When, as teachers, we learn to grapple with our implication in what Sedgwick calls the "interminable remediations"[34] that constitute the psychic lives of students—and theirs in ours—we may come some way toward radical reparation, toward making better on the various injuries education can compound in the name of learning.

CHAPTER 10

The Search for Wise
Love in Education
What Can We Learn from the Brahmaviharas?

ANN DILLER

May all beings be filled with joy and peace.
May all beings everywhere,
The strong and the weak,
The great and the small,
The mean and the powerful,
The short and the long,
The subtle and the gross:

May all beings everywhere,
Seen and unseen,
Dwelling far off or nearby,
Being or waiting to become:
May all be filled with lasting joy.

Let no one deceive another.
Let no one anywhere despise another.
Let no one, out of anger or resentment,
Wish suffering on anyone at all.

Just as a mother at the risk of her own life
Loves and protects her child, her only child,
So within yourself let grow
A boundless love for all living beings.

Let your love flow outward through the universe,
To its height, its depth, its broad extent,
A limitless love, without hatred or enmity.
Then, as you stand or walk,
Sit or lie down,
As long as you are awake,
Strive for this with a one-pointed mind;
This is said to be the sublime abiding. . . .
Metta Sutta ("Discourse on Love")[1]

What blocks the flow of wise, clear love in teaching and learning? What are some of the subtle, yet powerful barriers to love in classrooms? How might we work with these barriers? My approach in this essay rests on two key premises. I assume, first, that it is possible for a wise, clear love to occur in education but, second, that such love does not usually show up; it gets blocked in one way or another.

In this chapter I undertake to shed light on some of the obstacles to love in education which, unlike external conditions, such as institutional constraints, are more within our personal control as individual teachers. In order to do so, I draw upon an Asian, primarily Buddhist tradition, which says there are four interdependent aspects of "true love." Although translators disagree somewhat, the common renderings in English are: lovingkindness, compassion, sympathetic joy, and equanimity. Together they comprise the "Brahmaviharas," literally translated as the "Sublime Abodes" and often called "The Four Immeasurables" because, as the "Metta Sutta" (quoted at the beginning of this chapter) says, these qualities of love can "grow" into a "boundless love for all living beings" which is "limitless" in its "flow outward through the universe."

In addition to being viewed as interconnected facets of true love, each aspect has traditional "far-enemies" and "near-enemies." As we shall see in the last section of this chapter, not all Buddhist traditions endorse the longstanding traditional use of the word *enemy*. There are good reasons for this hesitation; it is easy to be misled by the term and misapply it. For example, we do not want to start thinking of these as "personal" enemies. The O.E.D.'s definition 1.d.*(b.)* for *enemy* expresses the central idea: "something that operates prejudicially upon, counteracts the action of."

The "far-enemies" represent strong opposing tendencies that "counter-act the action of" their corresponding aspect of love. Thus, hatred and ill-will stand as far-enemies to lovingkindness. Cruelty is compassion's far-enemy. Envy opposes sympathetic joy. Anxiety and restlessness "operate prejudicially upon" equanimity. We can begin to sense what this means if we continue the analogy and consider that any time our body–mind gets taken over or "captured" by one of these far-enemies, we lose our access to feelings of love, compassion, joy, and equanimity for the duration of our period of captivity, so to speak.

In contrast to far-enemies, with their obvious, blatant opposition, near-enemies come in disguise, as imposters that can be mistaken for the "real thing." For example, compassion's near-enemy is pity, which does seem similar, close (or "near") to compassion. Yet, according to the Brahmavi-haric tradition, pity stands as a "near-enemy" because it displaces or blocks true compassion. Likewise, the near-enemy of equanimity is indifference, which might mislead even its bearer into thinking he or she had achieved a state of equanimity. The standard near-enemies of love, or lovingkindness, are so prevalent that it may be difficult to imagine love or affection without them. These near-enemies of lovingkindness include what Buddhists call "attachments" of various sorts, such as our attachment to personal prefer-ences; likes and dislikes; our desires for control of people, of circumstances and of outcomes; as well as other forms of possessiveness. The near-enemy of sympathetic joy is affectation or hypocrisy, which may also be so auto-matic a reaction that it's difficult to detect or notice.

Because the near-enemies appear to be similar, or close in meaning, to their corresponding Brahmavihara, but are, nevertheless, marked off as distinctly and dangerously different, remembering the difference between each aspect of Brahmaviharic love and its traditional near-enemies may help us move beyond our conventional English-language connotations to a more precise understanding of the Brahmaviharas themselves. Identify-ing the near-enemies also provides illuminating clues to some subtle and elusive blocks to the flow of wise, clear love in educational settings. Let's turn now to a more in-depth look at what's entailed in each of the four Brahmaviharas.

The Four Brahmaviharas

The first of the four Brahmaviharas or aspects of true love is called *maitri* in Sanskrit and *metta* in Pali. The *Metta Sutta* selection at the beginning of this chapter contains what is probably the best known, most often quoted Buddhist discourse on Metta, attributed to the Buddha. Metta or maitri can be translated as "love" or as "lovingkindness"; most contemporary Buddhist teachers choose the term *lovingkindness,* as an understandable move designed to avoid the wide range of popular connotations associated with the word *love* in conventional English usage. But Thich Nhat Hanh, one of the few Buddhist scholars who retains the word *love* for his translation of *maitri,* says: "Words sometimes get sick and we have to heal them. . . . 'Love' is a beautiful word: we have to restore its meaning."[2]

I tend to agree with Thich Nhat Hanh's preference for translating *metta* or *maitri* as *love.* Yet I also realize it is no easy task to "restore its meaning." As Jeremy Hayward observes: ". . . love is so wrapped up with romanticism, sentimentality, pious religiosity, sex, and superficial Hollywood emotionalism that it is hard to use the word for anything genuine anymore."[3] Hayward himself does, nevertheless, use the word *love,* modified by *genuine,* long enough to give us something quite close to a Brahmaviharic definition. Hayward writes:

> Genuine love is the insight and affection that knows things as they are, that feels at one with things, that truly cherishes another. With that quality of love you can love anything. It could be a piece of bark from a tree, a bug, a piece of old iron, or another human.[4]

Hayward's conjunction of "insight and affection" matches Thich Nhat Hanh's insistence that true love requires cultivation of our capacities for clear seeing as well as loving intentions. Nhat Hanh points out that even if we have loving intentions, these may not be enough unless we also have the insight, or understanding, that comes from "looking and listening deeply so that we know what to do and what not to do to make others happy" (*TL,* p. 4).

Thich Nhat Hanh also tells us that the word for love, "*maitri* has roots in the word *mitra,* which means friend. In Buddhism, the primary meaning of love is friendship" (*TL,* p. 5). Of course, even with love in friendships, the near-enemies of "attachment" and "desire to control" can hang around on the perimeter of our personal relationships and occasionally assert themselves with vehemence.

The tendency for most personal relationships to be tainted by possessiveness and desires to control each other, in contrast to a love that is infused with the four Brahmaviharas, leads to the common interpretation that Brahmaviharic love is "impersonal" or "non-personal." But this is a misleading construal. I am inclined, therefore, to follow Heesoon Bai and Dhammika Mirisse, who choose to use the phrase "more-than-personal" as an English translation for the classical Buddhist concept of an "unobstructed love" that does not depend on personal likes and dislikes.[5] To speak of a love that is more-than-personal conveys the continued presence of a particular personal affection that also makes room for the more expansive love described in the Metta Sutta (quoted at the beginning of this chapter). Using the same analogy as the Metta Sutta, that of a mother's love for her child, Bai and Mirisse illustrate the "possibility of delinking love from liking":

> For whatever reasons, a mother may find herself disliking and disapproving what her child does or even how the child is. By the usual logic that equates love with liking, the mother is in danger of not loving the child. Indeed, she herself may think so and may feel guilty for having what would be considered an un-motherly attitude. But, the mother may also come to realize that her love for her child goes deep, beyond her dislikes and disapproval. She recognizes and reaffirms her undefeated commitment to care and wishes for her child's well-being.[6]

The phrase more-than-personal reminds us that a love that flows "outward through the universe, to its height, its depth, its broad extent," encompasses much more than persons. It embraces Hayward's trees, bugs, and old pieces of iron; it includes mathematics, mountains, moles, and molecules. A. H. Almaas describes it as "an ongoing love affair with the world and everything in it. You love your beloved, you love life, other people, truth, understanding—everything—sometimes with passion, sometimes with gentleness or with sweetness."[7]

The second Brahmavihara, *karuna* in both Pali and Sanskrit, is uniformly translated as "compassion," and literally means "experiencing a trembling or quivering of the heart in response to a being's pain."[8] Nhat Hanh defines karuna as "the intention and capacity to relieve and transform suffering and lighten sorrows" (TL, p. 5). Here again good intentions are not enough unless we also have the necessary understanding that comes from developing our capacities to "look and listen deeply" to the person who is suffering so we may be able to touch their pain in a way that "brings some relief" (*TL*, p. 6).

Indeed, according to Buddhists, good intentions accompanied by a lack of understanding is what often enmeshes us in the near-enemies. In the case of compassion, it feels like a Scylla and Charybdis dilemma where we are in danger, on the one hand, of being overwhelmed by, or ineffectually embroiled in, the suffering of others or else, on the other hand, of retaining a self-protective aloofness or condescension toward those who are suffering.

As we already mentioned, the traditional near-enemy of karuna, or compassion, is pity. Ayya Khema, a twentieth century Theravadan Buddhist nun, gives this account of why pity counts as the near-enemy of compassion: "Pity is called a near-enemy because it seems so similar. It is very close and yet it is an enemy. Pity arises when we are sorry *for* someone.

Compassion is when we are sorry *with* someone."[9] According to Ayya Khema, we get stuck in the near-enemy of pity because we want to hold on to "the delusion that everything is all right with oneself, that it's only other people who are having a bad time."[10] She and other Buddhists hold that ultimately our ability to be compassionate with anyone's suffering means a willingness to acknowledge or realize that everyone, ourselves included, suffers.

If pity is the Scylla, then being overwhelmed by feelings of "righteous anger, fear, or grief" may be the Charybdis of compassion's near-enemies. Salzberg says any of these "may disguise themselves as compassion." She notes that they can come upon us "when we do not feel in control" of circumstances:

> We may feel angry at injustice or outraged to see or hear of misuses of power. . . . We may become afraid ourselves when we witness the fear of others. We may feel sorrow and grief over the losses suffered by others. All of these feelings are similar to compassion, 'the trembling of the heart.' But compassion is quite different, in fact, from anger, fear, and grief. These [latter] states of aversion can drain us, perhaps destroy us (*LK*, pp. 107–108).

As one of the four Brahmaviharas, compassion is interconnected not only with love and joy, but also with the fourth aspect of equanimity. Thus, this Brahmaviharic "state of compassion as the trembling of the heart arises with a quality of equanimity. Can you imagine a mind state in which there is no bitter, condemning judgment of oneself or of others? This mind . . . sees only 'suffering and the end of suffering.' " (*LK*, p. 108)

Where near enemies serve to displace or prevent us from connecting with another's suffering, the compassion of karuna touches another's pain from a place of simply being with them. This does not, however, rule out taking appropriate action. What makes the difference is that instead of reactions representative of near-enemies, the actions one takes arise out of compassionate understanding. For example, Thich Nhat Hanh tells how his "love meditation" led to the social action he undertook to end the Vietnam War:

> During the Vietnam War, I meditated on the Vietnamese soldiers, praying they would not be killed in battle. But I also meditated on the American soldiers and felt a very deep sympathy for them. I knew that they had been sent far away from home to kill or be killed, and I prayed for their safety. That led to a deep aspiration that the war would end and allow all Vietnamese and all Americans to live in peace. Once that aspiration was clear, there was only one path to take—to work for the end of the war (*TL*, p. 37).

The third Brahmavihara, *mudita* in Pali and Sanskrit, again embraces everyone. This time we join in "joy with others," or in "sympathetic joy," as it is often translated. This translation can be misleading or misinterpreted if we do not include ourselves. We rejoice in the happiness of others and we feel joy about our own happiness as well. As with compassion, the joy of mudita is for everyone. The far-enemy of joy with others is envy, and the near-enemies can arise from attempts to handle or cover up the disconcerting feelings of envy. Ayya Khema gives us a succinct account of the common phenomenon:

> The near-enemy is affectation or hypocrisy, saying one thing and meaning another. For example, if someone has some good fortune and one feels obliged to offer congratulations, using just the words but not feeling anything; or worse using the words and thinking the opposite. Something like: "Why isn't it happening to me? Why always to someone else?"[11]

In contrast to the uncomfortable self-tortures of envy, Ayya Khema describes another possibility:

> One can also have joy with other people's abilities. . . . There are so many things other people can do better than ourselves. Some can sing and some can paint, some can dance and some can translate, some can make money and some can live without. Everybody has some ability. One can find innumerable occasions for being joyful.[12]

When we do experience these feelings of joy with others, we recognize that the "happiness of another . . . is not going to take away from us in any way. In truth, our happiness and that of others is inseparable" (*LK*, p. 133).

This understanding that "our happiness and that of others is inseparable" moves us directly into the fourth Brahmavihara, *upeksha* in Sanskrit and *upekkha* in Pali, translated as "equanimity" or "even-mindedness." The literal meaning of the Sanskrit term for equanimity, *upeksha*, comes from *upa*, which means "over" and *iksh*, "to look." Thus the equanimity of upeksha carries the ability to take a large view and to "look over the whole situation, not bound by one side or the other. . . ." (*TL*, p. 8).

The location of equanimity as last in the sequence makes sense in light of the traditional Buddhist approach, which calls upon us "to offer as much love, compassion, and rejoicing as we possibly can" and then, having done our best, to "let go of results" (*LK*, p. 147). In fact, it's often our inability to "let go of results" that feeds equanimity's far-enemy of anxiety and restlessness. This far enemy can be recognized when, for example, we find ourselves "careening back and forth, over and over again, between elation and despair, the violent movement for and against what our experience is" (*LK*, p. 143).

The near-enemy of equanimity is indifference, which may be more difficult to recognize since it can masquerade on the surface as even-mindedness. Indifference generally means that one has retreated into some form of denial, such as repression; inattention; or a disinterested, don't-care, can't-be-bothered attitude. Any of these variations on the near-enemy of indifference disconnects us from what's happening—either from what's happening with others, whether painful or joyful, or from what's happening with ourselves.

Implications for Love in Education

Having come this far, one may now have at least two questions: (a) Wouldn't someone have to be a Zen Master like Thich Nhat Hanh or at least an advanced practitioner of mindfulness training in order to have access to such "rarefied" or pure states as those described here in the Brahmaviharas? (b) Even if one could somehow attain these Brahmaviharic states, what does that have to do with a wise, clear love in educational settings? These questions go to the heart of the matter.

First, I would say from my own observations that if one were a Zen Master or at least an advanced practitioner of mindfulness training, it would give him or her a tremendous advantage in accessing and sustaining wise love in education. But, luckily, we do not have an all-or-nothing phenomenon here. Thich Nhat Hanh, writing a letter of encouragement to young Buddhists working on the front lines in the "School of Youth for Social Service" in South Vietnam in 1974, makes this crucial point in connection with the wisdom of "non-discrimination mind" (the basis for equanimity). He says, "This isn't some far-off, unattainable state. Any one of us—by persisting in practicing even a little—can at least taste of it."[13]

In his letter, Thich Nhat Hanh then goes on to describe an almost ordinary example, from his own everyday experience:

> I have a pile of orphan applications for sponsorship on my desk. I translate a few each day. Before I begin to translate a sheet, I look into the eyes of the child in the photograph, and look at the child's expression and features closely. I feel a deep link between myself and each child, which allows me to enter a special communion with them. While writing this to you, I see that during those moments and hours, the communion I have experienced while translating the simple lines in the applications has been a kind of non-discrimination mind. I no longer see an "I" who translates the sheets to help each child, I no longer see a child who received love and help. The child and I are one: no one pities; no one asks for help; no one helps.[14]

Such seemingly small acts of pausing long enough to give ourselves time to look closely at a child, a student, and/or at our own "internal reality" may be one of the crucial variables we need if we want to make room for moments of wise love.

Based on my own experience and observations, I would add that such moments may happen, at least to some extent, both with and without conscious intention. In fact, let's set Zen Masters aside, while we turn to look at a moment of seemingly accidental deep looking experienced by a New Hampshire public schoolteacher. Here's her own description of the experience:

> In my last year of teaching [before entering full-time doctoral study] I would have moments when I couldn't wait for the year to end, and a call from a student of "Msss. Spraaague," would make me cringe. But then I would have moments when something a student would do would appear to be the most beautiful thing on heaven or earth. One of these times was when 8-year-old Max sat eating his bag of popcorn for snack with his Brian Jacques text and messy 'reading reaction' paper in front of him. The popcorn kept hopping away from him because of static electricity. It was as if the popcorn had plans and ideas of its own, just like Max did. Suddenly I had this vision or feeling that the hopping popcorn, the long legged boy, and the smudgy paper were the very heart, the very essence of this child. I had to turn away and busy myself with my stapler to keep the tears away because if they'd come I think I would have been a sobbing heap. How could I have explained to my students that Max's snack made me cry?[15]

When I read Betty Sprague's description of her experience with Max and his snack, I see a clear instance of an elementary teacher in a busy classroom momentarily "looking deeply" and "seeing clearly" the "essence" of this student. Although she doesn't use the word *love* in her description, one certainly feels as if love was flowing freely during the time she was having a "vision or feeling" for the "very heart" or "essence of this child." In addition to the clear presence of metta, I infer a sense of "joy with others" from her evident delight over the "hopping popcorn." And I think it would be hard to miss the compassion she feels toward this "long legged boy" with his "smudgy paper" and out-of-control snack.

What may be less obvious is how much, in addition to these first three brahmaviharas, the fourth one, equanimity or even-mindedness, was also present for Betty Sprague in her classroom on that day and/or later when she wrote up these recollections. Recall that "even-mindedness is based on the wisdom that everything changes, on an understanding of total impermanence. No matter what happens, it will all come to an end."[16] Both the favorable and the unfavorable will come to an end. What Buddhists call the "eight worldly winds" of pleasure and pain, gain and loss, praise and blame, fame and infamy, all blow in and blow out again. Remembering this fact of impermanence in any given moment provides a context or space for more equanimity.

In her first sentence, Sprague alludes to her awareness that this was the "last year" and it would come to an "end," one that she sometimes longed for prematurely. When we read her first two sentences together, we can see her cognizance of the play of "worldly winds" in the ongoing flux between those classroom occasions that trigger "cringing" and those occasions that bring moments of sheer beauty. Another mark of equanimity can be noted in this classroom teacher's apparent ability to see the situation accurately, e.g., "hopping popcorn" and "smudgy paper" without having to be either for or against what's there. In other words, she is not "attached to" any particular judgment or "assessment."

In both our examples, when wise love arises it does so in a moment of clear seeing, with what Thich Nhat Hahn calls "deep listening and deep looking"—being able to be present with nonjudgmental insight. We see, hear, "listen to" where another person is coming from and who she or he "really is" at this moment, in this time and place. Toni Packer explicates "deep listening and deep looking" this way:

> When I talk about listening I don't mean just listening with the ear. "Listening" here includes the totality of perception—all senses open and alive, and still much more than that. The eyes, ears, nose, tongue, body, mind—receptive, open, not controlled. A Zen saying describes it as "hearing with one's eyes and seeing with one's ears." It refers to this wholeness of perception.[17]

It sounds simple, yet we are rarely able to do this, to be fully present and listen with a "wholeness of perception." Why not?

Working with the Obstacles

Now that we've explored what it might mean for the forms of love represented by the Brahmaviharas to show up, at least momentarily, in educational settings, it's time to return to our original question. What gets in the way, what blocks the flow of compassion, of sympathetic joy, of an even-minded lovingkindness in our work as teachers? The traditional answer tells us that the "enemies," both near and far, take over the territory that belongs to love. Thus, the key to unblocking the flow of wise love comes in being able to recognize and to deal with the particular enemies that hold sway over us as teachers. What does this mean?

Toni Packer takes up her own version of our question when she asks: "Why is it so inordinately difficult to listen . . . ?" In answer, she generates a list of "inner tapes of human conditioning [which] press hard to reel off and be heard—they do not want to make way for listening to others." Here are a number of entries from her list:

> How can I possibly hear you when I am dying to say something myself? How can I take the time and care to understand you when I think that I am right and you are wrong? When I'm sure that I know better? . . . Can I hear you when I have fixed images about how you have been in the past. . . . Can I listen freely when I would like you to be different from the way you are? Is there the patience to listen to you when I think I already know what you are going to say? Am I open to listen to you when I'm judging you?[18]

Most teachers can probably add a few more "inner tapes" of educational conditioning to Toni's list. For example: Can I engage in "deep looking and listening" when I have fixed ideas about who my students are or about what they can or cannot achieve? Can I listen openly when I carry images of how my students ought to be, what they should do or say? Am I preoccupied with my ideas or ideals about what ought to be happening in my classroom? Can I listen deeply to myself when I have set beliefs about what it means to be a good teacher? Do I have fixed self-images about who I am as a teacher—a very good one, an inadequate one, a struggling and well-intentioned one, and so on?

How do such seemingly harmless, even laudatory, beliefs serve to aid and abet the "enemies"? In the first place, it's not difficult to imagine from reading Toni Packer's list of questions how much static interference and smog get generated by the baggage of predetermined images and fixed beliefs we carry into any encounter. In addition, it's crucial to note that what these disparate "inner tapes of human [and educational] conditioning" have in common is that they bear the taint of what Buddhists call "attachment to views." The word *attachment* is pivotal here, for, of course, we all have views, beliefs, images, standpoints, perspectives, and the like. The difficulty arises because, instead of holding our beliefs lightly and acknowledging that our particular views represent just one of multiple possible perspectives, we get "attached" to, even sometimes identified with, certain beliefs. When any perspective turns into a "position" to "defend," we might suspect it's an "attachment."

Thus, not only do particular attachments, such as personal preferences and desires for control, constitute a formidable obstacle to lovingkindness, in addition the general phenomenon characterized as "attachment to views" undergirds and fuels virtually all the "enemies." How does this work? Consider a common situation for teachers—wanting to help students achieve certain desirable learning outcomes. Upon reflection we can see how quickly an admirable, appropriate aim can turn into an "attachment" to certain (probably elusive) outcomes, which leads to (probably futile) efforts to control what the students say, do, believe, think, and write. What happens in classrooms rarely coincides with a teacher's "lesson plans," envisioned outcomes, or general expectations.

Given this persistent mismatch between one's carefully wrought plans and their seemingly untoward results, it's easy for almost any teacher to fall prey to at least one near or far enemy. Some of us retreat into indifference with its façade of evenmindedness; others assume a mask of hypocrisy with its false affectation or become prone to outbursts of righteous anger; taken over by anxiety; overwhelmed by feelings of pity, resentment, envy or hatred toward one's students; or subject to attacks of guilt and self-hatred. In one sense it doesn't really matter which enemy has captured us;

they all block the flow of true love, thus, in effect, preventing us from either feeling or manifesting the qualities of a wise love interconnected with compassion, sympathetic joy, and equanimity.

Even though most of us probably acknowledge the force of these "enemies" in our lives outside the classroom, as teachers we may do our best to keep them at bay or "far" away from our work with students. When it comes to their overt expression in educational situations, placing appropriate restraints on our speech and actions is required from both an ethical and an educational perspective. The trouble arises not from inhibiting unethical behaviors or refraining from inappropriate "acting out" of such feelings as anger or hatred, but rather from the temptation to believe either that (1) we do not have any such feelings in relation to our students, or that (2) we should not have them. Both beliefs press one toward a false and untenable position. In the first instance, as we know, denial generally leads, sooner or later, to toxic leaks of negativity spilling out in seemingly unrelated behaviors. In the second case, believing that we should not experience the feelings associated with the far enemies could precipitate efforts to resist these feelings or attempts to will them out of existence, efforts that tend to strengthen their influence. So, what to do?

Here we can run into the danger of being caught in yet another "attachment to views," namely a view about how to proceed. For instance, Toni Packer tells us that when we want to move toward deep looking and deep listening, we start to question our own listening by: "Not asking, 'How can I achieve pure listening?' but rather, 'Where is my listening coming from this moment, in the light of all these questions?' [such as How can I possibly hear you when I am dying to say something myself?] Is it hampered by different ideas and attitudes or does it arise from a moment of being truly present—at one with you and your whole situation?"[19]

Along similar lines, the second century Buddhist philosopher Nagarjuna writes: "At the same time you practice the Immeasurable Mind of Love [Brahmaviharas], you must look deeply in order to face your anger and hatred." (quoted in *TL*, p. 14) But what exactly does it mean to "look deeply in order to face your anger and hatred"? How does one proceed? The short answer is that one stays alert, open, and allowing, without being carried along mentally by the "storyline" or pushed around physically by the reactive impulses. Let's consider two examples: first, the far-enemy of anger and second, the near-enemy of pity.

Anger often carries ferocious energy and gives the person who acts on it a momentary feeling of great power. Its ensuing harm can also be far-reaching and devastating. The Buddha is said to have compared anger with picking up hot coals in our bare hands so we can throw them at the object of our anger. When we reflect on what happens if we surrender to angry impulses and behave according to their dictates, we begin to understand the traditional designation of the term "enemies." Nevertheless, I am inclined to agree with those Buddhist teachers, such as Tarthang Tulku, who caution against the tendency to "categorize our experiences as good or bad."

Tarthang Tulku warns that "by splitting our experience in this way, by treating some experiences as friends and others as enemies, we separate ourselves from the richness of experience as a 'whole.' We become alienated from ourselves, and in the resulting conflict we stimulate energies which create new problems even while we are attempting to solve old ones."[20] When we take this perspective, negative emotions, including the so-called "far enemies," have the potential to be transformed.

This potential for transformation does not, however, occur easily or automatically. It requires, among other things, that one be "careful not to jump suddenly into the midst of negativity."[21] Dealing with our own strong feelings is challenging enough. Trying to help someone else who is caught in emotional turmoil puts us in an even more potentially volatile situation; and classroom teachers often find themselves in just such circumstances. Tarthang Tulku cautions against underestimating the dangers inherent in such situations:

> Handling intense emotions is not easy; emotions project a form of energy which makes it difficult for anyone near to maintain a balanced perspective. . . . If we are not careful, instead of helping, we may make the emotional imbalance even worse. Emotions, being in substance pure energy, tend to "soak up" any energy that is directed towards them. It works both ways: while our own energy may stir up the emotion, we may also be "infected" by the negative energy. The energy seems to intensify itself, as if it had a life of its own.[22]

Instead of jumping into negativity, we can learn to "accept our emotions as they come . . . make friends . . . and allow them to travel their natural course."[23] Here are some excerpts from Tarthang Tulku's instructions:

> What we can do is concentrate on the anger. . . . Concentrate on the feeling, not on thoughts about it. Concentrate on the center of the feeling; penetrate into that space. . . . Likewise, when anxiety or any other disturbing feeling arises, keep the feeling concentrated. It is important not to lose it. But it is also important not to think further about it or act on it; just feel the energy, nothing more.[24]

Thich Nhat Hanh gives the same basic advice. He emphasizes using mindful breathing in order to "put all our mind into observing our anger. . . . We avoid thinking about the other person, and we refrain from doing or saying anything. . . ." He summarizes five "steps" for "transforming" disturbing feelings: (1) recognize each feeling as it arises; (2) greet the feeling, "become one with it" and "chaperone" it with mindfulness; (3) calm the feeling down, using mindful breathing; (4) release the feeling, let it go; and (5) "look deeply into its causes."[25]

If we can follow these five steps, we not only avoid being taken over, caught in, or captured by the angry feelings, we also refrain from judging, suppressing, or pushing them away. Awareness "just looks after" the feelings. Nhat Hanh variously likens this awareness to "a mother tenderly holding her crying baby," to "a companion," and to "an older sister looking after and comforting her younger sister in an affectionate and caring way."[26]

Thich Nhat Hanh's similes for gentle nonjudgmental holding remind us of the four aspects of love and the basic belief that the ultimate "antidote to anger is love, compassion, and patience."[27] But before we return to them, let's look briefly at an example of what it means to contend with the obstacle of a "near-enemy." One reason for using mindful breathing to stay concentrated on the energy of disturbing feelings associated with "far enemies," and not to lose them until there's some "release" or "transformation," is that otherwise these obvious emotions may just get replaced by a newly recruited "near-enemy" who's much harder to detect.

As we noted earlier, with near-enemies, we may not only be relatively conscious of our feelings and reactions, we may also be "attached" to them, believing they lead to appropriate, indeed good and desirable, responses. For example, even though we might not use the word *pity*, as teachers we could notice ourselves "feeling sorry" for certain students because of their family environment, class, race, ethnicity, or "special needs." We generate feelings of sympathy and deplore their "situations." Without complete awareness, our demeanor and attitudes could be condescending (i.e., pitying) even as we "go out of our way" to help these "less fortunate" students. And the altruistic acts can indeed be outwardly helpful and supportive, even while they mask the underlying near-enemy of pity. In order to recognize the subtle signs of pity, one could endeavor to catch nuances of accompanying intentions; for instance, does one feel, think, or say things like "these people don't show any appreciation for all we do for them"?

In general, becoming aware of our intentions before we act or speak can be one way to spot an imminent near-enemy takeover. For example, as Jack Kornfield observes, "Even the simplest words can have a vastly different effect depending on our intention. The phrase 'What do you mean?' can sound accusing and judgmental or considerate and humble." Kornfield suggests, therefore, that we undertake a conscious practice "to see with eyes of compassion and act with our wisest intention." He claims that doing so "often has a surprising effect."[28]

In fact, being prepared for "surprising effects" comes with this whole territory of opening up to the four Brahmaviharas and learning how to deal with their enemies. One surprise may be that often the most direct route to a wise love comes from giving an open, nonreactive space to the so-called enemies both far and near, instead of engaging them in energy-draining skirmishes. For example, before she experienced a flow of clear love toward her student with his hopping popcorn, Betty Sprague had reported in a matter-of-fact way how she had moments when "a call from a student of 'Msss. Spraaague,' would make me cringe." Her account reads like a straightforward description of allowing this momentary "attachment to likes and dislikes" (one of metta's formidable near-enemies), to be recognized, acknowledged, and allowed to come and go without adding on judgments about herself or the plaintive students.

Another surprise is that, for most of us, experiences of the four Brahmaviharas come in unexpected moments and unpredictable ways. Earlier in this chapter we cited Toni Packer's advice, based on her own experiences and decades of work with meditation students; she says that "attentive listening may empty out the preoccupation with myself," thus opening us to the possibility of Brahmaviharic love. Toni also emphasizes the momentary and unpredictable nature of this experience: "So for unknown marvelous reasons, once in a while we are completely here. For a moment we hear, see, and feel all one. . . . The wholeness of being!"[29]

Just as we need to be alert to the possibilities for sudden "attacks" from near and far enemies, we also want to be ready for and welcoming to unexpected rushes of feeling from the four Brahmaviharas. And these can follow each other in quick succession, indeed much faster than any description can be given of the experiences. One more obstacle may, however, still stand in our way. In contrast to being misled by confusing the near enemies with facets of true lovingkindness, we can be misled by doubt or self-doubt.

If we assume that all we ever experience are more or less subtle versions of the near and far enemies and that we don't have, or cannot access, any capacities for Brahmaviharic forms of love, then doubt inhibits the growth of love. Such self-doubting beliefs not only constitute a serious obstacle to the flow of love in education, they may be even more insidious than most of the "enemies." In fact, Buddhists consider Doubt, as in doubting our own capacities for love, as one of the five classic "hindrances." As some Tibetan lamas are fond of saying: We need to bring the forces of doubt against Doubt itself.

In contrast to self-doubt, Buddhists insist that everyone contains the "seeds" of love, however deeply buried, tiny, and uncultivated these seeds of love might be. As one experienced meditation teacher says,

Many of us believe, in a vaguely post-Freudian sort of way, that large parts of ourselves are unconscious, and that these parts are probably rather dark and murky. My experience as a meditation teacher is that, on the contrary, much that is not 'on the surface' of our minds is positive.[30]

Another teacher in the same tradition observes that once we begin to direct lovingkindness toward ourselves and begin "to break up the hard crust of our negative self-view, we gain access to deep reserves of positive emotion."[31] This means that when we experience the love of metta, the joy of mudita, the oneness of upeksha, or the compassion of karuna arising, we do not turn away or trample on the feelings of softness or vulnerability they evoke. For example, here is a selection from Sogyal Rinpoche's strong encouragement to stay in touch with our feelings of compassion:

Don't waste the love and grief it arouses; in the moment you feel compassion welling up in you, don't brush it aside, don't shrug it off and try quickly to return to "normal," don't be afraid of your feeling or embarrassed by it, or allow yourself to be distracted from it or let it run aground in apathy. Be vulnerable: use that quick, bright uprush of compassion; focus on it, go deep into your heart and meditate on it, develop it, enhance, and deepen it.[32]

What if, as teachers, we could act on Sogyal Rinpoche's advice, not only when we experience the "bright uprush of compassion," but also when the other forms of Brahmaviharic love, joy with others, and equanimity well up in us? Would we then be able to meet our students in unexpected moments of loving appreciation for who they are, able to be with their sorrows and with their joys, with a balanced, clear seeing of what's there, without being captured by our judgments or captivated by our preferences?

Afterword

The world, East and West, would benefit from new and more all-embracing forms of love nuanced for many different contexts, including teaching and learning. The forms of love in the West and East are, as the religions and philosophies from whence they devolve, ancient. It is time to reconstruct these forms to serve the needs, desires, and purposes of a new era of human history. There is nowhere better to start than a rich dialogue across the differences and similarities between East and West on what it means to love well. Nor is there any place finer to begin such a conversation than with what loving well means in teaching and learning relationships, for that is the only way cultures pass on the wisdom, and folly, of humanity.

As we compiled this book, our nation was at war in the Middle East, thereby extending into a new century a conflict now over a thousand years old. Consuming hatred along with a fervent desire for wealth and power mask themselves as patriotism, devotion to democracy, and moral superiority. Yet, moral ends require moral means; war cannot conquer hate. The tired old aphorism that only love can cleanse the corruption of hate is true, though few hear and heed it message.

What holds for love and the world community also holds for schools, classrooms, and socially ameliorating teaching. Love must circulate or it stagnates and breeds pestilence. The forces that oppose the creative and curative flow of love are many; these powers seem always to prevail, but if it were so, we would not be here. Subtly, silently, and in many hidden ways the love that called us into existence sustains us every moment of our lives.

In calling together our community of authors, we sought to give voice to loving teaching; we wish it to speak its name aloud and in full view. The observant reader will recognize many omissions in topics treated and cultural voices included. Although not ignored, perhaps the most glaring topic calling for further consideration is the patriarchal construction of love in the West and its effects on teaching and learning. It is a gap whose presence cannot be denied.

Our task in this collection is to begin a conversation we wish to cultivate and continue so that we may build about it a community. Please help us, or let us know if we can help you. Our conviction rests on critical and creative hope in loving, caring, and learning communities.

Jim Garrison
400B WMH
Virginia Tech
Blacksburg, VA 24061-0313—USA
wesley@vt.edu

Dan Liston
School of Education CB249
University of Colorado
Boulder, CO 80309—USA
Listond@colorado.edu

Endnotes

Introduction: "Love Revived and Examined"

1. For useful analyses of Aristotle's theory of emotions, see S. Leighton, Aristotle and the emotions. *Essays on Aristotle's Rhetoric.* A. O. Rorty (Ed). Berkeley: University of California Press, 1996), 206–237; and J. Cooper, An Aristotelian theory of emotions, *Essays on Aristotle's Rhetoric.* A. O. Rorty (Ed). Berkeley: University of California Press, 1996, 238–257. See also Aristotle, *Rhetorica,* Vol. XI. *The Works of Aristotle,* W. D. Ross (Ed). Oxford: Clarendon Press, 1953; William James, The physical basis of emotion. *Psychological Review,* 1 (1894): 516–529; Jean-Paul Sartre, *The Emotions.* (New York: Philosophical Library, 1948; and *Sketch for a theory of the Emotions.* (London: Methuen, 1962; John Dewey, The theory of emotion. *The Early Works, 1882–1898,* J. A. Boydston (Ed). Carbondale: Southern Illinois University Press, 1971, 152–188; Iris Murdoch, *The Sovereignty of Good.* (New York: Schocken, 1971; Simone Weil, *Gravity and Grace.* London: Routledge and Kegan Paul, 1963.

2. See Ronald de Sousa, *The Rationality of Emotions.* Cambridge: MIT Press, 1987; Patricia Greenspan, *Emotions and Reasons.* New York: Routledge, 1988; Robert Solomon, *The Passions.* Garden City, New York: Anchor Press, 1976; Amelie Rorty, Explaining emotions. *Explaining Emotions,* A. O. Rorty (Ed.). Berkeley: University of California Press, 1980, 103–126; William Lyons, *Emotions.* New York: Cambridge University Press, 1980; and George Turski, *Toward a Rationality of Emotions.* Athens, Ohio: Ohio University Press, 1994.

3. See Michel Foucault, *The Order of Things.* New York: Vintage, 1970; Homi Bhabha, *The Location of Culture.* New York: Routledge, 1994; and Eve Sedgwick, *Epistemology of the Closet.* Berkeley: University of California Press, 1990.

4. Sara Ruddick, *Maternal Thinking.* Boston: Beacon Press, 1989; Alison Jaggar, Love and knowledge: Emotion in feminist epistemology. *Gender/body/knowledge.* A. M. Jaggar and S. R. Bordo (Eds). New Brunswick, N.J.: Rutgers University Press, 1989, 145–171; and Sandra Bartky, *Femininity and Domination.* New York: Routledge, 1990.

5. Max Scheler, *The Nature of Sympathy.* New Haven: Yale University Press, 1954; and Max Scheler, *Ressentiment.* Milwaukee: Marquette University Press, 1994; Norman Denzin, *On Understanding Human Emotion.* San Francisco: Jossey-Bass, 1984; Arlie Hochschild, Emotion work, feeling rules, and social structure. *American Journal of Sociology,* 85 (1979): 551–575; and *The Managed Heart: Commercialization of Human Feeling.* Berkeley: University of California Press, 1983.

6. Carol Gilligan, *In a Different Voice.* Cambridge, Mass.: Harvard University Press, 1982; George Mandler, *Mind and Emotion.* New York: Wiley, 1975; and Andrew Ortony, Gerald

Clore, and Allan Collins, *The Cognitive Structure of Emotions*. New York: Cambridge University Press, 1994.

7. Joseph LeDoux, *The Emotional Brain*. New York: Simon and Schuster, 1996; and Antonio Damasio, *Descartes' Error*. New York: Grosset/Putnam, 1994.

8. Jane Roland Martin, *The Schoolhome*. Cambridge: Harvard University Press, 1992; Nel Noddings, *Caring*. Berkeley: University of California Press, 1984; Megan Boler, *Feeling Power*. New York: Routledge, 1999; Daniel Goleman, *Emotional Intelligence*. New York: Bantam Books, 1995; Andy Hargreaves, The emotional practice of teaching. *Teaching and Teacher Education* 14 (1998): 835–854; Parker Palmer, *The Courage to Teach*. San Francisco: Jossey-Bass; 1998; and Vivian Gussin Paley, *White Teacher*. Cambridge: Harvard University Press, 1989.

9. For examples see: Boler, *Feeling Power*; Kerry Burch, *Eros as the Educational Principle of Democracy*. New York: Peter Lang, 2000; Woodrow Trathern and Michael Dale, Narratives in teacher education. *Literacy Conversations, Family, School, Community: Yearbook of the American Reading Forum*. R. J. Telfer (Ed). Whitewater, WI: American Reading Forum, 1999; Ann Diller, The Ethical education of self-talk, in *Justice and Care in Education*. M. Katz, N. Noddings, and K. Strike (Eds). New York: Teachers College Press, 1999; Ann Diller, "Pluralisms for Education: An Ethics of Care Perspective," http://x.ed.uiuc.edu/EPS/PES-Yearbook/92_docs/DILLER.HTM; Jim Garrison, *Dewey and Eros*. New York: Teachers College Press, 1997; Lisa Goldstein, *Teaching with Love*. New York: Peter Lang, 1997; Ursula Kelly, *Schooling Desire*. New York: Routledge, 1997; Rachael Kessler, *The Soul of Education*. Alexandria, VA: Association for Supervision and Curriculum Development, 2000; Daniel P. Liston, Love and despair in teaching. *Educational Theory*. 50 (2000): 81–102; Jane Roland Martin, *The Schoolhome* and *Reclaiming a Conversation*. New Haven: Yale University Press, 1985; and Elaine J. O'Quinn, Creative practices for reflective, active, and enduring learning. *The English Record* (Spring/Summer 2003: in press.

10. From Hesiod's *Theogeny* in Drew A. Hyland, *The Origins Of Philosophy*. New York: Capricorn Books, 73.

11. See S. Rosen, *Plato's Symposium*. New Haven: Yale University Press, 1987, 199.

12. Irving Singer, *The Nature of Love: Plato to Luther*. Chicago: The University of Chicago Press, 1984,13 and 22.

13. See Lisa Delpit, *Other People's Children: Cultural Conflict in the Classroom*. New York: The New Press, 1995.

14. Singer, *The Nature of Love*, p. 90.

15. Amazingly, most modern analyses of friendship still start with Aristotle and retain his general approach to the topic. Science has taken an extraordinarliy cognitive approach to love. Meanwhile, Freud reduces all forms of love, including friendship, to expressions of sublimated sexual love. He even extends this analysis to the love of parents for children, so it is easy to infer what he would say about a teacher's love of students. Interestingly, Irving Singer, whom we have cited on several occasions, seems stridently to reject feminist attempts to reconstruct the philosophy of love. See Singer, *The Nature of Love*, pages 418–425, among others.

16. Ibid., *106*.

17. Ibid., *106*.

Part 1 Introduction: Loving Gaps and Loving Practices
Chapter 1. "The Love Gap in the Educational Text"

1. George Boas, Love. *The Encyclopedia of Philosophy*. Paul Edwards (Ed.). New York: Macmillan, 1967, 90.

2. David L. Norton and Mary F. Kille (Eds). *Philosophies of Love*. Totowa, NJ: Rowman and Allenheld, 1983.

3. Irving Singer, *The Nature of Love*. Vols. 1–3. Chicago: University of Chicago Press, 1984–7.

4. White, Richard. Thinking about love: teaching the philosophy of love (and sex). *Teaching Philosophy* 25 (2002):111–122.

5. For example, White singles out the love of parents for their children but says only this: "The Virgin Mary is in many ways still the absolute ideal of motherhood." (Ibid., p.118.)

6. Martha Nussbaum, *The Fragility of Goodness*. Cambridge: Cambridge University Press, 1986, 167.

7. Among many other things, this means that if Ian Suttie's intimacy taboo is connected to the abuse of children, there is no room for this widely accepted, deep-seated cultural and psychological practice. See Mary Hamer, *Incest: A New Perspective*. Cambridge, UK: Polity Press, 2002.

8. On this issue see especially Sara Ruddick's pioneering work on preservative love and maternal teaching: Sara Ruddick, *Maternal Thinking*. Boston: Beacon Press, 1989 and Preservative love and military destruction: some reflections on mothering and peace. *Mothering: Essays in Feminist Theory*, Joyce Trebilcot (Ed). Totowa, NJ: Roman and Allenheld, 230–262). See also Susan Laird's essays on teaching and curriculum. (E.g., Susan Laird, Reforming "women's true profession": a case for 'feminist pedagogy' in teacher education? *Harvard Educational Review* 58 (1988): 449–463; and The ideal of the educated teacher—"reclaiming a conversation" with Louisa May Alcott. *Curriculum Inquiry* 21 (1991): 271–298.

9. In this connection it must be asked at what point the old adage "Spare the rod and spoil the child" stops representing sage advice and becomes a prescription for doing harm. It must also be asked if the intimacy taboo constitutes a perversion even if it is not implicated in sexual abuse.

10. See especially Carol Gilligan, *In a Different Voice*. Cambridge: Harvard University Press, 1982; Nel Noddings, *Caring*. Berkeley: University of California Press, 1984.

11. For a fictional description of a school that is guided by this form of love, see Louisa M. Alcott's *Little Men*. Laird has called the school Alcott depicts "a forgotten fictional precursor of Martin's 'schoolhome.' " Susan Laird, Who cares about girls?: rethinking the meaning of teaching. *Peabody Journal of Education* (1995): 82–103; 171; cf. Jane Roland Martin, *The Schoolhome* Cambridge, MA: Harvard University Press, 1992.

12. The material in this section is adapted from Jane Roland Martin, *The Schoolhome*, and Home and family, *Philosophy of Education: Encyclopedia*, J. J. Chambliss (Ed). New York: Garland Publishing, 1996, 275–277.

13. Virginia Woolf, *Three Guineas*. New York: Harcourt, Brace, and World, 1938, 18. In saying that western thought has located the kind of love at issue here in the private home, I do *not* mean to imply that throughout history all, or even most, private homes have in fact been loving.

14. Plato, *The Republic* (Trans. G. M. A. Grube). Indianapolis: Hackett, 1974, 464d.

15. Aristotle, *The Politics*. (Trans. T. A. Sinclair, rev. ed.). Harmondsworth: Penguin Books, 1981.

16. To be sure, Aristotle discusses philia at length in his works on ethics, and Nussbaum (*The Fragility of Goodness*, p. 354) maintains that although this is usually translated as "friendship," he used it to include all family relations, including the love of mother for child. Yet insofar as philia encompasses the love whose object is the growth and development of children, we have one more example of this latter being lost to view by being subsumed under another category. Moreover, given that philia emphasizes mutuality, one wonders how well it accommodates a form of love that obtains between people who are not equal.

17. Jean-Jacques Rousseau, *Emile*. New York: Basic Books, (Trans. Allan Bloom), 1979, 45.

18. *Ibid.*, 363.

19. *Ibid.*, 53.

20. Johann Heinrich Pestalozzi, *Leonard and Gertrude*. Boston: D. C. Heath, 1885, 118.

21. *Ibid.*, 135.

22. Johann Heinrich Pestalozzi, *How Gertrude Teaches Her Children*. London: Allen & Unwin, 1915, 182.

23. John Dewey, *The School and Society*. Chicago: University of Chicago Press, 1956.

24. Daniel Mulcahy (see Daniel Mulcahy, *Knowledge, Gender, and Schooling: The Feminist Educational Thought of Jane Roland Martin*. Westport, CT: Bergin & Garvey, 2002 defends Dewey from this criticism by citing two of Dewey's other works. I am only speaking here, however, of *The School and Society*. Mulcahy also cites passages in *The School and Society* in support of his defense of Dewey, yet these are the very places in which domestic affections, as opposed to domestic activities such as sewing, drop out of the picture.

25. Maria Montessori, *The Montessori Method*. New York: Schocken, 1964.

26. *Ibid.*
27. The discussion of the education-gender system in this section draws heavily on Jane Roland Martin, *The Schoolhome,* and *Cultural Miseducation.* New York: Teachers College Press, 2002. The discussion of Gilman draws on Jane Roland Martin, *Reclaiming a Conversation.* New Haven: Yale University Press, 1985 and *Cultural Miseducation.*
28. Woolf, 72.
29. Ivan Illich, *Deschooling Society.* New York: Harrow Books, 1972.
30. Martin, *The Schoolhome,* Chapter 4.
31. An earlier figure is Alcott, whose educational thought Laird has reconstructed. See, e.g., Laird, Susan, Teaching in a different sense: Alcott's Marmee In Audrey Thompson (Ed.) *Philosophy of Education 1993.* Urbana, Ill.: Philosophy of Education Society, 1994,164–172.
32. Charlotte Perkins Gilman, *Herland.* New York: Pantheon. 1979, 59.
33. This section draws heavily on Martin, *The Schoolhome,* and *Cultural Miseducation.*
34. This is not to say that it always performed that function well, only that the culture assigned it this task.
35. For more on this, see Martin, *The Schoolhome,* Chapter 1.
36. I do not mean to suggest that this should ever have been taken for granted.
37. cf. Ruddick, *Maternal Thinking.*
38. Plato, 377b–c.
39. Rousseau, 115.
40. John Stuart Mill, *Utilitarianism, On Liberty, Essay on Bentham.* New York: New American Library, 1952.
41. Jane Roland Martin, *Changing the Educational Landscape.* New York: Routledge, 1994, Chapter 8.

Chapter 2. "Loving Teacher Education"

1. Robert J. Sternberg, *The Triangle of Love.* New York: Basic Books, 1988.
2. Nel Noddings, *Caring: A Feminine Approach to Ethics and Education.* Berkeley, CA: University of California Press, 1984; Nel Noddings, Fidelity in teaching, teacher education, and research for teaching. *Harvard Educational Review* 56 (1986): 496–510; Nel Noddings, *The Challenge to Care in Schools.* New York: Teachers College Press, 1992.
3. Barbara Arnstine, Rational and caring teachers: reconstructing teacher preparation. *Teachers College Record* 92 (1990): 241–2.
4. National Commission on Excellence in Education, *A Nation at Risk: The Imperative for Educational Reform.* Washington, DC: National Commission on Excellence in Education, 1982.
5. Ruth S. Charney, *Teaching Children To Care.* Greenfield, MA: Northeast Foundation for Children, 1991.
6. Joan Dalton and Marilyn Watson, *Among Friends: Classrooms Where Caring and Learning Prevail.* Oakland, CA: Developmental Studies Center, 1997.
7. Morgan Daleo, *Curriculum of Love.* Charlottesville, VA: Grace Publishing, 1996.
8. Marilyn Gootman, *The Caring Teacher's Guide to Discipline.* Thousand Oaks, CA: Corwin Press, 1997.
9. James Henderson, An ethic of caring applied to reflective professional development," *Teaching Education* 2 (1988): 91–5; Jerry Rosiek, Caring, classroom management, and teacher education: the need for case study and narrative methods. *Teaching Education* 6 (1994): 21–30; Kevin Swick, Service learning helps future teachers strengthen caring perspectives. *The Clearing House* 73 (1999): 29–32.
10. Nel Noddings, Fidelity in teaching, teacher education, and research for teaching. *Harvard Educational Review* 56 (1986): 496–510.
11. Dwight Rogers and Jaci Webb, The ethic of caring in teacher education. *Journal of Teacher Education* 42 (1991): 173–81.
12. Robert Fried, *The Passionate Teacher.* Boston: Beacon Press, 1995.
13. Lisa Goldstein, *Teaching with Love: A Feminist Approach to Early Childhood Education.* New York: Peter Lang, 1997; Lisa Goldstein, Teacherly love: intimacy, commitment, and passion in classroom life. *Journal of Educational Thought* 32 (1998): 257–72; Lisa Goldstein, Meeting

at the classroom doors: motherly love, teacherly love, and parent–teacher partnerships. *Journal of Early Childhood Teacher Education* 20 (2000): 1–13.

14. Robert J. Sternberg, *The Triangle of Love*. New York: Basic Books, 1988.
15. *Ibid.*, 120.
16. *Ibid.*
17. See, for example, Sandra Acker, *The Realities of Teachers' Work: Never a Dull Moment*. New York: Cassell & Continuum, 1999; Andy Hargreaves, *Changing Teachers, Changing Times*. New York: Cassell & Continuum, 1994; Jennifer Nias, *Primary Teachers Talking*. London: Routledge, 1989.
18. Andy Hargreaves, *Changing Teachers, Changing Times*. New York: Cassell & Continuum, 1994, 145.
19. Dwight Rogers, Conceptions of caring in a fourth grade classroom. *The Tapestry of Caring*. A. R. Prillamin, D. J. Eaker, and D. M. Kendrick (Eds). Norwood, NJ: Ablex Publishing, 1991, 33–47.
20. Nel Noddings, *Caring: A Feminine Approach to Ethics and Education*. Berkeley, CA: University of California Press, 1984.
21. *Ibid.*, 201.
22. Nel Noddings, *The Challenge to Care in Schools*. New York: Teachers College Press, 1992, 17.
23. Nel Noddings, Fidelity in teaching, teacher education, and research for teaching. *Harvard Educational Review* 56 (1986): 496–510.
24. bell hooks, *Teaching to Transgress: Education as the Practice of Freedom*. New York: Routledge, 1994; Barbara Thayer-Bacon and Charles Bacon, Caring professors: a model. *The Journal of General Education* 45 (1996): 255–269; Barbara Thayer-Bacon and Charles Bacon, Caring in the college/university classroom. *Educational Foundations* 10 (1996): 53–72.
25. Lisa Goldstein, Teacherly love: intimacy, commitment, and passion in classroom life. *Journal of Educational Thought* 32 (1998): 257–72.
26. Nel Noddings, *Caring: A Feminine Approach to Ethics and Education*. Berkeley, CA: University of California Press, 1984, 4–5.
27. *Ibid.*, 82–3.
28. Robert Sternberg, *The Triangle of Love*. New York: Basic Books, 1988, 120.
29. See, for example, Carol Merz and Gail Furman, *Community and Schools: Promise and Paradox*. New York: Teachers College Press, 1997.
30. Ann Brown, Transforming schools into communities of thinking and learning about serious matters. *American Psychologist* 52 (1997): 411.
31. Kimberly Trimble, Building a learning community. *Equity and Excellence in Education* 29 (1996): 37–40.
32. Mara Sapon-Shevin, *Because We Can Change the World*. Boston: Allyn & Bacon, 1999.
33. Robert Bullough and Andrew Gitlin, Educative communities and the development of the relective practitioner. *Issues and Practices in Inquiry-Oriented Teacher Education*. B. R. Tabachnick and K. M. Zeichner (Eds). London: Falmer Press, 1991, 35–55.
34. Sharon Oja, Ann Diller, Ellen Corcoran, and Michael D. Andrew, Communities of inquiry, communities of support: the five year teacher education program at the university of New Hampshire. *Reflective Teacher Education: Cases and Critiques*. L. Valli (Ed). Albany, NY: SUNY Press, 1992, 3–23.
35. Michael Fullan and Andy Hargreaves, *What's Worth Fighting for in Your School?* New York: Teachers College Press, 1996.
36. *Ibid.*, 63.
37. Joel Westheimer, Communities and consequences: an inquiry into ideology and practice in teachers' professional work. *Educational Administration Quarterly* 35 (1999): 71–105.
38. Thomas Sergiovanni, *Building Community in Schools*. San Francisco: Jossey-Bass, 1994; Milbrey McLaughlin, What matters most in teachers' workplace context? *Teachers' Work*. J. W. Little and M. McLaughlin (Eds.). New York: Teachers College Press, 1993, 79–103; Carol Merz and Gail Furman, *Communities and Schools: Promise and Paradox*. New York: Teachers College Press, 1997. See also Sandra Acker, *The Realities of Teachers' Work: Never a Dull Moment*. New York: Cassell & Continuum, 1999; Andy Hargreaves, *Changing Teachers, Changing Times*. New York: Cassell & Continuum, 1994; Ann Lieberman and Lynne Miller, *Teachers, Their World, and Their Work: Implications for School Improvement*. (Alexandria,

VA: Association for Supervision and Curriculum Development, 1984; Jennifer Nias, *Primary Teachers Talking*. London: Routledge, 1989.

39. Robert Sternberg, *The Triangle of Love*. New York: Basic Books, 1988, 120.
40. bell hooks, *Teaching To Transgress: Education as the Practice of Freedom*. New York: Routledge, 1994.
41. Robert Fried, *The Passionate Teacher*. Boston: Beacon Press, 1995.
42. Andy Hargreaves and Elizabeth Tucker, Teaching and guilt: exploring the feelings of teaching. *Teaching and Teacher Education* 7 (1991): 491–505; Carol Weinstein, "I want to be nice, but I have to be mean": exploring prospective teachers' conceptions of caring and order. *Teaching and Teacher Education* 14 (1998): 153–163.
43. Ava McCall, Care and nurturance in teaching: a case study. *Journal of Teacher Education* 40 (1989): 39–44.
44. Dwight Rogers, Conceptions of caring in a fourth grade classroom. *The Tapestry of Caring*. A. R. Prillamin, D. J. Eaker, and D. M. Kendrick (Eds.). Norwood, NJ: Ablex Publishing, 1991, 41.
45. Lisa Goldstein, *Teaching with Love: A Feminist Approach to Early Childhood Education*. New York: Peter Lang, 1997.
46. Robert Fried, *The Passionate Teacher*. Boston: Beacon Books, 1995.
47. *Ibid.*, 1.
48. *Ibid.*, 17.
49. *Ibid.*, 18.
50. *Ibid.*, 6, italics in the original.
51. *Ibid.*, 23, italics in the original.
52. Jim Garrison, *Dewey and Eros: Wisdom and Desire in the Art of Teaching*. New York: Teachers College Press, 1997.
53. Maxine Greene, *Releasing the Imagination: Essays on Education, The Arts, and Social Change*. San Francisco: Jossey-Bass, 1995, 43.

Chapter 4. "Tales In and Out of School"

1. Ralph Ellison, *Invisible Man*. New York: Random House, 1952, 36.
2. *Ibid.*, 3.
3. William Finnegan, *Cold New World: Growing Up in a Harder Country*. New York: Random House, 1998.
4. Charles Dickens, *Hard Times*. New York: Penguin, 1997/1854, 11.
5. *Ibid.*, 283.
6. Jonathan Kozol, *Ordinary Resurrections: Children in the Years of Hope*. New York: Crown, 2000, 135.
7. *Ibid.*, 136–137.
8. Martha Nussbaum, *Poetic Justice: The Literary Imagination and Public Life*. Boston: Beacon Press, 1995, 26–27.
9. Dickens, *Hard Times*, 101.
10. *Ibid.*, 106.
11. *Ibid.*, 101.
12. *Ibid.*, 103.
13. *Ibid.*, 215.
14. Anne Carson, *Economy of the Unlost (Reading Simondes of Keos with Paul Celan)*. Princeton: Princeton University Press, 1999, 12.
15. *Ibid.*, 18.
16. Anny Gaul, The high school senior's numbers game. *The Charlotte Observer*, October 10, 2002.
17. Anne Carson, *Eros the Bittersweet*. Normal, Illinois: Dalkey Archive Press, 1998, 168.
18. *Ibid.*, 168.
19. Martha Nussbaum, *Love's Knowledge*. New York: Oxford University Press, 1990, 156.
20. *Ibid.*, 136.
21. Jo Anne Pagano, Moral fictions: the dilemma of theory and practice. *Stories Lives Tell: Narrative and Dialogue in Education*. Carol Witherall and Nel Noddings (Eds.). New York: Teachers College Press, 1991, 197.

22. Hilary Putnam, *Realism With a Human Face*. Cambridge: Harvard University Press, 1990, 183.
23. *Ibid.*, 166.
24. Iris Murdoch, *The Sovereignty of Good*. London: Routledge Classics, 2001/1970, 88.
25. Salmon Rushdie, *Haroun and the Sea of Stories*. New York: Penguin, 1990, 22.
26. Bernard Williams, *Shame and Necessity*. Berkeley: University of California Press, 1993, 13.
27. Nussbaum, *Love's Knowledge*, 47–48.
28. Tillie Olsen, *Tell Me A Riddle*. New York: Dell Publishing, 1994, 110.
29. *Ibid.*, 84.
30. *Ibid.*, 81.
31. Nussbaum, *Poetic Justice*, 172.

Part 2 Introduction: Love, Injustice, Teaching, and Learning

1. Walt Whitman, Democratic vistas. *Leaves Of Grass And Selected Prose*. Ellman Crasnow (Ed.). London: Orion Publishing Group,1871/1993, 505–559, 521.

Chapter 5. "Eros, Pedagogy, and the Pursuit of Happiness"

1. Specifically, I am struck by the reconstructive possibilities for educating democratic citizens latent in the idea that American identity contains no pre-given, stable essence. While such a perspective is nothing new, the value we attach to the "ontologically absent" quality of American identity, and what this means pedagogically for the formation of democratic personalities, is a psychical terrain that has not yet been expressly linked to the qualities of eros.
2. Jane Roland Martin, for one, "creatively repoliticizes" an "iconic meaning narrative" within the Constitution's Preamble. See her Education for domestic tranquility. *Critical Conversations in Philosophy of Education*. Wendy Kohli (Ed.). New York: Routledge, 1995, 45–55. The same interpretive creativity could be applied toward another phrase, the "right to revolution," as the *right to create new forms*, an activity deeply entwined with the eros concept.
3. Civic educators need to repoliticize this narrative in imaginative new ways. In another approach not tied to constitutional, state-centric language, the corporate images of happiness in the Disney mythology are problematized with great skill by Henry Giroux in his *The Mouse That Roared: Disney and the End of Innocence*. Lanham, MD:Rowman and Littlefield, 2001.
4. The discourse on eros in this essay is indebted mainly to those canonical figures who have contributed to the erotic underpinning of the western liberatory tradition: Plato, Rousseau, Dewey, Freire, and to certain authors associated with feminist theory and the Frankfurt School of Critical Theory.
5. Kerry Burch, *Eros as the Educational Principle of Democracy*. New York: Peter Lang Publishing, 2000.
6. For an analysis of the distinctions between various forms of love, in addition to those found in this volume, see Shin Chiba, Hannah Arendt on love and the political: love, friendship, and citizenship. *Review of Politics* Summer (1994), 505–35.
7. Jim Garrison, *Dewey and Eros: Desire and Wisdom in the Art of Teaching*. New York: Teachers College Press, 1997, xii–xiv.
8. Paulo Freire, *Pedagogy of the Oppressed*. New York: Continuum Books, 2000, 35.
9. *Ibid.*, 81.
10. Raymond Callahan, *Education and the Cult of Efficiency*. Chicago: University of Chicago Press, 1962, vii–x; 244–48.
11. For a full discussion of this Deweyan principle, see Robert Westbrook, *John Dewey and American Democracy*. Ithaca, NY: Cornell University Press, 1991, 38–51.
12. A brief but perceptive genealogy of eros can be found in Rollo May, Eros in conflict with sex. *Love and Will*. New York: Norton, 1969, 64–98.
13. Werner Jaeger, *Paideia: The Ideals of Greek Culture Vol. II*. New York: Oxford University Press, 1943, 192.

14. William Cobb, trans. *Plato's Erotic Dialogues: The Symposium and The Phaedrus.* Albany: SUNY Press, 1993. This book will be cited as *Sym.* in the text for all subsequent references.

15. Wendy Brown, Supposing truth were a woman: Plato's subversion of masculine discourse. *Feminist Interpretations of Plato.* Nancy Tuana (Ed.). University Park: Penn State University Press, 1994.

16. Susan Hawthorne, Diotima speaks through the body. *Engendering Origins: Critical Feminist Readings in Plato and Aristotle.* Albany: SUNY Press, 1994, 83–96.

17. Brown, Supposing Truth Were a Woman, 168.

18. Jean-Jacques Rousseau, *Emile.* Trans. Allan Bloom. New York: Basic Books, 1979, 226.

19. Theodor Adorno, Education after Auschwitz. *Critical Models: Interventions and Catchwords.* New York: Columbia University Press, 1998, 201.

20. Max Horkheimer and Theodor Adorno, *The Authoritarian Personality.* New York: Norton, 1950, 976.

21. Herbert Marcuse, Political Preface to *Eros and Civilization.* Boston: Beacon Press, 1955/1966, 19.

22. Abraham Lincoln, *The Collected Works of Abraham Lincoln.* Roy Basler (Ed.). Rutgers University Press, 1953. The "Fragment on the Constitution and the Union" (January 1861) will be cited as *CW* in the text for all subsequent references. My use of Lincoln requires a caveat. I do not dispute the politically dubious, racist elements of Lincoln's public career. However, I believe that it is possible to adopt a critical stance toward Lincoln yet appropriate for egalitarian purposes the often sublime imagery of his writings. Further, in my rather glowing assessment of the Declaration of Independence, I am not unmindful of the fact that the clauses attacking slavery were struck out in committee.

23. Elaine Pagels, *Adam, Eve and the Serpent.* (New York: Vintage Books, 1988), 98–126.

24. See, for example, W. E. B. Du Bois, "The Negro common school in Georgia." *W. E. B. Du Bois: A Reader.* Meyer Weinberg (Ed.). New York: Harper & Row, 1970, 111.

25. For further analysis, see Kerry Burch, A tale of two citizens: asking the *Rodriquez* question in the twenty-first century. *Educational Studies 32* (2001): 264–78.

26. Jonathan Kozol, *Ordinary Resurrections: Children in the Years of Hope.* New York: HarperCollins, 2000. This book will be cited as *OR* in the text for all subsequent references.

27. The idea of "inventing" a new meaning for the pursuit of happiness clause should not sound as suspect to readers as it probably does. For one of the greatest political inventions of all was the Fourteenth Amendment, which invented, against all prior Constitutional precedent *and* procedure, new definitions of national citizenship and new forms of national protection for individual rights. According to legal scholar Bruce Ackerman: "To the extent we have gained equality, we have won it through energetic debate, popular decision, and constitutional creativity. Once the American people lose this remarkable political capacity, it is only a matter of time before they lose whatever equality they possess—and much else besides." See Bruce Ackerman, *We The People.* Cambridge: Harvard University Press, 1991, 27.

28. James Baldwin, "A talk to teachers. *The Price of the Ticket: Collected Nonfiction, 1948–1985.* New York: St. Martin's Press, 1985, 332.

29. Aristotle, *The Nichomachean Ethics.* New York: Oxford University Press, 1990, 1125b. For a more substantive, gendered analysis of "Aristotle's Moral Anger," see Megan Boler, *Feeling Power: Emotions and Education.* New York: Routledge Books, 1999, 188–92.

30. For an analysis of how a psychoanalytic theory of love and learning can deepen and extend our philosophies of education, see Deborah P. Britzman, On making education inconsolable. *Lost Subjects, Contested Objects: Toward a Psychoanalytic Inquiry of Learning.* Albany: SUNY, 1998, 49–61.

31. John Dewey, The Democratic conception in education. *Democracy and Education.* New York: Macmillan Co., 1916/1938, 98.

32. Cornel West and Roberto Unger, The American religion of possibility. *The Future of American Progressivism.* Boston: Beacon Press, 1998, 12.

33. John Dewey, Creative democracy: the task before us. *The Essential Dewey: Pragmatism, Education, Democracy, Vol. 1.* Thomas M. Alexander and Larry Hickman (Eds.). Bloomington: Indiana University Press, 1939/1998, 341.

34. The etymology of idiot (*idios*) is instructive: In ancient Greek, an idiot was a "purely private" individual, one who could legally participate in the polis, but did not. I believe it is

also worth noting that an idiot, as a privatized identity, would be largely incapable of feeling anger at the sight of injustice. See, for example, Arlene Saxonhouse, The philosopher and the female in the political thought of Plato. *Feminist Interpretations of Plato.* Nancy Tuana (Ed.). University Park: Penn State University Press, 1994, 78–79.

35.   Pauline Maier, *American Scripture: Making the Declaration of Independence.* New York: Vintage Press, 1997.

36.   Alfred Young, *The Shoemaker and the Tea Party: Memory and the American Revolution.* Boston: Beacon Press, 1999, 147.

37.   John Dewey, Nationalizing education. *The Essential Dewey: Pragmatism, Education, Democracy, Vol. 1.* Thomas M. Alexander and Larry Hickman (Eds.). Bloomington: Indiana University Press, 1916/1998, 269.

Chapter 6. "The Allure of Beauty and the Pain of Injustice in Learning and Teaching"

1.   For an elaboration of some of these problems, see James Ladwig, *Academic Distinctions.* New York: Routledge, 1996.

2.   In earlier work I have attempted to portray and evoke a bit of this lure. See Love and despair in teaching. *Educational Theory* 50 (2000): 81–102; Daniel P. Liston, Despair and love in teaching. *Stories of the Courage to Teach.* Sam Intrator (Ed.). San Francisco: Jossey-Bass, 2002, 42–53; Daniel P. Liston and Sirat Al Salim, Race, discomfort, and love in a university classroom. *Race in the College Classroom.* Bonnie Tusmith and Maureen Reddy (Eds.). New Brunswick, N.J.: Rutgers University Press, 2002; and Daniel P. Liston *Love and Despair in Teaching: Feeling and Thinking in Educational Settings* (work in progress).

3.   Annie Dillard, *An American Childhood.* New York: Harper and Row, 1987; cited as *AC* in the text for all subsequent references.

4.   Anne Carson, *Eros the Bittersweet.* Normal, IL: Dalkey Archive Press, 1998, 71.

5.   Paulo Freire, *Pedagogy of the Oppressed.* New York: Seabury Press, 1973, 20.

6.   Sanyika Shakur, *Monster: The Autobiography of an L.A. Gang Member.* New York: Penguin, 1993; cited as *M* in the text for all subsequent references.

7.   George Jackson, *Soledad Brother.* New York: Bantam, 1970; cited as *SB* in the text for all subsequent references.

8.   Catherine McKinnon, *Toward a Feminist Theory of the State.* Cambridge: Harvard University Press, 1989. See especially Chapter 5, Consciousness Raising.

9.   While it is infrequently examined, there is a growing literature that examines the connections between thinking and feeling in learning, teaching, and schooling. Scholars include Megan Boler, Kerry Burch, Robert Fried, Jim Garrison, Daniel Goleman, Lisa Goldstein, Andy Hargreaves, Dwayne Huebner, Sam Intrator, Ursula Kelly, Nel Noddings, and Parker Palmer.

10.   Some intriguing and varied examples would include the work of Myles Horton, Robert Moses, and Rachael Kessler.

11.   See Simone Weil, *The Illiad or The Poem of Force,* Trans. by Mary McCarthy. Wallingford, PA.: Pendle Hill Pamphlet, #91, 1981. This also appears as The Illiad or the poem of might, the *Simone Weil Reader.* George Panichas (Ed.). Wakefield, RI: Moyer Bell, 1977, 153–83.

12.   Eric Springsted, *Simone Weil and the Suffering of Love.* Cambridge: Cowley, 1986, 23–24.

13.   *Ibid.,* 24.

14.   Martha Nussbaum, *Upheavals of Thought.* New York: Cambridge University Press, 2001, 4.

15.   Martha Nussbaum, Rational emotions, *Poetic Justice.* Boston: Beacon Press, 1995, 66.

16.   *Ibid.,* 74.

17.   *Ibid.*

18.   Oliver Sacks, *Uncle Tungsten: Memories of a Chemical Boyhood.* New York: Alfred A. Knopf, 2001; and Annie Dillard, *AC.*

19.   Richard Brown, Taming our emotions: Tibetan meditation in teacher education, *Nurturing our Wholeness.* John Miller and Yoshiharu Nakagawa (Eds.). Brandon, VT: Foundation for Educational Renewal, 2002.

20.   *Ibid.,* 6.

21.   *Ibid.,* 9.

Chapter 7. "Teaching for Hope: The Ethics of Shattering World Views"

1. James Loewen, *Lies My Teacher Told Me: Everything Your American History Textbook Got Wrong.* New York: New Press: Distributed by Norton, 1995.
2. Mark Epstein, *Going On Being: Buddhism and the Way of Change.* New York: Broadway Books, 2001.
3. *Ibid.,* 71.
4. Megan Boler, *Feeling Power: Emotions and Education.* New York: Routledge, 1999.
5. Peter McLaren, *Life in Schools: An Introduction to Critical Pedagogy in the Foundations of Education.* New York: Longman, 1984/1999.
6. Noam Chomsky, *Chomsky on Miseducation.* Donaldo Macedo (Ed.). Lanham, MD: Rowman & Littlefield, 2000, 10–11.
7. Jim Garrison, *Dewey and Eros: Wisdom and Desire in the Art of Teaching.* Teachers College Press, 1997, 109.
8. Maxine Greene, *Releasing the Imagination: Essays on Education, the Arts, and Social Change.* San Francisco: Jossey Bass, 1995, 23.
9. Jim Garrison, *Dewey and Eros: Wisdom and Desire in the Art of Teaching.* Teachers College Press, 1997, 139.
10. Maxine Greene, *The Dialectic of Freedom.* New York: Teachers College Press, 1988, 15.
11. Paulo Freire, *Pedagogy of the Oppressed.* New York: The Seabury Press, 1973, 106.
12. Mark Epstein, *Going On Being: Buddhism and the Way of Change.* New York: Broadway Books, 2001, 71.
13. Minnie Bruce Pratt, Identity: Skin/Blood/Heart. *Yours in Struggle.* Elly Bulkin, Minnie Bruce Pratt,and Barbara Smith (Eds.). New York: Longhaul Press, 1984.
14. Greene, *The Dialectic of Freedom,* 30.
15. Freire, *Pedagogy of the Oppressed.*

Part 3 Introduction: "Love's Losses and Love Regained"

1. Kahlil Gibran, *The Prophet.* New York: Alfred A. Knopf, 1992, 11.

Chapter 8. "Grief as a Gateway to Love in Teaching"

1. Naomi Naierman, Reaching out to grieving students. *Educational Leadership* 55 (1992), 62.
2. Based on the commonly known model of grief developed by Elizabeth Kubler-Ross, *On Death and Dying.* New York: Macmillan, 1969. In Kubler-Ross's text, the identified stages were: denial, anger, bargaining, depression, and acceptance.
3. Liz Sunnyboy, mimeographed copy, no date.
4. Personal communication.
5. Liz Sunnyboy, mimeographed copy, no date.
6. Naierman, 62.
7. Personal communication.
8. Please see the website www.jennadruck.org for many resources for families and students, including "The Compassionate Classroom" and the Teen Grief Curriculum for teachers and counselors created by Scott Johnson, MA, Child Bereavement Specialist.
9. Interview with Ken Druck, 9/11/02.
10. Please see my Web site for information on methods and training that support teachers creating safe and respectful community in the classroom where feelings can be shared: www.mediatorsfoundation.org/isel

Chapter 9. "The Place of Reparation: Love, Loss, Ambivalence, and Teaching"

1. Deborah P. Britzman, *Lost Objects, Contested Subjects.* Albany: SUNY Press, 1998, 20.
2. *Ibid.,* 47–8.

3. See, for examples, Paulo Salvo, The Teacher/Scholar as Melancholic. *Journal of Curriculum Theorizing* 14 (1998): 15–23; and various essays in Sharon Todd (Ed.), *Learning Desire: Perspectives on Pedagogy, Culture, and the Unsaid.* New York: Routledge, 1997 and also Jane Gallop (Ed.), *Pedagogy: The Question of Impersonation.* Bloomington: Indiana University Press, 1998.

4. Helen Humphreys, *The Lost Garden.* Toronto: Harper Flamingo Canada, 2002, 182.

5. Richard Johnson, Grievous recognitions 2: the grieving process and sexual boundaries. *Border Patrols: Policing the Boundaries of Heterosexuality.* Deborah Lynn Steinberg and Richard Johnson (Eds.). London: Cassell, 1997, 234, 235. See also Richard Johnson, Exemplary differences: mourning (and not mourning) a princess, *Mourning Diana: Nation, Culture and the Performance of Grief.* Adrian Kear and Deborah Lynn Steinberg (Eds.). London: Routledge, 1999, 15–39.

6. The description of Klein's theory offered here is quite encapsulated and focuses only on those points relevant to my discussion. For full accounts of Klein's theory, in particular, on points of love and reparation and mourning, see Melanie Klein, *Love, Guilt and Reparation and Other Works 1921–1945.* London: Hogarth Press, 1975. See also *The Selected Melanie Klein.* Juliet Mitchell (Ed.). London: Hogarth Press, 1986.

7. Madeline Grumet, *Bitter Milk: Women and Teaching.* Amherst: University of Massachusetts Press, 1988.

8. Todd, *Learning Desire*, 5.

9. Alice Pitt, Judith P. Robertson, and Sharon Todd, Psychoanalytic encounters: putting pedagogy on the couch *Journal of Curriculum Theorizing* 14 (1998): 3.

10. Britzman, *Lost Subjects, Contested Objects*, 41.

11. Lawrence O'Toole, *Heart's Longing: Newfoundland, New York and the Distance Home.* Vancouver: Douglas & McIntyre, 1994, 133.

12. E. Annie Proulx, *The Shipping News.* New York: Touchstone, 1993, 34. Proulx won numerous awards, including the Pulitzer Prize, for her Newfoundland-based novel. A film based on the novel—and enthusiastically endorsed by Proulx—was released in late fall, 2001.

13. Philip Sheldrake, *Spaces for the Sacred: Place, Memory, and Identity.* Baltimore: Johns Hopkins University Press, 2001, 20.

14. William F. Pinar, Curriculum as social psychoanalysis: on the significance of place. *Curriculum as Social Psychoanalysis: The Significance of Place.* Joe L. Kincheloe and William F. Pinar (Eds.). Albany: SUNY Press, 1991, 165–186.

15. O'Toole, *Heart's Longing*, 67.

16. Klein, *Love, Guilt and Reparation*, 333.

17. Gayatri Chakravorty Spivak, Thinking cultural questions in "pure" literary terms *Without Guarantees: In Honour of Stuart Hall.* Paul Gilroy, Lawrence Grossberg and Angela McRobbie (Eds.). London: Verso, 2000, 344–5.

18. Klein, *Love, Guilt and Reparation*, 319–20.

19. Doreen Massey, *Space, Place and Gender.* Cambridge: Polity Press, 1994, 230.

20. *Ibid.,* 110–12.

21. Jeanette Winterson, *Art Objects: Essays on Ecstasy and Effrontery.* London: Jonathan Cape, 1995, 157.

22. Jen Gilbert, Reading colorblindness: negation as an engagement with social difference. *Journal of Curriculum Theorizing* 14 (1998), 33.

23. Britzman, *Lost Subjects, Contested Objects*, 134.

24. Pinar, Curriculum as Social Psychoanalysis, 177.

25. Klein, *Love, Guilt and Reparation*, 330

26. Britzman, *Lost Subjects, Contested Objects*, 111.

27. *Ibid.,* 112.

28. Rinaldo Walcott, Pedagogy and truama: the middle passage, slavery, and the problem of creolization. *Between Hope and Despair: Pedagogy and the Remembrance of Historical Trauma.* Roger I. Simon, Sharon Rosenberg, and Claudia Eppert (Eds.). Lanham, MD: Rowman & Littlefield, 2000, 139.

29. *Ibid.,* 148, 149.

30. *Ibid.,* 147–149.

31. Humphreys, *The Lost Garden*, 50.

32. Alice Miller, *The Drama of the Gifted Child.* Trans. Ruth Ward. New York: Basic Books, 1997.

33. Eve Kosofsky Sedgwick, *A Dialogue on Love.* Boston: Beacon Press, 1999, 217.

34. *Ibid.,* 169.

Chapter 10. "The Search for Wise Love in Education: What Can We Learn from the Brahmaviharas?"

1. *Sutta Nipata,* Vol. I, Sutra 8. Translation adapted from Eknath Easwaran, *Meditation.* Tomales, CA: Nilgiri Press, 1991. For a detailed introduction to the canonical literature of Buddhism, see Sangharakshita, *The Eternal Legacy.* London: Tharpa Publications, 1985.
2. Thich Nhat Hanh, *Teachings on Love.* Berkeley, CA: Parallax Press, 5. This book will be cited as *TL* in the text for all subsequent references.
3. Jeremy W. Hayward, *Letters to Vanessa.* Boston: Shambala, 1997, 90.
4. *Ibid.*
5. H. Bai and D. Mirisse, The way of mindfulness and loving-kindness. *Learning Love.* Sonia MacPherson (Ed.) (unpublished).
6. *Ibid.*
7. A. H. Almaas, *Diamond Heart Book Two.* Berkeley, CA: Diamond Books, 1989, 193.
8. Sharon Salzberg, *Lovingkindness.* Boston: Shambala, 1997, 104. This book will be cited as *LK* in the text for all subsequent references.
9. Ayya Khema, *Being Nobody, Going Nowhere.* London: Wisdom Publications, 1987, 45.
10. *Ibid.*
11. *Ibid.,* 49.
12. *Ibid.* Hanh
13. Thich Nhat Hahn, *The Miracle of Mindfulness.* Trans. Mobi Ho. Boston: Beacon Press, 1976, 57.
14. *Ibid.*
15. Betty Sprague, unpublished term paper (University of New Hampshire, 2002).
16. Ayya Khema, *op. cit.,* 50.
17. Toni Packer, Finding a new way to listen. *The Wisdom of Listening.* Mark Brady (Ed.). Boston: Wisdom, forthcoming. Originally published in *Springwater Center Newsletter* (fall 2002), 1–3.
18. *Ibid.*
19. *Ibid.*
20. Tarthang Tulku, *Openness Mind.* Berkeley, CA: Dharma Publishing, 1990, 50.
21. *Ibid.,* 52.
22. *Ibid.,* 56.
23. *Ibid.,* 52.
24. *Ibid.,* 52–54.
25. Thich Nhat Hanh, *Peace Is Every Step.* NY: Bantam, 1992, 53–56.
26. *Ibid.,* 54, 57.
27. Tarthang Tulku, 54.
28. Jack Kornfield, *After the Ecstasy, the Laundry.* NY: Bantam, 2000, 252–253.
29. Toni Packer, 3.
30. Ratnapani, Introduction. *Metta: the practice of loving kindness.* Birmingham, England: Windhorse Publications, 1992 and 2000, 7.
31. Abhaya, Putting Oneself First, Ibid., 28.
32. Sogyal Rinpoche, *The Tibetan Book of Living and Dying.* Patrick Gaffney and Andrew Harvey (Eds.). NY: HarperSanFrancisco, 1994, 199.

Bibliography

Acker, Sandra. *The Realities of Teachers' Work: Never a Dull Moment.* New York: Cassell & Continuum, 1999.

Ackerman, Bruce. *We The People.* Cambridge: Harvard University Press, 1991.

Adorno, Theodor. "Education After Auschwitz." In *Critical Models: Interventions and Catchwords.* New York: Columbia University Press, 1998.

Alcott, Louisa M. *Little Men.* New York: Doubleday, 1960.

Allison, Dorothy. *Bastard Out Of Carolina.* New York: Plume, 1993.

Almaas, A. H. *Diamond Heart Book Two.* Berkeley, CA: Diamond Books, 1989.

Aristotle, *Rhetorica.* Vol. XI of *The Works of Aristotle,* edited by W. D. Ross. Oxford: Clarendon Press, 1953.

———. *The Politics.* Translated by T. A. Sinclair. Harmondsworth: Penguin Books, 1981.

———. *The Nichomachean Ethics.* New York: Oxford University Press, 1990.

Arnstine, Barbara. "Rational and Caring Teachers: Reconstructing Teacher Preparation." *Teachers College Record* 92 (1990): 241–2.

Bai, H., and D. Mirisse. "The Way of Mindfulness and Loving-Kindness." In *Learning Love,* edited by Sonia MacPherson (unpublished).

Baldwin, James. "A Talk to Teachers." In *The Price of the Ticket: Collected Nonfiction, 1948–1985.* New York: St. Martin's Press, 1985.

Bartky, Sandra. *Femininity and Domination.* New York: Routledge, 1990.

Bhabha, Homi. *The Location of Culture.* New York: Routledge, 1994.

Boas, George. "Love." In *The Encyclopedia of Philosophy, Vol 5,* edited by Paul Edwards. New York: Macmillan, 1967.

Boler, Megan. *Feeling Power.* New York: Routledge, 1999.

Britzman, Deborah P. *Lost Objects, Contested Subjects.* Albany: SUNY Press, 1998.

Britzman, Deborah P. "On Making Education Inconsolable." In *Lost Subjects, Contested Objects: Toward a Psychoanalytic Inquiry of Learning.* Albany: SUNY, 1998.

Brown, Ann. "Transforming Schools into Communities of Thinking and Learning About Serious Matters." *American Psychologist* 52 (1997): 411.

Brown, Richard. "Taming Our Emotions: Tibetan Meditation in Teacher Education." In *Nurturing Our Wholeness,* edited by John Miller and Yoshiharu Nakagawa. Brandon, Vermont: Foundation for Educational Renewal, 2002.

Brown, Wendy. "Supposing Truth Were a Woman: Plato's Subversion of Masculine Discourse." In *Feminist Interpretations of Plato,* edited by Nancy Tuana. University Park: Penn State University Press, 1994.

Bullough, Robert, and Andrew Gitlin. "Educative Communities and the Development of the Relective Practitioner." In *Issues and Practices in Inquiry-Oriented Teacher Education,* edited by B. R. Tabachnick and K. M. Zeichner. London: Falmer Press, 1991.

Burch, Kerry. *Eros as the Educational Principle of Democracy.* New York: Peter Lang, 2000.

———. "A Tale of Two Citizens: Asking the *Rodriquez* Question in the Twenty-first Century." *Educational Studies* 32 (2001): 264–78.

Callahan, Raymond. *Education and the Cult of Efficiency.* Chicago: University of Chicago Press, 1962.

Carson, Anne. *Eros the Bittersweet.* Normal, IL: Dalkey Archive Press, 1998.

———. *Economy of the Unlost (Reading Simondes of Keos with Paul Celan).* Princeton: Princeton University Press, 1999.

Charney, Ruth S. *Teaching Children to Care.* Greenfield, MA: Northeast Foundation for Children, 1991.

Chiba, Shin. "Hannah Arendt on Love and the Political: Love, Friendship, and Citizenship." *Review of Politics* Summer (1994): 505–35.

Chomsky, Noam. *Chomsky on Miseducation.* Edited by Donaldo Macedo. Lanham, MD: Rowman & Littlefield, 2000.

Coles, Robert. *The Call of Stories: Teaching and the Moral Imagination.* Boston: Houghton Mifflin, 1989.

Cooper, J. "An Aristotelian Theory of Emotions." *Essays on Aristotle's Rhetoric,* edited by A. O. Rorty (Berkeley: University of California Press, 1996).

Dale, Michael, and Daniel Liston. "Exploring Soul Through Literature in Teacher Education." Presentation at Holistic Learning: Breaking New Ground, The Third International Conference, October 2001.

Daleo, Morgan. *Curriculum of Love.* Charlottesville, VA: Grace Publishing, 1996.

Dalton, Joan, and Marilyn Watson. *Among Friends: Classrooms Where Caring and Learning Prevail.* Oakland, CA: Developmental Studies Center, 1997.

Damasio, Antonio. *Descartes' Error.* New York: Grosset/Putnam, 1994.

Delpit, Lisa. *Other People's Children: Cultural Conflict in the Classroom.* New York: The New Press, 1995.

Denzin, Norman. *On Understanding Human Emotion.* San Francisco: Jossey-Bass, 1984.

de Sousa, Ronald. *The Rationality of Emotions.* Cambridge: MIT Press, 1987.

Dewey, John. "The Democratic Conception in Education." In *Democracy and Education.* New York: Macmillan Co., 1916/1938.

———. *The School and Society.* Chicago: University of Chicago Press, 1956.

———. "The Theory of Emotion." *The Early Works, 1882–1898,* edited by J. A. Boydston. Carbondale: Southern Illinois University Press, 1971.

———. "Creative Democracy: The Task Before Us." In *The Essential Dewey: Pragmatism, Education, Democracy,* Vol. 1, edited by Thomas M. Alexander and Larry Hickman. Bloomington: Indiana University Press, 1939/1998.

———. "Nationalizing Education." In *The Essential Dewey: Pragmatism, Education, Democracy,* Vol. 1, edited by Thomas M. Alexander and Larry Hickman. Bloomington: Indiana University Press, 1916/1998.

Dickens, Charles. *Hard Times.* New York: Penguin, 1854/1997.

Dillard, Annie. *An American Childhood.* New York: Harper and Row, 1987.

Diller, Ann. "The Ethical Education of Self-Talk." In *Justice and Care in Education.* edited by M. Katz, N. Noddings, and K. Strike. New York: Teachers College Press, 1999.

———. "Pluralisms for Education: An Ethics of Care Perspective," http://x.ed.uiuc.edu/EPS/PES-Yearbook/92_docs/DILLER.HTM.

Du Bois, W. E. B. "The Negro Common School in Georgia." In *W.E.B Du Bois: A Reader,* edited by Meyer Weinberg. New York: Harper & Row, 1970.

Ellison, Ralph. *Invisible Man.* New York: Random House, 1952.

Epstein, Mark. *Going On Being: Buddhism and the Way of Change.* New York: Broadway Books, 2001. Finnegan, William. *Cold New World: Growing Up in a Harder Country.* New York: Random House, 1998.

Foucault, Michel. *The Order of Things.* New York: Vintage, 1970.

Fried, Robert. *The Passionate Teacher.* Boston: Beacon Press, 1995.

Freire, Paulo. *Pedagogy of the Oppressed.* New York: Seabury Press, 1973.

———. *Pedagogy of the Oppressed.* New York: Continuum Books, 2000.

Fullan, Michael, and Andy Hargreaves. *What's Worth Fighting For in Your School?* New York: Teachers College Press, 1996.

Furlong, Monica. *Wise Child.* New York: Alfred A. Knopf, 1987.

Gallop, Jane. (ed.) *Pedagogy: The Question of Impersonation.* Bloomington: Indiana University Press, 1998.

Garrison, Jim. *Dewey and Eros.* New York: Teachers College Press, 1997.

Gaul, Anny. "The High School Senior's Numbers Game." *The Charlotte Observer.* October 10, 2002.

Gibran, Kahil. *The Prophet.* New York: Alfred A. Knopf, 1992.

Gilbert, Jen. "Reading Colorblindness: Negation as an Engagement with Social Difference." *Journal of Curriculum Theorizing* 14 (1998).

Gilligan, Carol. *In a Different Voice.* Cambridge, Mass.: Harvard University Press, 1982.

Gilman, Charlotte Perkins. *Herland.* New York: Pantheon. 1979.

Giroux, Henry. *The Mouse That Roared: Disney and the End of Innocence.* Lanham, MD: Rowman and Littlefield, 2001.

Goldstein, Lisa. *Teaching with Love.* New York: Peter Lang, 1997.

———. "Teacherly Love: Intimacy, Commitment, and Passion in Classroom Life." *Journal of Educational Thought* 32 (1998): 257–72.

———. "Meeting at the Classroom Doors: Motherly Love, Teacherly Love, and Parent-Teacher Partnerships." *Journal of Early Childhood Teacher Education* 20 (2000): 1–13.

———. "Teacherly Love: Intimacy, Commitment, and Passion in Classroom Life." *Journal of Educational Thought* 32 (1998): 257–72.

Goleman, Daniel. *Emotional Intelligence.* New York: Bantam Books, 1995.

Gootman, Marilyn. *The Caring Teacher's Guide to Discipline.* Thousand Oaks, CA: Corwin Press, 1997.

Greene, Maxine. *The Dialectic of Freedom.* New York: Teachers College Press, 1988.

———. *Releasing the Imagination: Essays on Education, the Arts, and Social Change.* San Francisco: Jossey-Bass, 1995.

Greenspan, Patricia. *Emotions and Reasons.* New York: Routledge, 1988.

Grumet, Madeline. *Bitter Milk: Women and Teaching.* Amherst: University of Massachusetts Press, 1988.

Hamer, Mary. *Incest: A New Perspective.* Cambridge, UK: Polity Press, 2002.

Hahn, Thich Nhat. *The Miracle of Mindfulness.* Trans. Mobi Ho. Boston: Beacon Press, 1976.

———. *Peace Is Every Step.* New York: Bantam, 1992.

———. *Teachings on Love.* Berkeley, CA: Parallax Press, 1998.

Hargreaves, Andy. *Changing Teachers, Changing Times.* New York: Cassell & Continuum, 1994.

———. "The Emotional Practice of Teaching," *Teaching and Teacher Education* 14 (1998): 835–854.

Hargreaves, Andy, and Elizabeth Tucker. "Teaching and Guilt: Exploring the Feelings of Teaching." *Teaching and Teacher Education* 7 (1991): 491–505.

Hawthorne, Susan. "Diotima Speaks Through the Body." In *Engendering Origins: Critical Feminist Readings in Plato and Aristotle,* edited by Bat-Ami Bar On. Albany: SUNY Press, 1994.

Hayward, Jeremy W. *Letters to Vanessa.* Boston: Shambala, 1997.

Henderson, James. "An Ethic of Caring Applied to Reflective Professional Development." *Teaching Education* 2 (1988): 91–5.

Hesiod. *Theogeny.* In *the Origins of Philosophy.* Edited by Drew A. Hyland. New York: Capricorn Books, 1973.

Hill, Kathleen. "The Anointed." *Doubletake* Fall (1999): 79–89.

Hochschild, Arlie. "Emotion Work, Feeling Rules, and Social Structure." *American Journal of Sociology* 85 (1979): 551–575.

———. *The Managed Heart: Commercialization of Human Feeling.* Berkeley: University of California Press, 1983.

hooks, bell. *Teaching to Transgress: Education as the Practice of Freedom.* New York: Routledge, 1994.

Horkheimer, Max, and Theodor Adorno. *The Authoritarian Personality.* New York: Norton, 1950.

Horton, Myles, with Judith Kohl and Herbert Kohl. *The Long Haul : An Autobiography.* New York: Doubleday, 1990.

Huebner, Dwayne. *The Lure of the Transcendent: Collected Essays by Dwayne E. Huebner.* Edited by Vikki Hills (collected and introduced by William F. Pinar). Mahwah, NJ: Lawrence Erlbaum Publishers, 1999.

Humphreys, Helen. *The Lost Garden.* Toronto: Harper Flamingo Canada, 2002.

Huxley, Aldous. *Brave New World.* New York: Harper and Row, 1932.

Illich, Ivan. *Deschooling Society.* New York: Harrow Books, 1972.

Intrator, Sam M. (ed.) *Stories of the Courage to Teach.* San Francisco: Jossey-Bass, 2002.

Jackson, George. *Soledad Brother.* New York: Bantam, 1970.

Jaeger, Werner. *Paideia: The Ideals of Greek Culture,* Vol. II. New York: Oxford University Press, 1943.

Jaggar, Alison. "Love and Knowledge: Emotion in Feminist Epistemology." In *Gender/body/knowledge.* Edited by A. M. Jaggar and S. R. Bordo. New Brunswick, NJ: Rutgers University Press, 1989.

James, William. "The Physical Basis of Emotion." *Psychological Review* 1 (1894): 516–529.

Johnson, Richard. "Grievous Recognitions 2: The Grieving Process and Sexual Boundaries." In *Border Patrols: Policing the Boundaries of Heterosexuality.* Edited by Deborah Lynn Steinberg and Richard Johnson. London: Cassell, 1997.

———. "Exemplary Differences: Mourning (and Not Mourning) a Princess." In *Mourning Diana: Nation, Culture and the Performance of Grief.* Edited by Adrian Kear and Deborah Lynn Steinberg. London: Routledge, 1999.

Kelly, Ursula. *Schooling Desire.* New York: Routledge, 1997.

Kessler, Rachael. *The Soul of Education.* Alexandria, VA: Association for Supervision and Curriculum Development, 2000.

———. "Soul of Students, Soul of Teacher: Welcoming the Inner Life to School." In *Schools with Spirit: Nurturing the Inner Lives of Children and Teachers.* Edited by Linda Lantieri. Boston: Beacon Press, 2001.

———. "Eros and the Erotic Shadow in Teaching and Learning." In *Nurturing Our Wholeness: Perspectives on Spirituality in Education.* Edited by Jack P. Miller and Yoshiharu Nakagawa. Brandon, VT: The Foundation for Educational Renewal, 2002.

Khema, Ayya. *Being Nobody, Going Nowhere.* London: Wisdom Publications, 1987.

Klein, Melanie. *Love, Guilt and Reparation and Other Works 1921–1945.* London: Hogarth Press, 1975.

———. *The Selected Melanie Klein.* Edited by Juliet Mitchell. London: Hogarth Press, 1986.

Kornfield, Jack. *After the Ecstasy, the Laundry.* New York: Bantam, 2000.

Kozol, Jonathon. *Ordinary Resurrections: Children in the Years of Hope.* New York: HarperCollins, 2000.

Kubler-Ross, Elizabeth. *On Death and Dying.* New York: Macmillan, 1969.

Ladwig, James. *Academic Distinctions.* New York: Routledge, 1996.

Laird, Susan. "Reforming 'Women's True Profession': A Case for 'Feminist Pedagogy' in Teacher Education?" *Harvard Educational Review* 58 (1988): 449–463.

———. "The Ideal of the Educated Teacher—'Reclaiming a Conversation' with Louisa May Alcott." *Curriculum Inquiry* 21 (1991): 271–298.

———. "Teaching in a Different Sense: Alcott's Marmee." In *Philosophy of Education 1993.* Edited by Audrey Thompson. Urbana, Ill.: Philosophy of Education Society, 1994.

———. "Who Cares About Girls?: Rethinking the Meaning of Teaching." *Peabody Journal of Education* (1995): 82–103.

LeDoux, Joseph. *The Emotional Brain.* New York: Simon and Schuster, 1996.

Leighton, S. "Aristotle and the Emotions." In *Essays on Aristotle's Rhetoric.* Edited by A. O. Rorty. Berkeley: University of California Press, 1966.

Lieberman, Ann, and Lynne Miller. *Teachers, Their World, and Their Work: Implications for School Improvement.* Alexandria, VA: Association for Supervision and Curriculum Development, 1984.

Lincoln, Abraham. *The Collected Works of Abraham Lincoln.* Edited by Roy Basler. Rutgers University Press, 1953.

Liston, Daniel P. "Love and Despair in Teaching." *Educational Theory* 50 (2000): 81–102.

———. "Despair and Love in Teaching." In *Stories of the Courage to Teach.* Edited by Sam Intrator. San Francisco: Jossey-Bass, 2002.

———. and Sirat Al Salim. "Race, Discomfort and Love in a University Classroom." In *Race in the College Classroom.* Edited by Bonnie Tusmith and Maureen Reddy. New Brunswick, NJ: Rutgers University Press, 2002.

———. *Love and Despair in Teaching: Feeling and Thinking in Educational Settings* (work in progress).

Loewen, James. *Lies My Teacher Told Me: Everything Your American History Textbook Got Wrong.* New York: New Press (Norton), 1995.

Lyons, William. *Emotions.* New York: Cambridge University Press, 1980.

McLaughlin, Milbrey. "What Matters Most in Teachers' Workplace Context?" In *Teachers' Work.* Edited by J. W. Little & M. McLaughlin. New York: Teachers College Press, 1993.

Maier, Pauline. *American Scripture: Making the Declaration of Independence.* New York: Vintage Press, 1997.

Mandler, George. *Mind and Emotion* New York: Wiley, 1975.

Marcuse, Herbert. *Eros and Civilization.* Boston: Beacon Press, 1955/1966.

Martin, Jane Roland. *Reclaiming a Conversation.* New Haven: Yale University Press, 1985.

———. *The Schoolhome.* Cambridge: Harvard University Press, 1992.

———. *Changing the Educational Landscape.* New York: Routledge, 1994.

———. "Education for Domestic Tranquility." In *Critical Conversations in Philosophy of Education.* Edited by Wendy Kohli. New York: Routledge, 1995.

———. "Home and Family." In *Philosophy of Education: Encyclopedia.* Edited by J. J. Chambliss. New York: Garland Publishing, 1996.

———. *Cultural Miseducation.* New York: Teachers College Press, 2002.

Massey, Doreen. *Space, Place and Gender.* Cambridge: Polity Press, 1994.

May, Rollo. "Eros in Conflict with Sex." In *Love and Will.* New York: Norton, 1969.

McCall, Ava. "Care and Nurturance in Teaching: A Case Study." *Journal of Teacher Education* 40 (1989): 39–44.

McKinnon, Cattherine. *Toward a Feminist Theory of the State.* Cambridge: Harvard University Press, 1989.

McLaren, Peter. *Life in Schools: An Introduction to Critical Pedagogy in the Foundations of Education.* New York: Longman, 1984/1999.

Merz, Carol, and Gail Furman. *Community and Schools: Promise and Paradox.* New York: Teachers College Press, 1997.

Michaels, Anne. *Fugitive Pieces.* New York: Alfred A. Knopf, 1996.

Mill, John Stuart. *Utilitarianism, On Liberty, Essay on Bentham.* New York: New American Library, 1952.

Miller, Alice. *The Drama of the Gifted Child.* Translated by Ruth Ward. New York: Basic Books, 1997.

Montessori, Maria. *The Montessori Method.* New York: Schocken, 1964.

Moses, Robert, and Charles E. Cobb, Jr. *Radical Equations: Math Literacy and Civil Rights.* Boston: Beacon Press, 2001.

Mulcahy, Daniel. *Knowledge, Gender, and Schooling: The Feminist Educational Thought of Jane Roland Martin.* Westport, CT: Bergin & Garvey, 2002.

Murdoch, Iris. *The Sovereignty of Good.* New York: Schocken, 1971.

———. *Metaphysics as a Guide to Morals.* New York: Allen Lane, 1993.

Naierman, Naomi. "Reaching Out to Grieving Students." *Educational Leadership* 55 (1997): 62–65.

National Commission on Excellence in Education. *A Nation at Risk: The Imperative for Educational Reform.* Washington, D.C.: National Commission on Excellence in Education, 1982.

Nias, Jennifer. *Primary Teachers Talking.* London: Routledge, 1989.

Noddings, Nel. *Caring.* Berkeley: University of California Press, 1984.

———. "Fidelity in Teaching, Teacher Education, and Research for Teaching." *Harvard Educational Review* 56 (1986): 496–510.

———. *The Challenge to Care in Schools.* New York: Teachers College Press, 1992.

Norton, David L., and Mary F. Kille, ed. *Philosophies of Love.* Totowa, NJ: Rowman and Allenheld, 1983.

Nussbaum, Martha. *The Fragility of Goodness.* Cambridge: Cambridge University Press, 1986.

———. *Poetic Justice: The Literary Imagination and Public Life.* Boston: Beacon Press, 1995.

———. "Rational Emotions" In *Poetic Justice.* Boston: Beacon Press, 1995.

———. "Cultivating Humanity: A Classical Defense Of Reform" In Liberal Education. Cambridge: Harvard University Press, 1997.

———. *Upheavals of Thought.* New York: Cambridge University Press, 2001.

Oja, Sharon, Ann Diller, Ellen Corcoran, and Michael D. Andrew. "Communities of Inquiry, Communities of Support: The Five Year Teacher Education Program at the University of

New Hampshire." In *Reflective Teacher Education: Cases and Critiques*. Edited by Linda Valli. Albany: SUNY Press, 1992.

Olsen, Tillie. *Tell Me a Riddle*. New York: Dell Publishing, 1994.

O'Quinn, Elaine J. "Between Voice and Voicelessness: Transacting Silence in Laurie Halse Anderson's Speak." *ALAN Review* 29 (2001): 54–8.

O'Quinn, E. J. "Creative Practices for Reflective, Active, and Enduring Learning." *The English Record*. Spring/Summer (2003—in press).

Ortony, Andrew, Gerald Clore, and Allan Collins. *The Cognitive Structure of Emotions*. New York: Cambridge University Press, 1994.

O'Toole, Lawrence. *Heart's Longing: Newfoundland, New York and the Distance Home*. Vancouver: Douglas & McIntyre, 1994.

Packer, Toni. "Finding a New Way to Listen." In *The Wisdom of Listening*. Edited by Mark Brady. Boston: Wisdom, forthcoming). Originally published in *Springwater Center Newsletter* (Fall 2002), 1–3.

Pagano, Jo Anne. "Moral Fictions: The Dilemma of Theory and Practice." In *Stories Lives Tell: Narrative and Dialogue in Education*. Edited by C. Witherell and N. Noddings. New York: Teachers College Press, 1991.

Pagels, Elaine. *Adam, Eve and the Serpent*. New York: Vintage Books, 1988.

Paley, Vivian Gussin. *White Teacher*. Cambridge: Harvard University Press, 1989.

Palmer, Parker. *The Courage to Teach*. San Francisco: Jossey-Bass; 1998.

Pestalozzi, Johann Heinrich. *Leonard and Gertrude*. Boston: D. C. Heath, 1885.

———. *How Gertrude Teaches Her Children*. London: Allen & Unwin, 1915.

Pinar, William F. "Curriculum as Social Psychoanalysis: On the Significance of Place." In *Curriculum as Social Psychoanalysis: The Significance of Place*. Edited by Joe L. Kincheloe and William F. Pinar. Albany: SUNY Press, 1991.

Pitt, Alice, Judith P. Robertson, and Sharon Todd. "Psychoanalytic Encounters: Putting Pedagogy on the Couch." *Journal of Curriculum Theorizing* 14 (1998): 3.

Plato. *The Republic*. Translated by G.M.A. Grube. Indianapolis: Hackett, 1974.

———. *Plato's Erotic Dialogues: The Symposium and the Phaedrus*. Translated by William Cobb. Albany: SUNY Press, 1993.

Pratt, Minnie Bruce. "Identity: Skin/Blood/Heart" In *Yours in Struggle*. Edited by Elly Bulkin, Minnie Bruce Pratt, and Barbara Smith. New York: Longhaul Press, 1984.

Proulx, E. Annie. *The Shipping News*. New York: Touchstone, 1993.

Putnam, Hilary. *Realism with a Human Face*. Cambridge: Harvard University Press, 1990.

Ratnapani. "Introduction." In *Metta: The Practice of Loving Kindness*. Birmingham, England: Windhorse Publications, 1992 & 2000.

Rinpoche, Sogyal. *The Tibetan Book of Living and Dying*. Edited by Patrick Gaffney and Andrew Harvey. NY: Harper San Francisco, 1994.

Rogers, Dwight. "Conceptions of Caring in a Fourth Grade Classroom." In *The Tapestry of Caring*. Edited by A. R. Prillamin, D. J. Eaker, and D. M. Kendrick. Norwood, NJ: Ablex Publishing, 1991.

Rogers, Dwight, and Jaci Webb. "The Ethic of Caring in Teacher Education." *Journal of Teacher Education* 42 (1991): 173–81.

Rorty, Amelie. "Explaining Emotions." In *Explaining Emotions*. Edited by Amelie Rorty. Berkeley: University of California Press, 1980.

Rosen, S. *Plato's Symposium*. New Haven: Yale University Press, 1987.

Rosiek, Jerry. "Caring, Classroom Management, and Teacher Education: The Need for Case Study and Narrative Methods." *Teaching Education* 6 (1994): 21–30.

Rousseau, Jean-Jacques. *Emile*. Translated by Allan Bloom. New York: Basic Books, 1979.

Ruddick, Sara. "Preservative Love and Military Destruction: Some Reflections on Mothering and Peace." In *Mothering: Essays in Feminist Theory*. Edited by Joyce Trebilcot. Totowa, NJ: Roman and Allenheld, 1984.

———. *Maternal Thinking*. Boston: Beacon Press, 1989.

Rushdie, Salmon. *Haroun and the Sea of Stories*. New York: Penguin, 1990.

Sacks, Oliver. *Uncle Tungsten: Memories of a Chemical Boyhood*. New York: Alfred A. Knopf, 2001.

Salvo, Paulo. "The Teacher/Scholar as Melancholic." *Journal of Curriculum Theorizing* 14 (1998): 5–23.

Salzberg, Sharon. *Lovingkindness* Boston: Shambala, 1997.

Sangharakshita. *The Eternal Legacy*. London: Tharpa Publications, 1985.

Sapon-Shevin, Mara. *Because We Can Change the World*. Boston: Allyn & Bacon, 1999.

Sartre, Jean-Paul. *The Emotions*. New York: Philosophical Library, 1948.

———. *Sketch for a Theory of the Emotions*. London: Methuen, 1962.

Saxonhouse, Arlene. "The Philosopher and the Female in the Political Thought of Plato." In *Feminist Interpretations of Plato*. Edited by Nancy Tuana. University Park: Penn State University Press, 1994.

Scheler, Max. *The Nature of Sympathy*. New Haven: Yale University Press, 1954.

———. *Ressentiment*. Milwaukee: Marquette University Press, 1994.

Sedgwick, Eve Kosofsky. *Epistemology of the Closet*. Berkeley: University of California Press, 1990.

———. *A Dialogue on Love*. Boston: Beacon Press, 1999.

Sergiovanni, Thomas. *Building Community in Schools*. San Francisco: Jossey-Bass, 1994.

Shakur, Sanyika. *Monster: The Autobiography of an L.A. Gang Member*. New York: Penguin, 1993.

Sheldrake, Philip. *Spaces for the Sacred: Place, Memory, and Identity*. Baltimore: Johns Hopkins University Press, 2001.

Singer, Irving. *The Nature of Love: Plato to Luther*. Chicago: The University of Chicago Press, 1984.

———. *The Nature of Love, Vols. 1–3*. Chicago: University of Chicago Press, 1984–87.

Solomon, Robert. *The Passions*. Garden City, NY: Anchor Press, 1976.

Spivak, Gayatri Chakravorty. "Thinking Cultural Questions in 'Pure' Literary Terms." In *Without Guarantees: In Honour of Stuart Hall*. Edited by Paul Gilroy, Lawrence Grossberg, and Angela McRobbie. London: Verso, 2000.

Sprague, Betty. Unpublished term paper. University of New Hampshire: 2002.

Springsted, Eric. *Simone Weil and the Suffering of Love*. Cambridge: Cowley, 1986.

Sternberg, Robert J. *The Triangle of Love*. New York: Basic Books, 1988.

Sutta Nipata, Vol. I, Sutra 8. Translation adapted from Eknath Easwaran, *Meditation*. Tomales, CA: Nilgiri Press, 1991.

Swick, Kevin. "Service Learning Helps Future Teachers Strengthen Caring Perspectives." *The Clearing House* 73 (1999): 29–32.

Thayer-Bacon, Barbara, and Charles Bacon. "Caring Professors: A Model." *The Journal of General Education* 45 (1996): 255–269.

———. "Caring in the College/University Classroom." *Educational Foundations* 10 (1996): 53–72.

Todd, Sharon (ed.). *Learning Desire: Perspectives on Pedagogy, Culture, and the Unsaid*. New York: Routledge, 1997.

Trathern, Woodrow, and Michael Dale. "Narratives in Teacher Education." In *Literacy Conversations, Family, School, Community: Yearbook of the American Reading Forum*. Edited by R. J. Telfer. Whitewater, WI: American Reading Forum, 1999.

Trimble, Kimberly. "Building a Learning Community." *Equity and Excellence in Education* 29 (1996): 37–40.

Tulku, Tarthang. *Openness Mind*. Berkeley, CA: Dharma Publishing, 1990.

Turski, George. *Toward a Rationality of Emotions*. Athens, OH: Ohio University Press, 1994.

Walcott, Rinaldo. "Pedagogy and Truama: The Middle Passage, Slavery, and the Problem of Creolization." In *Between Hope and Despair: Pedagogy and the Remembrance of Historical Trauma*. Edited by Roger I. Simon, Sharon Rosenberg, and Claudia Eppert. Lanham, MD: Rowman & Littlefield, 2000.

Weil, Simone. *Gravity and Grace*. London: Routledge and Kegan Paul, 1963.

———. "The Illiad or the Poem of Might." In *The Simone Weil Reader*. Edited by George Panichas. Wakefield, RI: Moyer Bell, 1977.

———. *The Illian or the Poem of Force*. Translated by Mary McCarthy. Wallingford, PA: Pendle Hill Pamphlet #91, 1981.

Weinstein, Carol. " 'I Want to Be Nice, But I Have to Be Mean': Exploring Prospective Teachers' Conceptions of Caring and Order." *Teaching and Teacher Education* 14 (1998): 153–163.

West, Cornel, and Roberto Unger. "The American Religion of Possibility." In *The Future of American Progressivism*. Boston: Beacon Press, 1998.

Westbrook, Robert. *John Dewey and American Democracy*. Ithaca, NY: Cornell University Press, 1991.

Westheimer, Joel. "Communities and Consequences: An Inquiry Into Ideology and Practice in Teachers' Professional Work." *Educational Administration Quarterly* 35 (1999): 71–105.

White, Richard. "Thinking About Love: Teaching the Philosophy of Love (And Sex)." *Teaching Philosophy* 25 (2002): 111–122.

Whitman, Walt. "Democratic Vistas." In *Leaves of Grass and Selected Prose.* Edited by Ellman Crasnow. London: Orion Publishing Group, 1871/1993.

Williams, Bernard. *Shame and Necessity.* Berkeley: University of California Press, 1993.

Winterson, Jeanette. *Art Objects: Essays on Ecstasy and Effrontery.* London: Jonathan Cape, 1995.

Woolf, Virginia. *Three Guineas.* New York: Harcourt, Brace, and World, 1938.

Young, Alfred. *The Shoemaker and the Tea Party: Memory and the American Revolution.* Boston: Beacon Press, 1999.

Contributors

Megan Boler teaches feminist, media, and cultural studies. She received her Ph.D. from the History of Consciousness Program at the University of California. After spending time at the University of Auckland in New Zealand and Virginia Tech, she is now an Associate Professor at Ontario Institute of Studies in Education at the University of Toronto. Her book *Feeling Power: Emotions and Education* came out with Routledge in 1999. Her work has been published in such journals as *Cultural Studies*, *Educational Theory*, and *Hypatia*. She is currently working on a book entitled *Lost in Space: Exploring Bodies and Difference in Digital Education*.

Kerry Burch is Assistant Professor of Philosophy of Education at Northern Illinois University. His scholarly interests are centered on reinvigorating the democratic civic identity of teachers through the use of classical philosophy, American pragmatism, and critical theory. His publications have appeared in *Teachers College Record, Educational Studies, and Studies in Philosophy and Education*. His most recent book is *Eros as the Educational Principle of Democracy*.

Michael Dale is a Professor in the Department of Leadership and Educational Studies at Appalachian State University, Boone, North Carolina. His scholarly interests include philosophy of education and the relations between philosophy and literature in teacher education. Recent publications and presentations include "Exploring Soul through Literature in Teacher Education" (with Dan Liston) and "Narratives in Teacher Education" (with Woodrow Trathen).

Ann Diller is Professor of Philosophy of Education and the Director of Doctoral Studies in Education at the University of New Hampshire. She is a co-author of the book, *The Gender Question in Education: Theory, Pedagogy, and Politics*, and often writes about ethics and education. Professor Diller holds the UNH Lindberg Award for Outstanding Teacher-Scholar and is a past president of the Philosophy of Education Society.

Jim Garrison specializes in philosophy of education. His research and teaching interests center on philosophical pragmatism. Recent books include *Dewey and Eros*, Teachers College Press, 1997; *Constructivism and Education*, co-edited with Marie Larochelle and Nadine Bednarz, Cambridge University Press, 1998; and *William James and Education*, co-edited with Ronald L. Podeschi and Eric Bredo, Teachers College Press, 2002. Jim is a past president of the Philosophy of Education Society.

Lisa S. Goldstein is an Associate Professor in the Department of Curriculum and Instruction at the University of Texas at Austin, where she teaches in the Early Childhood Education and Curriculum Studies programs. Lisa's scholarly work situates the ethic of care in the contexts of classroom life and teacher education, examining the ways that caring manifests itself in the lived experiences of teachers and students. Her most recent books are *Teaching with Love* and *Reclaiming Caring in Teaching and Teacher Education*.

Ursula A. Kelly is the author of *Schooling Desire: Literacy, Cultural Politics and Pedagogy* (Routledge) and *Marketing Place: Cultural Politics, Regionalism, and Reading* (Fernwood), as well as several book chapters and articles that address issues of desire, knowledge, culture, and teaching. She is a Professor in the Faculty of Education of Memorial University of Newfoundland, St. John's, Newfoundland, Canada.

Rachael Kessler is the director of The PassageWays Institute, where she conducts training, consultation, research and curriculum development for schools, districts, individual educators, and youth development professionals. She is the author of *The Soul of Education: Helping Students Find Connect, Compassion and Character at School* (ACSD, 2000), as well as co-author of *Promoting Social and Emotional Learning: Guidelines for Educators* (ASCD, 1997) For more information, see www.passageways.org.

Daniel Liston is Professor of Education at the University of Colorado at Boulder. He recently completed *Love and Despair in Teaching* and is the author of books and articles in teacher education and curriculum theory, including *Teacher Education and the Social Conditions of Schooling* (with Ken Zeichner) and *Curriculum in Conflict* (with Landon Beyer). His research interests include education and social justice, reflective deliberation and contemplation in teaching, and reason and emotion in teaching and learning.

Jane Roland Martin, Professor of Philosophy Emerita at the University of Massachusetts, Boston, is the author of numerous books and articles. The publications most relevant to this project are *The Schoolhome* (1992) and *Cultural Miseducation* (2002), but see also "Romanticism Domesticated: Maria Montessori and the Casa dei Bambini" in her 1994 volume of essays *Changing the Educational Landscape*.

Elaine J. O'Quinn is Assistant Professor in the Department of English at Appalachian State University. She teaches courses in Secondary English Methods, Young Adult Literature, and Issues of English Studies. Her scholarly interests include the teaching of writing and literature, as well as the democratic implications for teaching as seen in the work of poet Walt Whitman. Her work has appeared in the *ALAN Review, National Women's Studies Association Journal, The English Record, The Language Arts Journal of Michigan,* and the *Virginia English Bulletin.*

Index